THE CO BOOK OF THE .22

A GUIDE TO THE WORLD'S MOST POPULAR GUNS

WAYNE VAN ZWOLL

The Lyons Press
Guilford, Connecticut
An imprint of The Globe Pequot Press

Also by Wayne van Zwoll

Modern Sporting Rifle Cartridges
The Hunter's Guide to Ballistics
The Hunter's Guide to Accurate Shooting
The Gun Digest Book of Sporting Optics
America's Great Gunmakers
Mastering Mule Deer
Elk Rifles, Cartridges and Hunting Tactics
Elk and Elk Hunting

First Lyons Press paperback edition, 2006

The Lyons Press is an imprint of The Globe Pequot Press.

10 9 8 7 6 5 4 3 2 1

Printed in the United States of America

ISBN-13: 978-1-59228-896-0
ISBN-10: 1-59228-896-0

The Library of Congress has previously cataloged an earlier (hardcover) edition as follows:

Van Zwoll, Wayne.
The complete book of the .22 : a guide to the world's most popular guns / Wayne van Zwoll.
p. cm.
ISBN 1-59228-047-1
1. Firearms. I. Title.

TS534.V36 2004
683.4-dc22

2004048896

CONTENTS

INTRODUCTION

The best gun isn't always the biggest, or the newest. The .22 rimfire was decades old before the first successful centerfires appeared, and even older when smokeless powder came along. The accuracy, economy, and versatility of the .22 Long Rifle have made it an all-time best-seller. Its quiet report and low recoil, and the trim rifles (and pistols) in which it is chambered, keep it chugging along while more potent centerfires come and go.

Because .22 rifles and ordinary .22 cartridges can be had for a song, many youngsters start hunting with a rimfire. And the light recoil and soft report enable beginners to concentrate on the fundamentals of shooting. The low weight of these rifles and ammunition also makes them easier to lug around on long hikes afield. Still, a .22 is not just a rookie's hunting rifle. Some people even claim it's not a good rifle for a novice at all. "The cartridge is so small and the report not much louder than the snap of a spring-piston pellet rifle," said one fellow. "Kids don't take these rifles seriously. Careless handling results. I'd rather start them on a 20-gauge shotgun."

The shotgun is arguably safer, and it's surely less lethal at a distance. It also delivers a bigger bang and kicks harder—factors that make anyone more mindful of each shot. But marksmanship can't be learned with a scattergun. And shotgunning is expensive. At two cents a round, anyone can burn enough .22 ammo to become somewhat skilled with a rifle or handgun, provided they focus on fundamentals. Pursuing small game with a .22 is probably the best training anyone—novice or veteran—can get for hunting big game.

I took my first game with a borrowed Remington, walking fencerows for cottontails and sitting for squirrels on October mornings.

The .22 is a first rifle—properly dangerous but gentle, difficult to master but tractable.

Decades later, there's still nothing more enchanting to me than Midwest woods awakening to the chirrs of fox squirrels and the hollow squawks of cruising crows.

Among the best of my .22s was an Ithaca autoloader. I stoned the sear to improve the trigger pull and took too much off. Each squeeze loosed two bullets as the disconnector failed to engage. The rifle had a fetching profile and fine wood. But the plastic pyramid on the front ramp proved a neon barricade to fine aim. Though I missed a lot of fox squirrels and barn pigeons with that rifle, I wish I had kept it. It still looked new when I sold it in college for forty-five dollars.

An Anschutz 1413 made me a competitive rifleman. In 1969 it cost me $325, with a free-rifle stock and adjustable sights. It brought me a state prone championship and a berth in the 1972 Olympic tryouts. The English match at that event comprised sixty shots at black targets the size of a golf ball. Fifty meters away, the black, representing most of the scoring rings, appeared as a dot in the iron sights. If your rifle was precisely zeroed and you shot perfectly, the bullet would take out the *real* dot in the middle. You had to hit that to score a ten. The 9-ring was smaller in diameter than a .22 bullet. My Anschutz helped me to a 591/600 in the preliminaries, not far short of the score that later won Olympic gold.

By then I was shooting a Browning BL-22 lever-action where I lived in rural Oregon. It wore a receiver sight, which was good for close shots. One morning I tried the rifle on a distant crow, holding the big front bead well over its back. Confident to the point of arrogance as

One of the author's favorites is this Browning BL-22, with which he once shot a crow at more than 140 yards.

only crows can be, that bird was surely as astonished as I when the bullet struck home. I paced 145 yards. Good luck is responsible for most celebrity.

After graduate school I married and moved to eastern Oregon, land of the Belding ground squirrel. Standing upright in the alfalfa they ravaged, these rodents looked like the picket pins used to stake out horses. And so they were called. Farmers welcomed young riflemen with .22s. A month's shooting in one field netted me several hundred squirrels. I killed most of them with a rifle I'd bought so my wife could join me in an indoor rimfire league. The Winchester 52A wore a 1930s-vintage barrel not quite as heavy as those on later 52s. The 10x Fecker scope had external adjustments. I no longer hunt Belding ground squirrels with a big tally in mind, but I wish I'd kept that 52.

These days it's hard to find .22s with the lithe but solid feel of the Remington 121 and Winchester 61 pumps, both pre-war designs. For bolt-gun connoisseurs Winchester briefly resurrected the 52 Sporter. Kimber's bolt-action is also a fine rifle; same goes for the Anschutz, Cooper, and Sako sporters. Remington recently got back in the game with the Model 504 bolt-action, after discontinuing its accurate 541S in the 1980s. If you want a classy lever-action, the choices are few. Marlin's 39 and the Winchester 9422 get my vote as the best lever-action .22s ever built, but the Browning BL-22 is even smoother and quicker. Among self-loaders, Thompson/Center's new .22 offers a look of sophistication not seen since Weatherby's Mark XXII, discontinued in 1990.

You don't need a thoroughbred .22 to enjoy rimfire shooting. Cheap fun is what .22s are all about. The .22 Long Rifle is an ideal round for a simple blowback mechanism, the heart of all popular .22 autoloaders from Remington's Nylon 66 to the Marlin Model 60. They are lightweight and reliable, and most are inexpensive. Low-priced .22 bolt guns abound. You'll get minute-of-squirrel accuracy with almost any rimfire rifle and economy-brand ammo.

Left to right: .22 CB, .22 Short, .22 Long, .22 Long Rifle. The latter, announced in 1887, has become far and away the most popular.

While the cost of .22 match ammunition has risen steadily over the last decades, "plinking" fodder is still ridiculously cheap. I bought some on sale in the late 1970s and paid almost as much as you'll spend on the same cartridges now. Think about that. An accurate, low-recoil target and small-game round for less than three cents. Better bargains are hard to find, unless you shop the farm and garage sales and gun shows that offer up useful rimfire guns for the price of a new pickup tire. Indeed, affordability may be the .22's most appealing facet. Anyone can shoot a .22 rifle or pistol enough to get good. And when you're good, shooting is more fun.

But while shooting .22 cartridges is indeed a lot of fun, the family of .22 rimfires, and the .17 HMR, also have plenty of utility. Not only are they premier small-game cartridges (the only practical choice for squirrels and by far the best pick for many other animals), they help you develop and hone shooting skills. The .22 is accurate enough for Olympic shooting events, so in sporting rifles it's the ideal practice round. You can learn to shoot with centerfires, but at much greater cost, and you won't shoot as much because you'll find the shooting less comfortable. It's easy to ferret out a place to shoot a .22, not as easy to find a spot where you can bang away with that .30 magnum.

Because many, if not most, shooters who use .22s also hunt big game, I've taken the liberty of discussing centerfire rifles as well as .22s in several sections of this book. The principles of marksmanship apply to both, while differences in bullet shape and speed and their effect on ballistic performance merit explanation. Besides, I've yet to meet a rifleman whose interest lies solely in the history and use of a single cartridge—or a rabbit hunter whose aspirations end at the briar patch.

Part 1

Beginnings

Chapter 1

FIRST OBSESSION

If you didn't grow up with a .22 rifle, you probably pined for one. I did. A tall, dusty rack on the south wall of the local hardware store held a bolt-action Winchester 67, which I visited as regularly as if it were a rich uncle about to draw up a will. But the little single-shot listed for sixteen dollars. It might as well have cost a grand. Even plunking down a nickel for a red cardboard tube of BBs once every two weeks was difficult.

The Daisy had been a gift—a stretch for my parents, who didn't hunt or have any use for firearms. Consequently, my natural interest in guns soon blossomed into an obsession. Had I not been denied access to a trigger early on, I might have grown up normal.

The store was as narrow as a cattle chute, but long enough to accommodate rows of shelves laden with bolts and nails and screws, ordinary hand tools and implements that youngsters these days might not recognize. The Model 67 stood with a handful of more expensive guns against faded yellow wallpaper on a ledge that towered above the scarred hardwood floor. A moose shot before the Second World War peered dolefully from the other side, across a huge ceiling fan. Fishing poles (yes, we called them poles) were stacked vertically in a corner. They shadowed a glass counter covering lures, knives, and ammunition, along with Marble's compasses and a used Colt Single-Action Army revolver I could probably have picked up for the price of a new double-bit axe.

The men shuffling about that store came to know me and to tolerate my fondling of the 67. I got used to asking for it. They always obliged. In those days, you had to have a reason to keep a kid from a .22.

Times are different now. To some people, firearms are alien, reminders of the violence television exaggerates for our entertainment. No longer fixtures in every den or in every closet, guns have taken on a sinister character to the increasing number of people not raised with them. Pity. The perversion and criminal menace we must deal with on our streets, and the paranoia we've chosen to tolerate in our classrooms and air terminals might well evaporate if instead of watching contrived shoot-'em-ups on screen, children would again take to the hills and hedgerows, .22 rifle in hand. Life, cheap as it is shown on camera, becomes precious when we see eyes glaze and feel warm blood grow cold.

Not that killing is the daily function of a rifle. After proving that they can kill, youngsters mature by staying their hand. Those who have never killed cannot know why they must refrain from killing. And they cannot be as aware of the woods noises made only by the living. Those who've never heard the snap of a .22 and watched a fox squirrel tumble cannot know as keenly the waking sounds of an October dawn *without* rifle fire.

Early on, humans evolved as predators, and burying that instinct has left us oddly separated from the pulse of nature. Even our kindnesses are ill conceived. They protect wild animals to the detriment of

This spare but sleek Remington is one of many .22s that delights veterans and beginners alike.

fragile habitats, which at last give way under unsustainable populations. Of course, we blame winters for the resulting die-offs. We deny our children firearms and the opportunity to explore the natural world, providing instead mindless electronic entertainment that presents no physical challenge and demands no ethical decision.

Perhaps my age is showing. Perhaps in the final tally, rap music will emerge as the salvation of generations yet unborn, and guns will be remembered only for the havoc they caused.

But I suspect not. Firearms have never caused havoc without our help. Like automobiles that can be both delightful and deadly, guns simply do our bidding. And like automobiles, they engender romance.

The Chipmunk rifle was developed to enable very small shooters to handle a .22.

Who can imagine a frontier West without Colt revolvers on cartridge-studded belts, or Winchester lever rifles in saddle scabbards? Half a century later, deer camps and Savage 99s saw us through the Great Depression. We came out of World War II aiming through scopes on glitzy Weatherby Mark Vs and homely but efficient Remington 721s. A culture developed around Winchester's Model 70, "the rifleman's rifle."

And through it all, we leaned on .22s. A nation that had beaten the British army with squirrel rifles before the advent of cartridge guns sent its youth to learn at nature's knee with one of the first successful cartridges. The .22 rimfire is nearly 150 years old now. Many versions have appeared since Horace Smith and Daniel Wesson came up with the first blackpowder .22 cartridge in 1857. More rifles and handguns have been chambered for it than for any other round. It is still an inexpensive cartridge to make, at least in the quantities pumped out annually by major ammo firms. (More than 20 million rounds ship every year.) It is inherently accurate and easy to shoot well because it is quiet and barely nudges you in recoil.

Rimfire rifles and pistols have evolved, too. The Model 67 that caught my eye forty years ago is no longer made. And you won't find any new .22 rifles listed for sixteen dollars. But the pleasures and life lessons to be had from shooting and hunting with modern rimfires are as poignant as ever, the skills as easily learned as in the days before television when traveling exhibition shooters left audiences open-mouthed in astonishment. Whether you spring for a collector-quality Winchester 61 pump, a battered second-hand bolt-gun from Stevens, or a new Marlin lever-action with a century-old profile, you'll have chosen well.

In debates over the best .22 pistols, you'll find nobody denigrating the Smith & Wesson rimfire revolver developed during the 1920s. In 1930 the firm introduced its K22 Outdoorsman, cannily named to draw sportsmen as well as target shooters to the counter. The six-shot revolver featured a six-inch barrel, checkered grips of Circassian walnut, target sights, and a crisp trigger that broke at about three pounds. It weighed thirty-five ounces and was advertised to keep bullets in an inch and a half at fifty yards. The gun sold well, but in 1939, after a produc-

The grin says it all.

tion run of just seventeen thousand, S&W overhauled it. A faster action and micrometer rear sight improved the K22. The new model, called the K22 Masterpiece, retailed for forty dollars in 1940. It became significant not only in .22 circles, but as the predecessor of the big-bore hunting handguns that later gave S&W a virtual lock on that market.

Among autoloading pistols, the pre-war Colt Woodsman commanded the same respect as the K22 did in the wheel-gun crowd. A vintage Woodsman or Outdoorsman might be beyond your reach, but autoloading pistols by Browning and Smith & Wesson and Ruger's Single Six revolver will milk all the fun you can get from a soup can on a sand bank. If that's too easy, try plastic film cans, or even walnuts. You can't find a better first gun than a .22, nor a better place to raise a youngster than under the beech trees on crisp October mornings.

Thompson/Center's Contender accommodates both rimfire and centerfire barrels on one breech.

The .22 is more than a cartridge type or a lightweight, light-recoil firearm that whispers when you pull the trigger. It's an American icon. From the "bicycle guns" at the turn of the last century to modern sporting rifles and pistols and super-accurate match guns, .22s have fed our pioneers, trained our soldiers, brought us glory in Olympic games, and taught our youth the hunter's skills and responsibilities.

Topped with a Kahles scope, this Cooper in .17 qualifies as a carriage-class sporting rifle.

Chapter 2

THE SHEEP PENS

My hunting career began at a barn. It belonged to a farmer named A. I. Root. He and his wife, Dorothy, raised sheep and farmed a few acres of corn and oats on poor soil south of Albion, Michigan. A. I. might have done better on better ground. Then again, he didn't show much enthusiasm for progress. Near sixty at that time, he and Dorothy seemed content with what they had, which wasn't much. The house and barn showed no evidence of having ever been painted; had you walked up the warped planks to the long, covered porch, you'd have thought the place was abandoned. A single light bulb hung from the ceiling in the center of a kitchen notable for its lack of color. Bare cupboards hung over countertops void of anything resembling food. No cookie jar, no cracker box, no fruit—none of the items common to kitchens.

A. I. had a pretty fair tractor, a two-lung John Deere 720 with lots of paint left. Most of the time it sat in a ragweed patch behind the sheep pens. The pens were a mix of split rail and salvaged wire barricades that kept the sheep—perhaps fifty in all—between the house and the barn. Years had passed since the barn door had been closed. It was imbedded hip-deep in sheep manure that ramped up from the yard to form an indoor mound on which the sheep lounged and slept out of the weather, nearly bumping their heads on the ceiling. Rats tunneled in the clay-like surface under their feet, emerging periodically from vertical boards at the barn's hem, which were spread by the pressure of the manure, giving the walls a look of imminent collapse.

A Remington 121 gave the author his first taste of hunting with a .22.

Because the rats raided the corncrib, they were considered vermin. While A. I. may have owned a rifle, he probably had no money for ammunition. So the rats proliferated. A friend of mine, who lived a mile down the road on a more prosperous farm, was lucky enough to have an assortment of rifles and shotguns around the house. We'd used air guns to trim mouse numbers in his family's granaries, switching on flashlights at night when we heard them scampering along the boards that separated oats from wheat. One day his father decided we were responsible enough to turn loose with a .22. He handed us a Remington 121 pump wearing a dim Weaver J4 the diameter of a dime and allowed that A. I. could use some help with his rats.

In the ensuing weeks, I found myself alone at the sheep pens. My friend Jon was lukewarm about guns, so I happily assumed his part of the mission, perching on split rails twenty steps north of the barn. The 121 was an expensive rifle it its day, and accurate. I knew nothing about scopes, so I marveled at the big image presented by the J4. Firing .22 Shorts, I became reasonably adept at head-shooting rats as they peeked out or catching them through a hole in the pack that served as a window to a main tunnel. One rat that ventured out from behind a rock at the corner of the barn flopped spasmodically when my bullet struck,

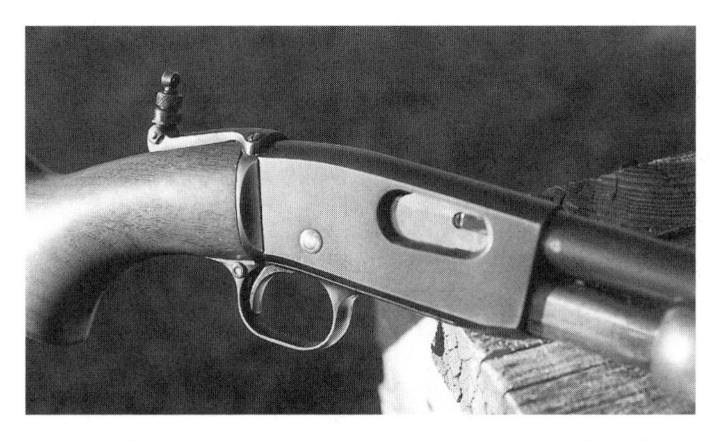

Decades after he shot in the sheep pens, the author found this lovely Remington 121 at a gun show.

spraying blood over the rock. Shortly another rat appeared and began licking the blood off the rock. Another shot.

Rats hardly qualify as glamorous game, but I was as excited as if they'd been trophy-class deer. They taught me the value of waiting to fire until a kill was assured, of getting ready for a follow-up right away. I learned about bullet placement and animal reaction to hits. Eventually my muscles learned to behave so the reticle stayed on target most of the time. I'd examine carcasses to confirm where my bullets had struck, even reaching into tunnels to grab rats whose death spasms had carried them back into their lairs. I don't think I'd do that now.

A. I. and Dorothy may have appreciated my chipping away at the rat population under the barn. More likely, they just enjoyed having a youngster around. Hunched on the split rail, that Remington .22 clutched tightly in my hands, I was the child they never had. The mischievous snap of a .22 Short meant more than dead vermin. It echoed off the weathered barn boards in defiance of age, senility, and the sameness of a life watching generations of sheep cycle poor-quality hay. Unlike the hollow, dolorous pop of A. I.'s vintage John Deere, it carried a note of optimism. Not everyone heard that, of course, as it was still the sound of a small explosion. You had to know that a .22 wasn't just for killing.

Chapter 3

IN THE BIG WOODS

It skittered along the limb of a red oak, then vaulted onto the corncrib roof, where it paused. I pressed the trigger as soon as the thick cross-wire shadowed the eye. To my astonishment, the squirrel collapsed to the pop of my .22 Short and tumbled, lifeless, into an apron of brown leaves and husks.

A first killing is like a first love—poignant in memory and different from all subsequent events. You can have only one first kill, and it sticks with you partly because it amounts to an irretrievable loss of innocence. Taking a life changes you. Do it with nothing more than a shrug, and you are still changed because you had a chance to prove your civility and failed. A casual killing is what we've come to call "cold-blooded." It is no more a lethal act than killing with remorse—the victim is still dead—but a killer unmoved has nothing of substance to leave others to whom life is sacred.

This first killing moved me. The elation lasted through a pang of regret. Pride remained until the farmer whose corncrib had been bloodied told me red squirrels didn't do as much damage as crows on the seeded furrows or deer in the growing corn. Killing vermin could be justified; killing wild creatures with no criminal record seemed less defensible. I may have looked uncomfortable, if not crestfallen. "Of course, any critter that sets up housekeeping in the crib can cause mischief," the farmer said kindly.

This was a red squirrel, known as a pine squirrel in some quarters. Michigan didn't give them much respect; I can't even recall now if the

Squirrel hunting with a .22 is the best practice you can get for whitetail hunting in the big woods.

state listed them as game. Fox squirrels, double their size, were another story.

These denizens of mixed hardwoods have salt-and-pepper backs that blend with the beech trees and, somehow, with the darker walnuts and maples. The rising sun gleams on the bellies of fox squirrels as they are perched high to cut nuts at first light. The nuts tick down through colored leaves and frost-stiff twigs to plop onto the forest floor. Your muscles tense and you strain to see movement through the branches, or that spot of orange, or the glint of a new day in the squirrel's eye. And if you're very careful with the trigger and have zeroed your rifle so it hits where you look at fifty yards, forty-five degrees above level, the squirrel comes hurtling down, landing with a thud. And through the scope you make sure it is dead, but you leave it until the echoes of silence have subsided and the forest has forgotten about the .22. A distant crow calls, then a woodpecker hammers and a chipmunk scurries along a hickory log. Somewhere cuttings start to fall again.

Squirrels are my favorite .22 quarry. Big, fat fox squirrels that bend the boughs when they leap from tree to tree. The smaller southern gray squirrel ranks a close second—though you'll often find your hunting partners ready to pursue them with shotguns and squirrel dogs. Trained to bark "treed," dogs can find squirrels you'd miss. But they also change the character of the hunt. Instead of listening and watching for squirrels, you're focused on the dog. It's the difference between upland gunning with a setter and sneaking through the woods solo after deer. I prefer the latter.

Squirrel hunting teaches patience. It gives you an awareness of nature that's hard to achieve by other means. You learn to listen when you hunt squirrels. And to look. Aggressive squirrel hunters may later succeed in business, but they don't shoot many bushytails. The woods reward the humble, those who accede to the rhythms of nature rather

A Remington 504 accounted for these West Virginia bushytails.

than impose upon it the loud step and hurried cadence of the workaday world.

Whether you still-hunt, moving slowly through the hickories, or park yourself at the base of a giant beech and wait, motionless, for movement in the branches above, squirrel hunting will throttle you back. It will freshen your perspectives, change your priorities. It's a good activity for youngsters who need to know what matters in life, and for those of us who need to be reminded.

Chapter 4

RUN, RABBIT, RUN

It was a big magazine, with a square back and a map-size trim; bigger than magazines today. It cost fifty cents, almost half again as much as *Outdoor Life* or *Field & Stream*. Oddly, I can't remember the exact title. *Hunting*, I think. The year was 1962—I recall that clearly—and a twelve-year-old boy couldn't help but turn page after oversized page, ogling photos of plaid-clad hunters straddling huge whitetails or stacks of moose and caribou antlers and sheep horns perched atop grizzly hides as broad as a tool shed, with the wilderness of Alaska for a backdrop. All in black and white, of course.

With barely enough change in my pocket, I'd have to review carefully even this bonanza of hunting stories and photos. A magazine a month and a twenty-five-cent arrow to shoot at starlings represented the limit of my investments. The content of this issue would have to pass muster before I'd dig out any coins.

Then I spied a two-page spread on rabbit hunting by Joe Linduska. I was hooked. The magazine went home with me and was dog-eared in a week. Linduska had *hunted* rabbits. You could tell by the way he wrote. He hadn't just shot a few; he'd been afoot where cottontails had trampled paths in the snow, and had tried to swing the sights fast enough to catch them jetting from hedgerows and streaking through the winter thistles. He'd pushed through the swamp edges and the willow patches, in grass thick enough to trip a horse, and through storm-toppled corn that lay kinked over heavy ears too low for the picker but

A Marlin 39 with receiver sight gives you fast aim and repeat shots at bunnies.

just right to hide rabbits. He'd heard the patter of an autoloading .22 rifle lose itself in mounds of soft snow, listened to the whine of bullets careening off stones in rusty honeysuckle. By ear, he'd tracked his beagles—those in the opening photo spread—as they swung toward him, lumbering after the nut-colored blur he knew would not be herded, but which often returned to the start of the chase. Joe had gripped the walnut of his .22 as tightly as I gripped that magazine, reading of his Midwest adventures. And I wanted mightily to share them.

Cottontail rabbits were made to order for .22 rifles. Self-loaders fired with more enthusiasm than care will, by virtue of firepower alone, deliver the hasenpfeffer. Beagles give you more shooting and add another facet to the hunt. Whether you use dogs or kick along fencerows by yourself, sprinting cottontails hone your reflexes like no other small game. Spotting them before they jump will sharpen your eye for other wildlife. "Look for that gleaming eye or a patch of white, or the backline behind grass against new snow," wrote Joe. "Bunnies pour out of their burrows to bask in bright sun on newly fallen snow." Like an Indian summer dawn is meant for the squirrel woods, an iron-cold December morning with powder crisp enough to sparkle should find you cradling a .22 and scanning the brush for rabbits.

Midwestern cottontails proved no match for this hunter's .22.

I've also hunted jackrabbits with rimfires. As a tune-up for mule deer hunting, you can't beat a day on the prairie, still-hunting for these lanky hares. Galloping deer come easy after you've trained on jacks. Tumble every third jackrabbit on the scoot, and you'll have to wait for quail to catch up with your shotgun bead.

One long-ago day in Kansas a friend and I ran into herds of jackrabbits; after a bit of shooting, we eventually got leads figured out. My Winchester 75 Sporter accounted for one jack that was blitzing

Browning handgun or Winchester rifle, rabbit hunting on new snow is a pleasure.

through the sage at sixty yards. More difficult were the bunnies that alternately ran and stopped motionless by cover. Swing with the ardor of a skeet shooter at station eight, and you'll kill jacks that run smoothly. But few are so considerate. You'll miss ahead of a jack that suddenly slows as you pull the trigger. After a few botched attempts, your velvet swing is ruined; your confidence in shambles. The rifle moves in fits and starts as you anticipate those maddening pauses.

Jackrabbits, incidentally, are fine table fare. They won't match cottontails for tenderness, but they're much bigger. Hollowpoint bullets are a must for jacks, which can run after taking a solid bullet through the vitals. Quick kills on any small game come more often when you use expanding bullets.

There's nothing imperative about rabbit hunting. Only those who have never hunted rabbits will assume your rifle indicates only a mission to kill. Joe Linduska knew that rabbits can be enjoyed when they run, whether they tumble or not, and that the feel of a .22 rifle in the hand is reward enough when cottontails hide.

Targeting jackrabbits with a .22 pistol can be quite a challenge.

Chapter 5

LITTLE BEARS

I wasn't thinking of small game, only shade. The turbocharger whined in relief as I throttled down and slipped the mammoth John Deere into neutral. A great plume of dust settled over the tractor. Jumping off, I grabbed my Thermos and trudged into the trees.

This homestead had once sheltered a pioneer; now all that remained was the tilted, weathered shell of a house. Barn, shed, fences were gone, victims of the green diesel I'd left idling under June's hot sun. The house stood only because trees had been established around it. Planted Russian olives claimed for the farm a place in history, a security that would not be breached. Even ambitious young men tilled around them.

I didn't see the animal peering at me from behind. It had crawled to the roof's sagging spine to better observe my actions. Suddenly it shrieked, a warning that jammed a slug of lemonade down my windpipe. Sputtering, I turned to see *Marmota flaviventris* slide from view behind the tattered shingles. Its claws raked audibly down the back of the roof; there was a thud, then silence.

This half-acre brush-closet would hold a deer or two, probably some rabbits. It would attract coyotes and hawks looking for mice in the surrounding wheatfield. But I hadn't expected rockchucks. Poking about the house, I found signs of a big colony. They'd burrowed between stones in the crumbling foundation, sunned themselves on the roof, and worn runways in the dirt beneath flooring that nowhere

Rockchucks make use of abandoned farmsteads, especially if there is alfalfa nearby.

covered more than half the joists. Grass near the old house had been cropped close; pencil-thick sections of dung lay scattered about.

A few days later, when the field had been worked and the rockchucks had had time to forget about me, I sneaked into that copse of planted trees with a bow and arrow. I broke two shafts on stones, lost another as it ricocheted off a floorboard and caromed into the brush, then decided to give my quarry a reprieve. The 'chucks didn't appear unnerved by this assault; it was only to salvage my dignity that I gathered my splintered arrows and retreated, vowing to come back with a .22.

We like to think of big mammals as contributing most of the color to nature. Still, more than half of all living mammal species are rodents. While we have roughly half a million elk in North America and 5 million deer, rodents number in the billions. Population densities vary, but some species "swarm" at twelve thousand to the acre. Multiply 640 acres per square mile by the 8,664,860 square miles in the U.S. alone, and even conservative estimates of rodent densities seem beyond belief. One scholar wrote that between 10 billion and 10 trillion rodents live in North America.

An Anschutz sporter in .17 HMR accounted for this Washington rockchuck.

Nine of the thirty rodent families are represented in North America. Comprising those nine are forty genera and more than three hundred species. Western rockchucks, or yellow-bellied marmots, grow to about two feet in length, and adults weigh around twelve pounds. They're roughly the same size as Eastern woodchucks (*M. monax*) but nearly a third smaller than the hoary marmot (*M. caligata*), a timberline dweller. Two other marmots, the Olympic (*M. olympus*) and Vancouver (*M. vancouverensis*), prefer high rock too, and like the hoary marmot are protected. They're found only in Washington's Olympic Mountains and on Vancouver Island, respectively.

A European relative, the alpine marmot, inhabits the Alps—and stores hay for winter food. One animal reportedly piles cut

Hunting woodchucks, young shooters can learn safe gun handling and field shooting fundamentals.

vegetation on the belly of another, lying on its back. The supine marmot and its load are then dragged into a storage burrow where the burden is taken off and stashed. Lots of people don't buy this; the marmots aren't talking. Bobaks, or Himalayan marmots, have no such reputation. In fact, they avoid agriculture, living on virgin steppe or grassland. As farms have encroached on their native range, the bobak has disappeared.

North American marmots hibernate during winter. They also "estivate," becoming dormant for a period in midsummer to escape high temperatures and drought at low elevations. Timing of estivation depends on habitat and weather conditions.

Because they gobble lots of alfalfa and other succulent crops, both rockchucks and woodchucks have been hunted hard. But now game agencies are classifying marmots as small game. My home state of Washington has a rockchuck hunting season to protect the young until they're able to forage for themselves.

As a lad, I hunted woodchucks as if they were bears. The plump, boxy form and waddling stride of my quarry encouraged such fantasy. But the cornfields and brushlots of southern Michigan didn't offer many opportunities—certainly not the cornucopia in Pennsylvania's rolling hay country. So scarce were woodchucks that they might as well have been bears, and when I did find one, the animal ducked into a hole before I got within .22 range. Crows were plentiful but just as smart. I satisfied my blood lust on barnyard rodents, fox squirrels, and cottontails.

My first recollection of a successful woodchuck hunt was in Vermont, where as a college student I worked for the Student Conservation Association. The project leaders there were a cerebral couple who taught at a local school. They, and their teenage daughter, Sandra, held a preservationist view of nature but knew more about it than did most preservationists. My Midwest views on hunting had been shaped by farm boys in sweatshirts thumbing shotgun slugs into magazines by flashlight as they planned the first October deer drive. I'd killed pheasants and ducks, grouse and woodcock. My .22 had claimed rabbits and squirrels and stray cats. With a .303 SMLE that I'd brought to hunt Maine's bears, I arrived in Vermont bug-eyed by its beauty. And just as impressed by the picturesque patches of alfalfa ringed by stone hedgerows. Here I'd find my "little bears."

Young Sandra said she'd very much like to ride with me to hunt woodchucks. She probably had no idea that hunting woodchucks sometimes involved killing woodchucks, but she must have figured that a few miles in a 1965 Mustang with a four-barrel 289 couldn't be altogether regrettable. We went for a spin and eventually spotted a woodchuck. It wasn't far from the road. I stopped behind some trees, slipped the .303 from its case, chambered a 180-grain softpoint and tiptoed back to the field edge. Peeking over a board fence, I saw the 'chuck was still there. I lined up the iron sights and shattered the bucolic Vermont stillness. Dangling the bloodied marmot in one hand and my rifle in the other, I must have looked a bit less debonair than Sandra had imagined. She kept a lid on it though, as I tossed the animal in the trunk.

"Do you eat woodchucks?" she finally asked, timidly.

I hadn't given that much thought, but by now the gulf between Midwest and bedroom New York was becoming clearer. "Uh, yes," I managed. "We'll have this one for supper."

Expecting the worst from her parents, I gave them little opportunity to object. Sandra watched as I field-dressed the woodchuck, then carefully washed the meat.

"Can we help?" The couple was fascinated. They'd already found a recipe. In short order, they'd marinated the woodchuck in wine and were up to their elbows in side dishes. We dined that evening on a marmot stew that everyone proclaimed delicious. Actually, it was.

Some of my best rockchuck hunting has come in eastern Oregon, near irrigated high-desert cropland threaded with basalt bluffs that give the 'chucks security and visibility. I've also found colonies of marmots along central Washingon's Columbia River, near dams and blasted roadways. Nearby orchards provide water and grass.

Rockchuck den entrances, commonly shielded by rocks, but rarely by vegetation that compromises a good view, lead to a labyrinth of tunnels. Some serve as toilets. Marmots don't store food, so dig no food caches. Many tunnels lead to other entrances, giving a 'chuck several alternatives for escape. A nest chamber, up to two feet across, lies deep, often several yards of tunnel from daylight. Rockchucks change nest material in October before hibernation and again when the adults emerge, typically in March.

With .22 and .17 rimfires, use hollowpoint, softpoint, or polymer-tipped bullets for 'chucks.

From four to eight young are born in April, after a gestation of forty-two days. They're naked at birth and remain blind for a month. They stay in the den until early summer, and by June start to feed aggressively to put on weight. They commonly strike off on their own before hibernation to dig burrows. Sexually mature at age two, marmots don't live long in the wild.

Sunning 'chucks are hard to approach because they lie where they can spot danger at a distance, and are seldom far from a den entrance. Hunters looking for shots in rimfire range have their best chance during dawn and dusk feeding times. Because rockchucks are primarily slope-dwellers, the best stalk route is from above. A rim will hide you, and when you pop over it, you'll likely see more rockchucks than you'd ever spot from below. You'll also see more of each animal, so your shot will be easier. Sneaking in the back door, you'll cripple less, too. The shots will be short, and the bullet impact will drive the animal down on its perch, not back into its den, as is often the case when you shoot from below. But you'll have to polish your sneak. Unlike deer, marmots routinely look up (raptors are a major threat), and their eyes are positioned to catch movement topside even if they're not facing up.

A marmot that spots you across a hayfield may peer at you; one that sees you or your shadow close by will hit its den entrance so fast the hole will smoke. A .22 Long Rifle hollowpoint is adequate for rockchucks, provided you hit them in the vitals. It lacks the explosive punch of a centerfire bullet that can kill a 'chuck instantly with a peripheral hit. Consequently, I take great care to place my shots when hunting marmots with rimfires. Even the .22 Magnum and .17 HMR can let you down. One big rockchuck I threaded through the lungs with a .17 bullet kept walking as though nothing had happened. Within a few feet the animal collapsed and died—the reaction you might expect of a deer struck with a bullet of marginal power. It's unethical, in my view, to shoot game unless you're all but certain of a quick kill. Rockchucks that pack bullet wounds to the den and dive before you can finish them topside are lost. Avoid this by getting close and hewing to a "3-for-3" rule: Shoot only if you could be reasonably

A heavy-barreled Kimber 22 and a Savage 93, both in .22 LR, make excellent 'chuck rifles.

assured of hitting a golf ball three times with three tries from that hunting position and distance.

The piercing chirp of spring's first marmot is a couple of months away as I write this. It waits in the bullet-scarred rubble bordering Foster Creek. I'm sure I'll smash hollowpoints on those rockchuck ramparts again. It's the price of hunting little bears.

Rockchucks and woodchucks eat the same forage that packs meat on steers and can be good table fare. Here are two of my recipes.

PASTURE POODLE STEW

1–2 lbs. meat, cut in 1-inch cubes
½ cup flour
¾ teaspoon salt
¼ teaspoon pepper
2 tablespoons oil
1 large onion, sliced
1 bay leaf
6 potatoes, quartered
6 carrots, cut in chunks
2 beef bouillon cubes

Dredge meat in flour, salt, and pepper. In Dutch oven, brown meat in hot oil. Add onion, bay leaf, and one cup water. Cover and cook slowly for two hours, adding water as needed. Add potatoes, carrots, bouillon, and water to almost cover vegetables. Cover and cook until vegetables are tender. Remove bay leaf and serve.

ROCKSLIDE STROGANOFF

1¼ pounds of meat, sliced in thin strips
2 tablespoons oil
2 cups sliced fresh mushrooms
2 onions, sliced
2 beef bouillon cubes
1 cup hot water
½ teaspoon salt
¼ teaspoon pepper
2 tablespoons catsup
3 tablespoons flour
½ cup water
½ to 1 cup sour cream

In a large fry pan, cook meat, mushrooms, and onions in hot oil until brown. Add bouillon, water, salt, pepper, and catsup. Cover and simmer thirty minutes or until tender. Combine flour and water. Stir into meat mixture. Cook, stirring constantly. When mixture comes to a boil and thickens, reduce heat and stir in sour cream. Heat, but do not boil. Serve over rice or egg noodles.

Chapter 6

EARL

He was a big-boned heron of a man with a long mop of orange hair. He talked softly, sucking on a cigar the size of a bratwurst between sentences. He was a plumber by trade, but I never saw him at his trade. To me, he was simply Earl. And he taught me how to shoot.

No mean feat, this. I'd had no experience with rifles when a classmate at high school told me of his Tuesday evenings at Earl's. My parents didn't like guns, and they had none in the house. They didn't know what to make of my insatiable appetite for anything having to do with shooting. I read about it and made wooden guns, including a blackpowder musket from a 2x4; fortunately the lock was faulty and this bomb never went off. I saved my money to buy a toy gun that shot plastic bullets from spring-loaded cases. It cost $3.67, a princely sum that for years later I wished I'd saved for a real rifle.

Working on area farms, I came across .22 rifles and shotguns and envied the youngsters allowed to accompany their fathers on hunts. When my friend Bruce returned from a short November absence to say he'd been in deer camp in the U.P. and had killed an eight-point buck with his own .30–30, I could feel myself turning green. Other boys were clobbering pheasants with shotguns and sniping at squirrels with .22s. In a fit of frustration one day I asked the parents of a chum if I could please *clean* the guns stacked in their closets. They demurred; perhaps they considered such an offer a mark of mental instability.

So with great enthusiasm, but no experience, I accompanied Greg to Earl's basement one cold, dark Tuesday in the middle of a Michigan winter. We descended as if into water, the blue haze from Earl's cigar engulfing us as our feet touched the concrete at the bottom of the staircase. Earl had bright eyes, frank and not unfriendly, but not warm either. "Want to shoot?" he said.

I nodded and said please. The eyes softened just a bit, and I'd later remember the broad smile. "Then you got the right address. It's fifty cents a box for ammo, but the first night's on me. Let's fit you up." He pulled a target rifle from among a dozen on the rack and handed it to me. "Have you shot before?"

"Uh, a little." I'd shot a farmer's Remington .22 pump at rats in a barnyard. I'd fired a 12-gauge shotgun once (one shell) at a can in the middle of the sandlot baseball diamond behind a neighbor's house. I'd even fired a Krag rifle—and remembered vividly the steel buttplate. But really, I'd not shot.

Earl understood.

Over the next weeks, I worked hard to follow Earl's instruction on building a solid position, using the sling to transfer rifle weight to my

Earl donated thousands of hours of coaching to youngsters who showed an interest in rifles.

torso, squeezing the trigger when the globe front sight ringed the tiny black target and holding pressure when it wavered. I learned to control my breathing if not that trigger, and I learned to focus.

"Most good shooting comes from between your ears," said Earl. "And all bad shooting. Make your body into a platform, then think the shot into the target. Don't doubt yourself. Call every shot, and keep your eye in the sights until the echoes fade."

It was good advice, and I progressed quickly. Earl didn't hover. Instead, he ghosted up and down the shooting line, silently assessing technique. If you showed bad form, he told you; if you made a bad shot he let you chastise yourself. Horseplay was not tolerated. Youngsters who came to goof around or flirt got no return invitation. Once, as the Beach Boys crooned "Barbara Ann" through Earl's radio, I remember watching willowy Nancy, Earl's daughter, nip 10s with a target-weight Remington 513. But I was too shy to ask how she held that heavy rifle still in any position higher than prone. Or suggest a Saturday movie. My pick of the rack, a Remington 40x, was always available. Looking back, I imagine other shooters would have used it had Earl not reserved it for me.

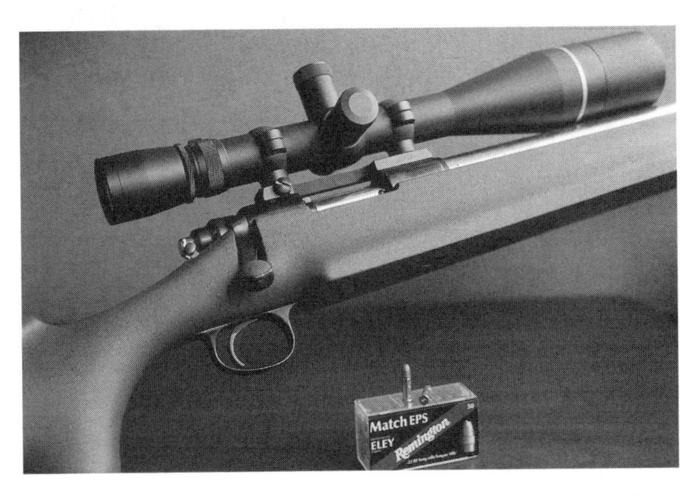

This 40x is a modern version of the Remington that gave the author a grounding in marksmanship.

Earl and that DCM .22 taught me about being honest with myself. Holes in paper can't be moved. They can't be fabricated or erased. They're the measure of a marksman, cleanly punched, no interpretation required. You can make excuses—blame the equipment or the referee on a close plug—but only *you* make the hole; you alone have the power to put it elsewhere. In that sense, every shot is an acknowledg-

The plug is unequivocal. At Earl's range, shooters learned how to keep bullets in the middle.

ment of responsibility. More important than learning how to hit the middle of those black bull's-eyes was learning to behave with maturity and grace when you didn't. It took me less time than most students to become adept at building a position, and in reasonably short order I was shooting as well as any waif on the Tuesday line. That's because I earnestly, feverishly, wanted to shoot well. I was much longer coming to grips with errant shots and accepting my failings as a shooter. Once I learned the fundamentals, I expected to improve even more quickly. But the truth is, the better you shoot, the harder it is to make significant progress. It's easy to tally 389 in a four-position match if your average is, say, 385. It's much harder to shoot 399 with a 395 mean.

Starting with DCM .22s and cheap ammo, the author came to shoot Eley Match in competition.

Later, shooting for the Michigan State University rifle team, I'd cry after a poor performance. The intensity of competition heightened both my sense of accomplishment and failure. No doubt my classmates wondered about sharing the line with someone who'd bawl if he let a seven slip out offhand. I eventually was able to put a lid on my post-mortems and behave as if I were normal. Fortunately, Earl had seen that I wasn't, and in that haze of cigar smoke, rifles cracking, and bullets clanging as they danced on quarter-inch plates, he saw to it that I got what I so desperately wanted: a grounding in marksmanship. To other adolescents, evenings at Earl's were mostly a diversion, and they had more fun. But in years following, as I managed reasonable scores in open competition and made a career of the shooting sports, I remembered Earl's investment in me.

He got a copy of my first book. By then he'd been divorced and was much older, living in the same town but not in the nice house with the basement range and his big game trophies from Wyoming. I phoned around until I got him on the line at home, most of a country

In Earl's basement, the author learned skills that would shape his career and reward his time afield.

away. "I *thought* that was you I'd been reading," he beamed. He told me he was hunting pigs in New Guinea with a bow and arrow and said it was great fun and asked if one day I'd join him there. I didn't commit, but was grateful for the invitation. He must have known the proposition was a little bizarre; he knew I'd consider it.

Perhaps other shooters who cut their teeth in the blue fog of Earl Wickman's basement in Alma, Michigan remember him as fondly as I do. Perhaps they too see in retrospect the extent of his dedication to young marksmen. Selfless and kindly, but demanding as a coach, he gave me the best start I could have had. Here's to you Earl, and the 40x you managed to save every night just for me.

PART 2

Rimfires in Retrospect

Chapter 7

WHAT IS A .22?

Rimfire cartridges evolved in big-bore rifles. But these days, only .22s and the .17 HMR are so assembled. Small doses of fast-burning powder generate modest pressures to push tiny bullets from lightweight cases. The rimfire hull is a study in simplicity: Instead of a tapered case web and a machined extractor groove fronting a stout rim, the rimfire case is simply a cup of thin brass. Between the base and the forward fold of the rim, there's a pinch of priming compound. The rifle's striker hits the case rim, crushing this compound against the rim's forward fold, abutting the breech end of the barrel. (As a lad, I made firecrackers with spent .22 cases by stuffing them with match heads, pinching the mouth closed, then hitting the hull squarely with a hammer on a concrete barn floor.)

The .22 rimfire clan is so old as to make the grizzled .30-30 appear a newcomer. The first of these diminutive cartridges popped up just before the Civil War, but their origin dates to the start of the eighteenth century, when chemists discovered fulminates—compounds that detonated under a sharp blow. For the next hundred years that discovery was of no benefit to shooters. Then, in 1807, Scotch clergyman Alexander John Forsyth patented the application of percussion ignition to firearms. Seven years later, an immigrant sea captain named Joshua Shaw devised a percussion cap in his Philadelphia shop. After that, the race to perfect and market internal ignition accelerated as fast as flintlocks became obsolete. By the time Shaw had discarded steel and

Winchester's 9422 is beautifully made.

pewter caps in favor of copper, flintlock shooters were ready for the quicker, more reliable percussion spark.

To modern marksmen, designing a mechanism to fire fulminates seems a simple task. It was not. Many inventors spent many years deciding where to put the sensitive charge, then building guns around their ideas. In 1808, a Geneva gunmaker named Pauly devised a paper percussion cap that was pierced by a long-nosed pin to fire. Because of the internal location of the priming charge, this seemed a prudent notion even after Shaw's copper cap. Lefaucheux's breechloading "pinfire," with the firing pin set inside the cartridge and at right angles to its axis, evolved from the Pauly gun in 1836. Two years later Dreyse of Sommerda introduced a unique breechloading "needle gun" in which the firing pin penetrated the paper case and powder charge to strike the fulminate on a shot wad or bullet base.

Much of the early work on breechloading guns should be called cartridge development, because inventors were trying to build mechanisms that would accommodate paper cases, and to find better case material at the same time. First used in the late sixteenth century, paper cases were vulnerable to moisture, varied in dimension, would bend or break if forced by steel parts, and did nothing to contain breech pressures.

When percussion caps became available, LePage, a Frenchman, tried to fit one to a paper case. The primer and its thick wad proved too difficult to extract after firing. Shortly thereafter, in 1847, a Parisian named Houllier fashioned a metal case for use in Lefaucheux's pinfire gun. The metal slid smoothly into the chamber, expanded on firing to help seal gas, and extracted easily. About this time in the U.S., Steven Taylor patented a hollow-base bullet housing its own powder charge. A perforated end cap admitted sparks from an outside primer. A year later,

This Remington 504 is one of several high-quality .22 bolt guns now available.

Walter Hunt developed a similar bullet, with cork sealing the base. Hunt, a New Yorker who was over fifty years old at the time, had impressive credentials as an inventor, but no interest in business. He developed but did not patent a lockstitch needle, which would spawn the sewing machine. His other inventions ranged from stoves to the safety pin.

Hunt's "rocket ball" cartridge was really only one step on the road to a more ambitious goal. In 1849 the prolific inventor was awarded a patent for an ingenious breechloading rifle: the "Volitional" repeater. But he lacked money to further develop it. Fellow New Yorker George Arrowsmith chipped in with some cash and business savvy, hiring skilled gun mechanic Lewis Jennings to troubleshoot the complex rifle. The brilliantly conceived tubular magazine and delicate pill-lock primer advance had glaring weaknesses, but by year's end Jennings had made several improvements. He assigned patent rights to Arrowsmith, who decided to sell the rifle. Arrowsmith found a buyer in Courtlandt Palmer, a leading New York hardware merchant and financier. Palmer paid one hundred thousand dollars for all rights and immediately sought a manufacturer to assemble five thousand guns so he could recoup his investment. The Vermont firm of Robbins & Lawrence contracted to build the Hunt-Jennings repeater. The project soon ran into several problems. Company mechanic Horace Smith solved some, but by completion of the contracted production run in 1851, many flaws remained. In fact, feeding inconsistencies prompted Robbins & Lawrence to modify the mechanism and market part of the run as single-shots.

That year a Washington dentist, Dr. Edward Maynard, introduced a cylindrical brass cartridge case with a wide, flat base soldered to one end. There was a hole in the middle of the base. Maynard's own "tape primer" advanced on a spool and shot sparks through this hole to ignite the main powder charge. (Previously the tape primer had been used on an external nipple, the sparks blasting into paper or linen cases; later it was resurrected for use in toy cap guns.) The Maynard case had an advantage over Hunt's rocket ball: It came out after firing, leaving no base wad residue in the bore. It could also be made in any size, to hold more powder.

Meanwhile, sales of Hunt-Jennings rifles were so slow that Palmer decided not to build more. And there the project might have died. But in 1852 Horace Smith met Daniel Wesson while both were working at the Massachusetts plant of Allen, Brown, and Luther. They discussed an alternative to the Volitional repeater. Wesson, who had studied the work of French gun designer Flobert, considered using Flobert's self-contained ammunition in the Hunt-Jennings mechanism. Seating a ball atop a metallic primer, Flobert had produced ammunition that worked in French parlor pistols. Incorporating the primer in the case would eliminate the repeater's troublesome primer feed. Adding powder in a case longer than Flobert's would adapt the idea to repeating rifles.

With Palmer's backing, Smith and Wesson explored this idea. Patents issued to Flobert in 1846 and 1849 limited the partners in their work, but by 1853 they had patented a disc to cover the priming compound in such a cartridge. The disc would also serve as an anvil against which the fulminate could be pinched by the blow of the striker. Two weeks after that filing, Smith and Wesson sought patents on an extractor for the Flobert-style case and on a cocking mechanism that readied the hammer on the bolt's rearward travel.

The first guns built for Smith and Wesson's new cartridge were pistols, partly because the small size of the case was best suited for short ranges and partly because the Hunt-Jennings rifle had become a public failure. The pistols must not have worked well, as none of the 250 built in 1853 and 1854 are known to have survived. The partners adapted a few to a modified rocket ball that featured a fulminate of mercury primer in a glass cap in the cork cap's inner face. The cap rested on an iron anvil. There were still cork crumbs in the bore after firing, however, and the cork cushioned the striker, sometimes resulting in misfires.

While Smith and Wesson had found the Flobert-style cartridge hard to make, they considered its design the most promising of any in their day. By 1857 they were working on it again, and late that year had designed what we still know as the .22 Short. The case was fashioned much as it still is now: A disc punched from thin sheet metal was drawn into a tube with one closed end. Next, a rim was "bumped" onto that

Rimfire pistols and revolvers have a place in competition and the hunting field.

end, and the fold filled from inside with fulminate of mercury. This fulminate exploded when the case rim was crushed against the breech end of the barrel by the striker.

Smith and Wesson adapted the round to a new revolver and went on to manufacture handguns. But the .22 rimfire cartridge proved one of their most important contributions to the firearms industry. It became a prototype for a tide of rimfire rounds during the 1860s, among them the .44 Henry cartridge (in a modified Hunt-Jennings rifle) and the huge .56 Spencer (in another repeater). These raised battle to a deadlier level during our Civil War and, with similar cartridges, fueled the development of repeating rifles and new companies like Winchester Repeating Arms.

But the most important and longest-lived rimfire to evolve from the Short was the .22 Long Rifle, a product of the J. Stevens Arms and Tool Company in 1887.

By 1900, seventy-five rimfire cartridges had been loaded by American ammunition firms. But centerfire priming and smokeless powder eventually killed off many big rimfire rounds. Their thin, soft, folded-head cases could not contain the pressures bottled in a centerfire with a solid case head. By the end of World War I, Remington was listing only thirty-two rimfires; by the middle of the Great Depression, Winchester was down to seventeen. Today only a handful of rimfire cartridges remain, and most are .22s.

The smallest .22 is the BB Cap (BB for "bullet breech"). It is essentially the Flobert round that prompted Smith and Wesson to experiment with bigger cases. Several American companies loaded the BB Cap until World War II, but now I believe it is marketed only by the German firm of RWS. Intended for indoor target shooting, BB Caps

The .22 Long Rifle is accurate, versatile, and easy to shoot.

launch 16-grain bullets at 750 feet per second (fps), for a muzzle energy of 26 foot-pounds. They can penetrate up to an inch of soft pine at close range. Conical bullets replaced the original round ball before U.S. ammunition firms dropped this cartridge, but it still packs only one-fifth the energy of a .22 Long Rifle.

The .22 CB (conical bullet) Cap is a grownup BB Cap, born in 1888. The original loading called for a 29-grain .22 Short bullet in a BB Cap case, with a pinch of black powder. But most CB Cap cases were longer than the BB Cap's. Still loaded by RWS, the CB Cap delivers about the same velocity as its little brother, but ten ft-lbs more energy due to the heavier bullet.

The .22 Short that Smith and Wesson pioneered was initially charged with four grains of black powder. In 1887 it became available with semi-smokeless powder, to be followed shortly by a smokeless loading. Remington announced "Kleanbore" priming for the .22 Short in 1927, several years after German cartridges had first featured "Rost-frei" (rust-free) noncorrosive priming. All ammunition companies that load rimfire rounds still list the .22 Short. Its high-speed 29-grain solid bullet leaves a rifle muzzle at 1,125 fps, high-speed hollowpoints fractionally faster. Energy comes in at about 80 ft-lbs; the bullets drop about 4.3 inches at 100 yards with a 75-yard zero.

When I was a shy lad ogling gingham-skirted girls at county fairs, I lost a truckload of quarters at shooting booths, trying to punch diamonds out of cards with battered Remington pump guns so I could win a teddy bear and then a girl. The type of ammunition used escapes my memory, but probably it was the 15-grain gallery Short, listed at 1,750 fps. The bears, incidentally, were dusty enough to have perched above those shooting booths for months. I've since determined that three 22-caliber bullet holes cannot be arranged on one of those diamonds without missing a corner—but I digress.

Some shooters think the .22 Long resulted when the Long Rifle case was married to the Short bullet. But while the bullets and cases do check out dimensionally, the Long, introduced in 1871, predated the Long Rifle by sixteen years. The .22 Long's original loading of 5 grains of blackpowder gave its 29-grain bullet a little more sauce than the Short, though the difference did not pull the Long past its parent in the marketplace. High-speed loads for the Long kick a bullet downrange at 1,240 fps, generating 99 ft-lbs.

The .22 Long bullet drops 3.8 inches at 100 yards, given a 75-yard zero, and in rifling designed for the Long Rifle, it is not nearly as accurate. The blunt bullet it shares with the Short has a ballistic coefficient, or "C," of .083, laughable when compared to hunting bullets in modern centerfire cartridges, but not far off the .115 C of the Long Rifle's 40-grain bullet. Those low numbers guarantee quick deceleration and an arc that yields to the slightest breeze. Higher velocity won't save you, because to get it you must reduce bullet weight, which lowers sectional density and, thus, the ballistic coefficient. Boosting speed also increases wind resistance and the *rate* of deceleration. Lag, or the difference between starting and terminal speed, goes up as a result, and you get more drift.

The proliferation of special-purpose Long Rifle loads for hunting and competition has all but killed off the .22 Long. Announced in 1887, the .22 Long Rifle was first loaded with a 40-grain bullet in front of 5 grains of black powder. Semi-smokeless and smokeless loads followed quickly, as did a crimp for the heeled bullet. Peters is said to have been the first manufacturer to list this cartridge, while Remington is credited with the first high-velocity load (in 1930).

For as long as I can remember, high-speed solids from the .22 Long Rifle have been leaving rifles at 1,335 fps, delivering 158 ft-lbs at the muzzle. That's twice the energy claimed by the .22 Short and 60 percent more than you'll get with the Long. Flat flight is a bonus; high-speed Long Rifle bullets drop 3.3 inches at 100 yards, given a 75-yard zero. Recent hypervelocity loads straighten the arc even more. To be honest, Long Rifle bullets I've shot don't quite deliver listed velocities. And they drop a bit faster. High-speed ammunition from three manufacturers averaged 1,247 fps from a 22-inch barrel over my Oehler screens. I have no recent data for Short and Long cartridges, but I expect similar discrepancies.

Among other .22 rimfire rounds that went public are the .22 Remington Automatic, developed in 1914 for that company's Model 16

The huge Smith & Wesson .500 is a direct descendant of the K22 Outdoorsman.

autoloading rifle and discontinued in 1928. Like the similar .22 Winchester Automatic, made until 1932 for Winchester's Model 1903 self-loader, it had a 45-grain, inside-lubricated bullet. As both cases had to be substantially bigger in diameter than their .222 bullets, they couldn't be chambered in guns bored for the Short, Long, or Long Rifle, with case-mouth diameters of only .224. Why bother with these oddballs? Well, at that time, rimfire cartridges were loaded with black, semi-smokeless, and smokeless powders. By making new smokeless cartridges for autoloaders, armsmakers ensured that shooters wouldn't gum up those guns with blackpowder ammo.

While the .22 Automatics were milk-toast rounds, clocking 1,000 fps, the Winchester .22 WRF manufactured for the company's Model 1890 pump rifle fired its 45-grain solid and 40-grain hollowpoint bullets at an impressive 1,450. Case length was .960—half again that of the

Automatics and the .22 Long Rifle. An inside-lubricated bullet made for a fat case and a chamber too big for other .22 ammunition. Shooters who used Shorts, Longs, and Long Rifles in WRF guns got split cases and spotty extraction. Remington made an interchangeable cartridge and called it the .22 Remington Special.

Between 1880 and 1935 some ammunition firms offered the .22 Extra Long, a round with the Long Rifle's 40-grain bullet in a case a tad longer. Initially, it held 6 grains of blackpowder. It was hawked as a two-hundred-yard target cartridge—but blunt 40-grain bullets don't do well at two hundred yards, especially when launched at 1,050 fps. As the .22 Short, Long, and Long Rifle established themselves in the post–World War I marketplace, gunmakers fashioned mechanisms that handled all three and even functioned with mixed magazine loads. Because the .22 Short bullet shoots best in barrels rifled one turn in twenty-four inches, it didn't perform well in guns chambered and rifled 1-in-16 for the Long Rifle. A Short bullet also had to jump some distance into the rifling of one of these barrels. Rumor had it that the jumps would deposit enough lead on the land corners to cause eventual problems. I didn't shoot enough Shorts to find out.

Winchester's .22 Magnum Rimfire, introduced in 1959, offered significantly more power than earlier .22s. Essentially a .22 WRF case stretched to 1.052 inches, with a 40-grain jacketed bullet at 2,000 fps, the WMR was initially chambered in pistols. Ruger and Smith & Wesson sold Magnum revolvers right away; Winchester was slow in bringing out its first WMR rifle, the Model 61 pump. Since then the cartridge has trundled along steadily, but it has never threatened the .22 Long Rifle.

In 1977 CCI had a better idea. Its Stinger had the overall length of a Long Rifle cartridge, but its hollowpoint bullet, about 6 grains lighter and backed by a stiffer charge of powder, reached 1,680 fps. Winchester soon brought out the Xpediter, Remington its Yellow Jacket. Now these super Long Rifle rounds and their clones are quite popular.

Next to centerfire varmint cartridges, any .22 rimfire looks puny. Those blunt lead bullets, which may be plated, waxed, or greased to prevent barrel leading, are hardly aerodynamic. Compare their ballistic

The .22 WMR delivers 50 percent more speed than the more popular .22 Long Rifle.

coefficients with the C of .400 for a sleek hunting bullet from a .270 or .30–06. Wind blows .22 rimfire bullets around as if they were scraps of newspaper. Gentle, oblique puffs of air, loafing across the range during a match, have kicked my bullets three inches out at a hundred yards.

Higher speeds are not the answer because extra velocity is only a benefit if it can be sustained. Low ballistic coefficient guarantees a quick deceleration, and "hypervelocity" Long Rifle rounds that look good on ballistics charts get much of their speed from lighter bullets with lots of lag (the difference in velocities at the muzzle and at the target). Match bullets are loaded modestly in part to keep them subsonic. Accuracy suffers when bullets break the sound barrier.

Someone once wrote that a disadvantage of rimfires is that you cannot reload them. That may be a liability if you own a .44 Henry. But why would you want to reload cartridges that cost a couple of pennies each? And even if you could reassemble .22 ammo, you'd hardly achieve the accuracy of match cartridges. At the fifty-yard mark in competition, I've shot many, many five-shot groups too small to easily accept a .30-caliber bullet. Several at one hundred yards have measured under a half minute of angle. Eley Match ammo in my McMillan-barreled Remington 37 shoots so consistently that any hole outside the X-ring is unquestionably my fault.

I still marvel at the accuracy of plinking loads—the least costly cartridges available for rifles and pistols. Unlike centerfire ammo, .22 rounds haven't changed much in price since I was a boy. I recall buying Long Rifle solids for fifty-eight cents a box—just over a penny a shot—

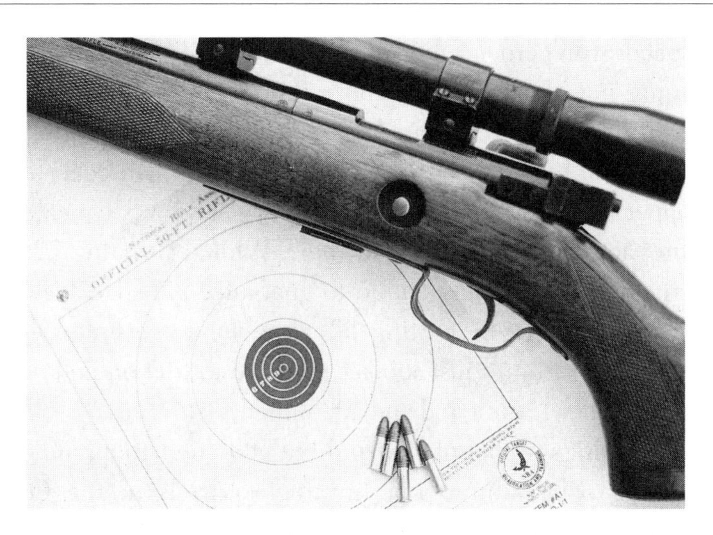

The Winchester 75 Sporter offered shooters a classy bolt gun at a lower cost than the Model 52.

in the 1970s. Thirty years later you can still find them for under a buck. No wonder more .22 cartridges have been cycled through sporting rifles than any centerfire round. Remember that low cost is more than a convenience. Shooters who burn the most ammo in conscientious practice invariably bring home the match medals and limits of squirrels. A marksman well trained with a .22 is also likely to score consistently on big game with centerfire rifles and pistols.

Another asset of .22 rimfires is their light report and recoil. The older I get, the more I like gentle rifles. And a lot of good small-game hunting is on farms, where noise, reach, and penetration can be liabilities. The standard caution about safe backstops still applies to rimfires, however; a .22 Long Rifle bullet will travel over 1,600 yards if you elevate the gun thirty-one degrees. A .22 Short bullet will go 1,200. Each will be clocking over 200 fps when it noses into the ground or anything else it finds. Because of its construction and relatively low velocity, a .22 bullet will also ricochet more readily than a softpoint game bullet from a centerfire gun.

Still another often-overlooked benefit of the .22 rimfires is their treatment of rifle and pistol bores. The small powder charges and low bullet speeds won't erode rifling. The spartan dose of priming mix and fast-burning powder leaves little bore residue. Because they are not moving at high speed (compared to centerfire varmint and big game bullets), rimfire bullets need not wear jackets that can coat the bore with copper fouling. The thin plating, grease, and wax typically used on rimfires actually help preserve the bore. While I clean my .22 match rifle frequently during competition to guarantee gilt-edge accuracy, I usually leave the bores of sporting .22s alone for a year unless they get wet. Frequent brushings just subject the bore to friction and possible damage from the cleaning rod and attachments.

A surprising number of load and bullet combinations are offered in .22 Long Rifle ammo. For hunting squirrels in the October beech woods, where you can shoot for head or lungs, standard- or high-velocity rounds with solid bullets usually suffice. The slightly more expensive hollowpoints work best if you're walking up rabbits and taking body shots. Hollowpoints are more destructive than solids, so you'll lose more meat; but quick kills should be the top priority.

Because small game doesn't require gnat's-eye accuracy, and because high velocity sells, the folks at CCI developed a "hyperspeed" .22 Long Rifle in 1977. The Stinger fired a 32-grain bullet at 1,600 fps. It got rave reviews and was soon copied at Winchester (Xpediter) and Remington (Yellow Jacket). The hollowpoint bullets opened explosively and could be used in almost any rifle or handgun chambered for the .22 Long Rifle cartridge. Hyperspeed ammo is still popular, and the list of offerings in this category has grown. According to my count, forty-two rimfire loads are currently offered by Federal, Remington, and Winchester. CCI, PMC, Fiocchi, and Lapua catalog many others.

The .22 rimfire family includes a few rounds that don't fit the chambers of guns chambered for the .22 Long Rifle. The .22 Winchester Magnum Rimfire (WMR), introduced in 1959, is the most potent. Its thin-jacketed 40-grain bullet leaves the muzzle at roughly 2,000 fps, delivering more energy and a flatter flight than any Long Rifle bullet. It is the modern equivalent of the .22 Winchester Rimfire (1890), whose bullet clocked 1,440 fps. The cases of both are bigger in diameter than

High-capacity tube magazines, like the one on this Marlin 39, are ideal for .22 rimfires.

those of other .22s. They grip the bullet's full-diameter shank, not a recessed heel. The .22 Winchester Automatic (1903) and .22 Remington Automatic (1914) were less powerful and were developed mainly to prevent use of blackpowder .22 ammo in specific autoloading rifles.

The most accomplished shooters in history have demonstrated their prowess with rimfires. Exhibition shooters from Ad Topperwein to Tom Frye have worked magic with .22 rifles. In earlier days, a comely

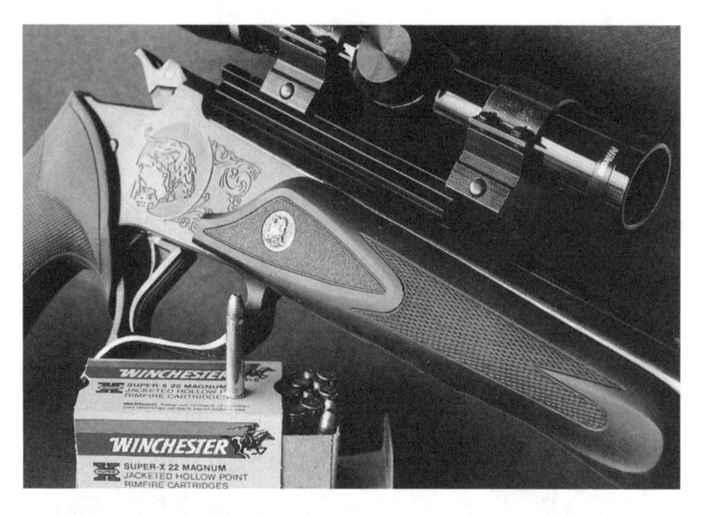

In Thompson/Center's Contender pistol, the .22 WMR delivers quite a crack. Wear ear protection when shooting.

Annie Oakley not only snared a shooting career with her keen eye and a .22, she landed a husband as well. When she was in her sixties, Annie could still hit twenty-five hand-tossed pennies in a row with her Marlin rifle. Tom Knapp, who now shoots for Benelli, spices his shotgun routines with .22 stunts. "I can sometimes keep a golf ball airborne for up to three shots by hitting it on the underside," he says. "I'm about two for three on hand-tossed aspirin." The hardest targets? Airborne BBs. "Oh, the onlookers can't see 'em, but I do. And the bullet whines off the BB when it hits, so there's audible proof!"

No matter the rifle or handgun you choose, hunting with a .22 will hone your stalking skills as well as your shooting and wind-doping abilities. If you're a bit gray around the edges like I am, it might bring you memories of cottontails or fox squirrels from seasons long past and hunters who can't be with you anymore. And it might remind you of how much fun it was to put a hole in a soda can or sneak really close to a chattering bushytail. The .22 rimfires are a piece of American history, gentle rounds that shoot straight and kill efficiently for any marksman or hunter bold enough to embrace their limitations.

Chapter 8

SQUIRREL RIFLES

It's been said that squirrel hunting is a good training ground for young hunters. That is so, though not just for the reasons usually given. Yes, it is more affordable than hunting Stone sheep. It does offer Easterners and Midwesterners a lot of field time close to home. Hunting solo for squirrels, a young hunter can safely tend his rifle; and the deliberate shooting can sharpen the skills of any marksman. But the main reason to get a beginning hunter into the squirrel woods is to let him (or her) feel nature's pulse. Finding a target comes after the sifting—after the interference is sorted out, piece by piece, each subtle sound and slight movement labeled and discounted. The target appears after time no longer has a clock face, after the beech trunk stops biting into your back and the wet has gone from your socks; when frost has left your fingers and the woods have adopted you.

"If you keep aholt of yer baggage," an old farmer once told me, "you'll look, smell, and sound like a human. Good way to save ammo."

This fellow had something, and I eventually figured out what it was. There's more to shooting game than going where game lives and looking for it. To get it in your sights with any regularity, you must become a native. "Most hunters don't know how to act local," said the farmer, thumbs hitched in his coveralls. "Act foreign, and warning lights start flashin' from the trees. You don't see 'em, but you can bet the critters do."

Well, I had to try *something*. I'd been prowling the woods for days, the borrowed .22 pump rifle in my hands. I'd seen fox squirrels leaping through the treetops and sprinted after them. I'd seen them easing along branches and sat rock-still. Neither method had won me a shot. The only kill I'd claimed had been a red squirrel raiding a corncrib as I shuffled by on my way out of the woods. That squirrel was slow, and I had been lucky.

The next morning I got up extra early and eased into the big woods beyond the corncrib, sliding my sneakers through the carpet of russet oak and beech leaves. "Step on top, and you'll sound like what you are," the farmer had cautioned. "Go slow. Don't move anything above your belt 'cept your eyes." It had sounded easy but it wasn't, and by the time I'd reached the trunk of a beech straight enough for a bowsprit, the eastern sky had gone incendiary. I slid my back down the bark and carefully picked leaves from around my feet until I could shift my position from time to time without making noise. Then I tried hard to follow his last bit of advice: "Peel off everything that you'd look for if you wanted to avoid hunters."

It was, he said, like shedding a skin. You couldn't become a good hunter unless you became what the squirrels didn't expect you to be. "You're not ordinarily a hunter. You're somethin' else, mostly. You get lots of practice out of the woods *bein'* somethin' else. You got a *habit* of bein' somethin' else. When you step into the woods, send that somethin' else away." Animals, he added, are quick to spot an invasion. "What you want to do is slip in with nothin' to prove, kind of humble, and be somethin' you ain't. Think of what you'd be if you weren't out to kill somethin', if you just wanted to fit in. Don't think about rifles."

I'd listened because I was desperate for any advice that would bring me shooting. The woods won't accept you right away. And that first morning of becoming something else, I didn't shoot a squirrel. But several mornings later—I can't recall how many—it came to me that for some minutes I hadn't felt wet or cold or anxious, and that the nearby pattering of nut hulls had sneaked up on me. Moving only my eyes, I looked up. An orange-bellied fox squirrel the size of a raccoon was perched above me, cutting an acorn. Somehow, a crosswire appeared against its pepper-colored shoulder. The Remington's crack surprised me almost as much as the thud of the animal hitting the ground.

First deer, first elk, first Cape buffalo—they were all follow-ups. My first game was that squirrel. In the waking time of an October morning, I learned just enough about hunting to get a shot, just enough to know what the farmer meant by becoming something else in the woods. Hunting isn't about shooting. Shooting is what you do after you've become a hunter. And that's why squirrel rifles don't interest me like they used to.

I've used a variety of .22s and enjoyed them all, especially old ones that hide history in scarred walnut and silvered barrels. Squirrel hunting, you don't need the most accurate .22 or one with a lot of firepower. You don't need an expensive sight, either, though it's a mistake to buy the cheapest. The Remington 121 that collected my first squirrels wore a Weaver J4 scope. It had a crosswire as thick as concrete reinforcing bars, in a 3/4-inch tube. The sight picture was seawater-gray in good light. In deep shade it inked up, erasing the dark blur you knew to be the target.

Inexpensive but a tack-driver, this Savage in .17 HMR makes a fine squirrel rifle.

One of my favorite squirrel rifles was an Ithaca X-15 autoloader. It had a lovely walnut stock that fit me just right. After a little trigger work, it shot well too. A 4x Herter scope, sharp and underpriced, made this .22 lethal. But in a fit of stupidity I sold it. Another rifle would have become a keeper, had I the sense to buy it. "A dandy," said the man behind the table at the gun show. It had been years since I'd owned a first-cabin .22, but $575 was two months' rent. I shuffled off and told a friend about the rifle. He bought it, a Winchester 52 Sporter restocked by Al Biesen. The memory still stings. You have to brace yourself for disappointments like that.

Autoloaders aren't my choice for the squirrel woods. Repeat shots can help you take squirrels, but if you need them more than occasionally, you're shooting when you shouldn't. Instant repeat shots are about as useful as they'd be hunting woodchucks. Like long-range varminting, squirrel shooting is a sniper's fare, an exercise in precision. That said, you don't need a one-hole target rifle or match ammo. More important is a trigger of reasonable weight and clean, consistent letoff. Autoloaders have notoriously poor triggers, although Ruger's 10/22 has been refined in custom shops to give a match-trigger pull. Some other

Reliable and surprisingly accurate, the Ruger 10/22 is among the most popular autoloaders ever produced.

self-loader triggers can be adjusted. Be warned that stoning or filing can make the rifle unreliable.

Autoloaders are not all cheap rifles. The classic Browning takedown, with its butt-housed tube magazine, is a delightful rifle: solid and quick. But for me, the sights are too low for the comb, and I can't shoot this rifle well. Browning's newer Buckmark Sporter, built on a pistol frame, is easier to shoot, if less aesthetically pleasing. One of the best looking and most accurate rimfire self-loaders to come along in years is the Thompson/Center 22 Classic. Weatherby's glitzy .22 autoloader, retailing for less than $90 in the days of $2,700 Ford

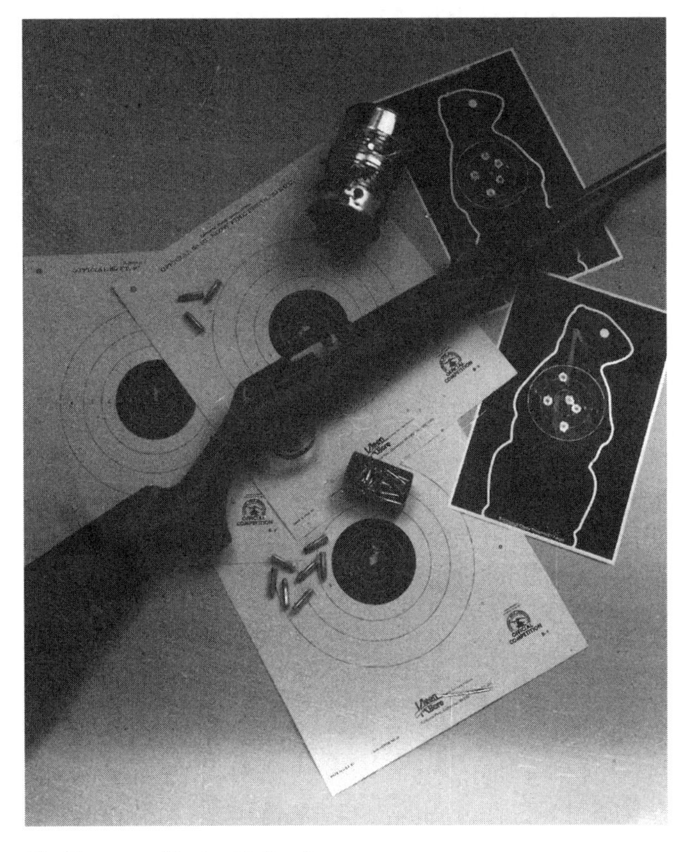

The Thompson/Center 22 Classic.

Mustangs, appeared last in 1990. It has the heft of a centerfire and is a fine pick for squirrels. Secondhand specimens remain hard to come by.

Lever-action .22s began life in 1891, with a rifle designed for Marlin by L. L. Hepburn. A take-down screw on the right side of the Model 1891's receiver was destined to remain on Marlin lever-action .22s for more than a century. It was included for ease in cleaning. Early .22 rimfire cartridges used black powder that left a lot of bore residue. Also, grease on the first .22 bullets melted when the rifle got hot and could gum up the mechanism. During a twenty-five-year production run, the Model 1891 earned fame in the hands of "Little Miss Sure Shot," Annie Oakley, and was followed in 1895 by the Model 1892 Marlin. In 1897 along came an improved Model 1892, the Model 1897.

After World War I, John Moran formed the New Marlin Firearms Corporation, whose first catalog in 1922 featured a new lever-action .22 rifle called the Model 39. It was touted as "the choice of expert shooters for hunting small game such as rabbits, squirrels, crows, foxes, etc., and for target shooting up to 200 yards." Initially priced at $28.40, the Model 39 (essentially the pistol-grip Model 97 revived) became more affordable during the Great Depression. When an improved 39 appeared, it listed for only twenty-five dollars. In 1954 Marlin gave the rifle Micro-Groove rifling, with sixteen shallow grooves. Cosmetic changes followed, but the 39, as manufactured today, has the fit, finish, and feel of pre-war .22 rifles. So does the 1897T, a slender, straight-grip version with octagon barrel.

Other lever guns worth a look: Winchester's 9422 and Browning's BL-22. I've owned and liked both. The Winchester has the gunny feel of a Model 94, that inexplicable combination of heft, balance, and dimensions that has made its .30-30 forebear legendary. The BL-22 has an exceptionally smooth, short lever cycle that leaves your finger on the trigger. Parts in both mechanisms fit as if they were honed and assembled by little old men with files under metal lamps with Tommy Dorsey on the Victrola. By some stroke of good fortune, neither .22 is afflicted with a crossbolt safety. The traditional hammer catch is, of course, sufficient.

Using a gun you're comfortable with will pay off in the squirrel woods.

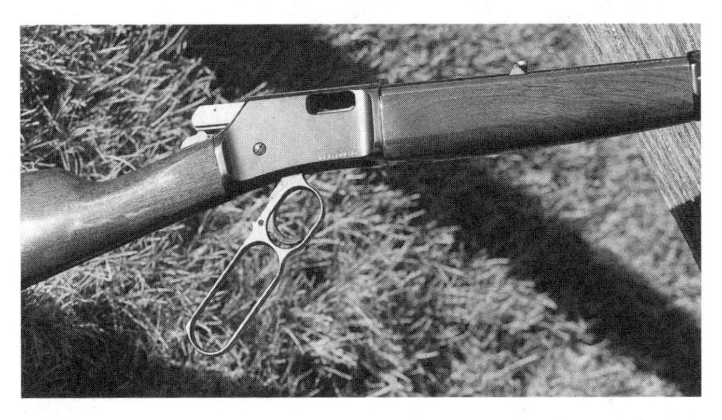

A smooth, quick-shucking .22, Browning's BL-22 is among the trimmest lever guns around.

One more lever rifle of note is the Henry (the current brand, www.henryrepeating.com). This carbine has the Winchester 1894 profile, but a lower price. It's made in the U.S. and comes in a youth version, too. If you want a .22 that looks somewhat like an original Henry, there's the Golden Boy, a bit heavier and more costly. The company also manufactures pump rifles and an updated version of the AR-7 self-loading rifle.

Perhaps because I started with a pump rifle, I still favor them. There's really no other reason. The forend on a slide gun can clack and rattle in carry or as you lift it to shoot; and in the woods, you must be quiet. No pump gun can match a good bolt gun for accuracy. And slide-action .22s have always cost more than mid-level bolt-actions. Still, a handful of truly fine .22 rifles have been built with trombone forends.

In my view, the best pump .22s were the Remington 121 (discontinued in 1954) and Winchester 61 (last made in 1963). Remington's 572 Fieldmaster is a worthy successor to the 121. There's not much else available in slide-operated .22s these days. A pity. Savage's Model 29, which retailed for $44.95 in my youth, died without heirs; so too the Miroku-built Browning BPS, manufactured from 1977 to 1982.

The receiver sight on this Remington 121 adds challenge to the shooting.

The Winchester exposed-hammer Model 62 pump has been copied successfully and imported. Not long ago, browsing gun-show tables, I spied on the shadowed side of a rack the slender forend of a Model 121. It wore a lovely peep sight and showed only honest wear. I paid more than I should have for it but don't regret it. A Winchester 61 in .22 Magnum remains at the top of my "wish I had one" list. Can't say why. You don't always need a reason to like a gun.

At one time a lot of single-shot .22s were manufactured with the dropping-block action best known in the Stevens Favorite. Savage has revived the Favorite, but it has little competition. Break-action single-shots are available from New England Firearms. Neither of these designs appeals to me, partly because the rifles have short forends, and I'm long-armed, with big hands. Nor are they well adapted for scopes. If you want a single-shot squirrel rifle, a bolt gun is still best. Unless, that is, you're shopping for a survival rifle. Springfield Armory's .22/.410 break-action gun has a folding, detachable buttstock and rifling in both tubes so you can use .45 Colt cartridges with effect. A muzzle attachment keeps rotation from disturbing shot patterns. The M6, like Armalite's Autoloading AR-7, enables you to pack a firearm in small baggage crannies. Hollow stock compartments serve as ammo reservoirs.

Simple bolt-action .22s are still bargains. Gone are the days when you could buy a new Model 15 Savage for $13.85, but Savage's Mark I is a fine pick for the present, even if it does cost ten times as much. Winchester and Remington have left most of the entry-rifle business to others, but Marlin is still in that arena, with short-stocked single-shots and, like Savage, a host of box- and tube-fed .22 rifles at reasonable prices. I like tube magazines better than straight-stack detachable boxes, by the way, because they hold more rounds and give me a smooth stock line forward of the trigger, for easier one-hand carry. Box magazines for .22s are notoriously easy to fumble and can be difficult to load. Many don't eject readily. A much better alternative is the recessed spool pioneered on the Ruger 10/22. Ruger's bolt-action 77/22 is also a fine squirrel gun, with its ten-shot spool and "big rifle" feel.

Ruger's 77/22 in .22 WMR is a potent squirrel rifle that also works well on woodchucks.

Many .22 sporting rifles are hard to shoot because they have rough, heavy, inconsistent triggers. A consistent trigger that breaks like a slim glass shard is invaluable. To my mind, if it's not adjusted light enough to be a hazard in careless hands, it's not light enough! I like a two-pound trigger on a hunting rifle. A two-pound letoff is stiff enough to prevent a cold, insensitive finger from prematurely tripping the sear. But it's responsive enough that you can easily fire within four seconds of touching the trigger. If you hold the sight on target too long, you lose clear vision, and your muscles start quivering. Then you panic and tense up. You want to end the tension. As your sight picture deteriorates, you try to time the ever-more-violent oscillations of the sight. When you see the reticle dive toward the middle, you yank the trigger. The rifle, already moving, reacts to the sudden pressure, and your bullet goes, well, anywhere but in the middle.

Costly .22 bolt rifles like the Kimber, the Cooper, the new 504 Remington, and the old Winchester 52 can help you shoot better because they have crisp, consistent triggers that can be adjusted for reasonable weight of pull. The contribution of such triggers to accurate shooting can hardly be overestimated, especially on lightweight rifles.

This Sako Finnfire offers the fine accuracy and crisp trigger pull hunters look for in squirrel rifles.

While some types of rimfires have succumbed to high production costs, the bolt-action repeater has improved since I started hunting squirrels. OK, the Winchester 52 Sporter is gone, and you'll pay dearly for a target rifle action like the old Remington 37 (picture a *machined* box magazine) around which to build a custom rifle. If money matters not, the easier route is a Remington 40x Sporter, still available from the firm's custom shop. Hunters with a budget like mine and a taste for earlier models can find, on the used market, classic mid-century bolt rifles like the Winchester 75 and Mossberg 340 series. You'll pay a little more than the 1964 price of $38.95 for the tube-fed 346K, but the wonderful thing about .22 ammo is that the slow, soft bullets don't eat barrels. Even well-used .22 rifles can shoot like new.

If you want the best of .22 bolt-actions, seek out a Kimber 22 (yes, that's the model number). The Classic and Hunter versions have the clean, elegant lines you'd want in a big game rifle and the side-swing safety made popular on the Winchester 70. The magazine box is recessed. A youth version features a short stock and barrel. The HS, intended for rimfire silhouette, wears a very high comb—too high for shooting from head-forward hunting positions. The SVT version, with

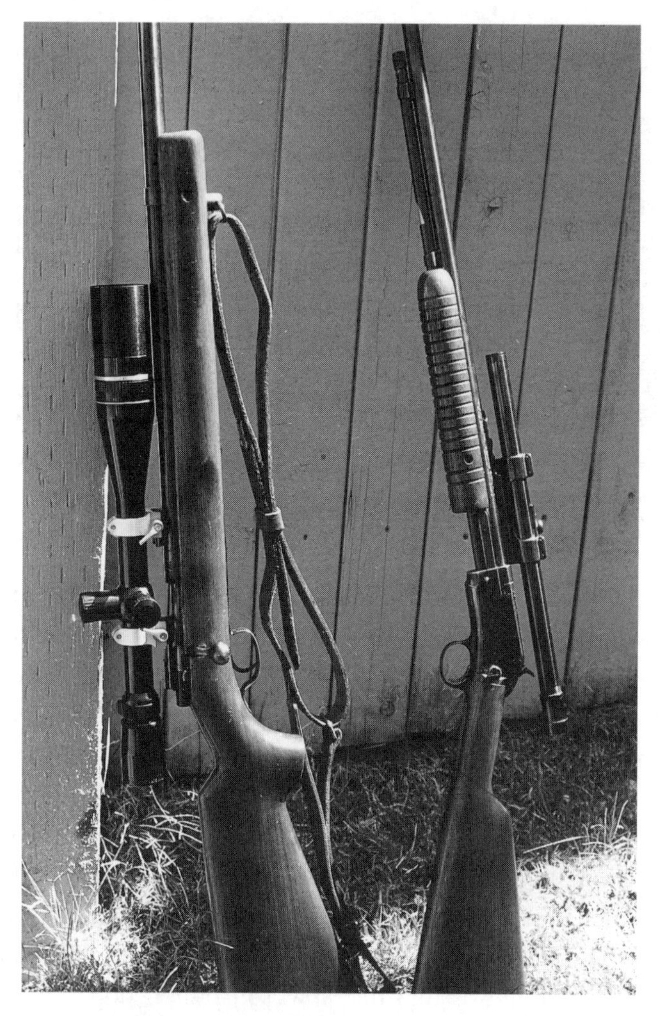

The Winchester Model 75T (left) is a great rifle for stand hunting, while the 62 is ideal for stalking.

its short, heavy barrel, has a laminated stock, deep in the forend with a thick, vertical grip. It's not a rifle to carry, but the balance is perfect for offhand shooting, and a fine trigger makes any Kimber 22 easy to shoot well.

To make the most of any rifle's inherent precision, you need a sight that helps you see a tiny target clearly in shadow-dappled foliage. I like a 6x scope best for squirrel hunting. It has magnification enough for seventy-five-yard shots, but gives me a bright image at dawn and doesn't bounce around too badly when I must shoot offhand. A 4x works for most shots; a compact 3–9x adds versatility without bulk. Keep the scope small so it looks good on your rifle, and so it doesn't impair balance. Pay particular attention to scopes parallax-corrected at seventy-five yards and designated for use on rimfires. Some rifles were meant to be shot with iron sights. I use 'em that way. No, I'm not as effective looking over iron; but squirrel hunting isn't just about killing squirrels. And shooting is still what you do after you've become a hunter.

Chapter 9

THE TINY .17

New rimfire cartridges don't come along often. The latest came many years after the .22 Winchester Magnum Rimfire. In 2001, Hornady introduced the .17 Hornady Magnum Rimfire on a necked-down .22 WMR case. It fired a 17-grain polymer-tipped bullet at 2,550 fps. One of the first to have a rifle in this chambering was Dave Emary, Hornady ballistician. When Dave told me about his rifle, he dashed any hopes I had of impressing anyone with tight groups from the .17 HMR.

"Half inch at one hundred. I've managed an inch at two hundred."

It's hard to top that with centerfire varmint rounds, though I knew the minuscule .172 Hornady spitzer would have a tough time in the gentlest breeze beyond two hundred yards. "I got a squirrel at an honest 225," said Dave, as if reading my thoughts over the phone. "But that's a stretch. Drift gets you if that bullet swipes the slipstream of a horsefly." In addition to working for Hornady, Dave is an accomplished rifleman. He had a lot to do with developing the .17 HMR, arguably the biggest headliner in the cartridge world since Remington came out with its 7mm Magnum forty years ago. It wouldn't be long, prophesied the scribes, before anyone building .22 Magnums would lay in a supply of .17 barrels. And that turned out to be true.

Within weeks of the .17's debut, Hornady (and Speer/CCI, which loaded the Hornady bullet), had a backlog of ammunition orders totaling 12 million rounds. I was lucky to get a couple of boxes of the first .17s. The CCI .22 WMR cases had been necked down by Hornady,

Hornady's polymer-tipped 17-grain bullet leaves the muzzle at over 2,500 fps.

then charged with Hodgdon's new Li'l Gun propellant and capped with Hornady's tiniest V-Max bullet. The .17 bullet leaves nearly 600 fps faster than the blunt-nosed .22 WMR bullet, and its pointed profile offsets the .22's momentum advantage. At a hundred yards, the velocity spread is about the same as at the muzzle: 550 fps. At 200 it's narrowed to roughly 450 fps, and at 250 to about 350 fps. While the .22 Magnum goes subsonic before reaching the 200-yard mark, the .17 is still comfortably supersonic at 250—well beyond the distance most hunters deem practical for rimfire shooting.

Here's some ballistic data from the Hornady lab:

Range (in yds)	muzzle	50	100	150	200
Velocity (fps)	2,550	2,212	1,902	1,621	1,380
Energy (ft-lbs)	245	185	136	99	72
Arc (inches)	−1.3	1.5	2.5	1.1	−3.6
Deflection, 10 mph wind (inches)	0.8	3.3	8.0	15.3	

Obviously, this isn't an ordinary rimfire. With its high speed and sleek ogive, the bullet delivers a much flatter trajectory than the .22 Magnum. Ballistics programs tell us that a .17 rifle zeroed at 100 yards prints about 8 inches low at 200 and 20 inches low at 250. An ordinary .22 WMR bullet falls nearly 2 feet during its first 200 yards of travel, and another 2 feet in the next 50. Drift is about 15 inches less for the .17 (in a 10-mph full-value wind at 200 steps). Still, wind has its way with this tiny bullet. You can't expect something that weighs as much as a paperclip to cut neatly through the breeze.

My first shooting sessions with the .17 came by way of background work for an article I published in *Guns & Ammo* magazine. Rounding up the .17 HMR rifles that had been announced by mid-April was like

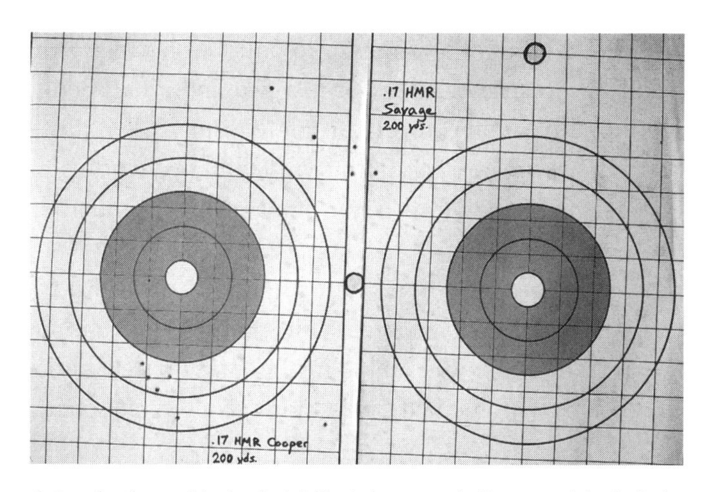

A 7-mph, three-o'clock wind drifted these .17 bullets surprisingly little. (Aiming points circled.)

collecting prototypes of a new Maserati. Demand from the press had sucked up the few Anschutz .17s in the country. And even the inexpensive models, quick to produce because they're essentially rebarreled .22 Magnums, were in short supply. Three rifles came from Savage pronto. So did a Chipmunk from Rogue Rifle Company, and a beautiful Cooper. A Marlin followed. The boxes from Anschutz, H&R, and T/C arrived later. Ruger's bolt-action and M96 lever-action .17s seemed reluctant to visit central Washington. So I scoped up what I had and hied off to the range.

My chronograph confirmed what Hornady claimed: ten shots over the screens averaged 2,545 fps from the twenty-one-inch barrel of a Savage .17. Nine of the readings ranged between 2,528 and 2,594, most of them close to the middle. One shot registered 2,444. Omitting that one from the series boosted the average to 2,556.

Curious about the effect of barrel length on velocity, I fired ten rounds from the sixteen-inch barrel of a Chipmunk from Rogue Rifle Company. Originally based on the Rogue River in southwest Oregon, this company now makes its home in Lewiston, Idaho. There it turns out single-shot .22 bolt rifles scaled to very young shooters. Hardly elegant, these rimfires do have walnut stocks (11½-inch butt). The cocking piece can be a bit hard for a youngster to pull, but having to engage it by hand adds a measure of safety. At just two and a half pounds, the standard Chipmunk weighs less than many pistols. Chambering this Lilliputian rifle to .17 was natural; it will enable youngsters to shoot high-speed jacketed bullets from a rifle of manageable proportions, and without noticeable recoil.

Chronograph readings from the Chipmunk followed the pattern of the Savage. Nine shots ranged from 2,400 to 2,480 fps. The anomaly: 2,333. Average for all ten was 2,446. Tossing out the slow bullet, I got 2,459. A drop of 100 fps seemed modest for a six-inch reduction in barrel length.

Most handloaders would gnash their teeth over a load that spread velocities 70 to 80 fps—let alone one that handed them a 120-fps blip in every 10-shot string. But with the exception of costly match ammo, rim-

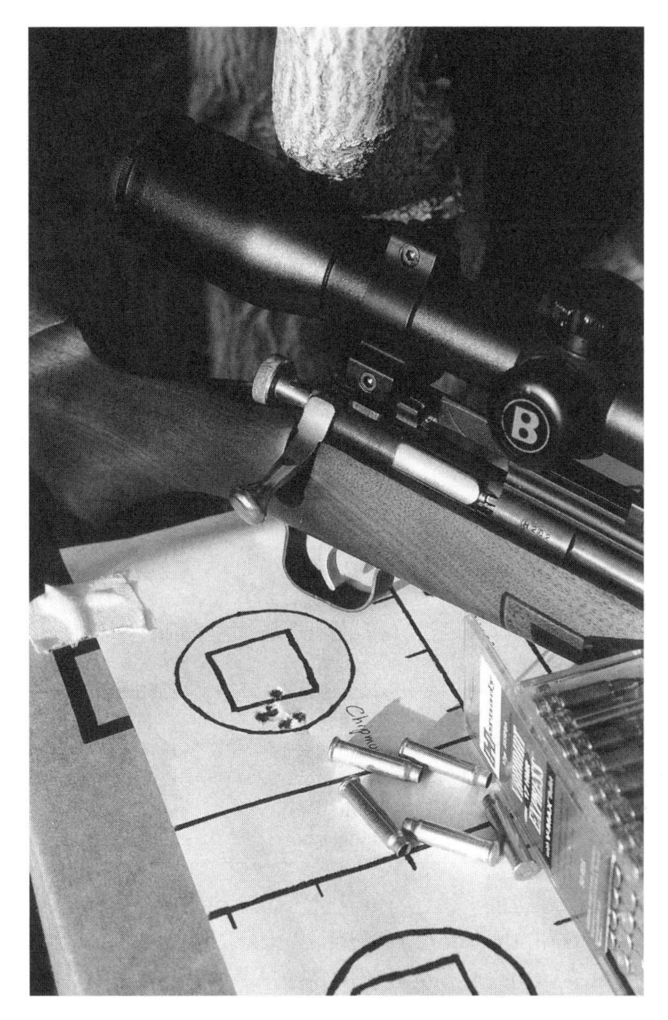

Even the lightweight, short-barreled Chipmunk from Rogue Rifle Company shoots the .17 HMR well.

fire cartridges aren't known for consistency. And subsequent shooting showed the .17 HMR as accurate as even the optimists had expected.

"We like to think it's the bullet," Dave Emary says. A pointed, jacketed bullet made just like the centerfire bullets designed for accurate long-range shooting would indeed enhance rimfire precision. But I'd have to shoot to determine the benefit.

Right away I ran into trouble. The triggers on the least expensive rifles proved as stubborn as a Missouri mule. I do believe some would have lifted a bale of alfalfa. Shooting them accurately, even from the bench, took all my concentration. Often I watched the crosswire move as the shot broke. The problem was particularly acute with the lightweight rifles. Another handicap was imposed by the mounts and optics on hand. Heavy barrels prevented use of big scope objectives with ordinary rings. And lightweight rifles like the Chipmunk didn't match up well with high-power glass. So rather than wring each rifle out under a target scope, I used a variety of scopes.

Here's the line-up, with barrel lengths and magazine capacities:

rifle	mag. capacity	scope
Anschutz 1717 HB 23"	4 rounds	6x44 Cabela's
Cooper 24"	4 rounds	3–9x42 Kahles
H&R SS1-017 22"	single-shot	6–18x Swarovski
Marlin 17VS 22"	7 rounds	6x40 Tasco
Rogue Chipmunk 16"	single-shot	4x32 Bushnell
Ruger 77/17RM	9 rounds	3–9x42 Sightron
Savage 30GM Favorite 21"	single-shot	1.5–4.5x32 Bushnell Banner
Savage 93 bolt (synthetic) 21"	5 rounds	6x36 Leupold
Savage 93 bolt (wood) 21"	5 rounds	24x44 Sightron
T/C Contender 14"	single-shot	2x28 Sightron

I don't think the scopes affected group sizes as much as the triggers did. I fired sub-minute groups with the 2x Sightron on Thompson/Center's Contender, and though two rifles wore powerful target scopes, my best two groups—both well under half an inch—were shot with a 6x Leupold and a 6x Cabela's. I fired five 5-shot groups from each rifle, using Wally Brownlee's excellent rest. If I pulled a shot far enough to embarrass myself, I re-fired the group. But only one per series. Here are the results:

Anschutz 1717 HB: 1.0, 0.35, 0.9, 1.0, 0.9; average: 0.8
Cooper: 0.6, 0.8, 0.9, 1.0, 1.1; average: 0.9
(best 4-shot groups: 0.7, 0.3, 0.6, 0.7, 0.9; average: 0.64)

H&R SS1–017: 1.0, 1.3, 1.3, 1.4, 1.8; average: 1.4
Marlin 17VS: 0.8, 1.0, 1.2, 0.6, 0.8; average: 0.9
Rogue Chipmunk: 4.0, 2.0, 2.4, 4.0, 3.0; average: 3.1
Ruger 77/17RM: 0.8, 0.8, 0.9, 1.2, 0.8; average: 0.9
Savage 30 R17 "Favorite": 2.3, 2.8, 2.8, 2.6, 1.4; average: 2.4
Savage 93 R17FV (synthetic): 2.4, 1.3, 1.7, 2.0, 1.3; average: 1.7
Savage 93 R17GV (wood): 1.8, 1.3, 1.1, 0.9, 0.35; average: 1.1
T/C Contender: 1.3, 0.6 (doubled to 1.2), 1.4, 0.9, 2.0; average: 1.4

The Contender's best group was ruined by one bad letoff. Instead of scotching the first four shots, which clustered inside 0.6 inch, I arbitrarily doubled the measure to 1.2. Reason: I was running low on ammunition. Without doubt, the Contender was capable of shooting better than its groups indicated. Sub-minute clusters with a pistol and a 2x scope are hard to shoot. Given my experience with Contenders in the past, I wouldn't be surprised if, from a machine rest, the .17 T/C delivered the highest level of precision.

Dan Cooper's rifle has a fine trigger and shows the fit and finish normally seen only on expensive custom guns. It is by a wide margin the

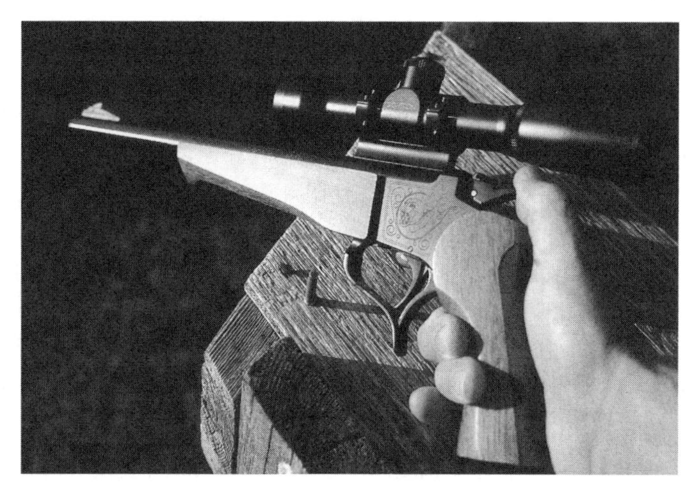

In .17 HMR, Thompson/Center's Contender is capable of very fine accuracy.

most appealing of the .17 rifles in this battery. Of course, it also costs a lot. The Anschutz delivered equal accuracy but was harder to shoot because the trigger needed adjustment. It had far too much creep and broke at over three pounds. Having used Anschutz rifles to win prone matches, I like the brand. While the European stock style of this rifle leaves me cold, both wood and metal show the superb finish I've come to expect of Anschutz, and the barrel is beautifully crowned. Groups included one just under 0.4 inch, and the average beat all comers.

But it would be a mistake to say you have to spend lots of money for an accurate .17. The Savage 93 R17GV fired an honest one-hole group, measuring 0.35. If you think one-hole groups are good but not exceptional, try sticking five .17-caliber spitzers in the same tear. Center-to-center, the outside hits must be within 0.89 inch (these were closer). A 30-caliber rifle shooting into one hole can span up to 1.23 inch between centers; and five 45-caliber bullets can cut a single window if the outside hits are 1.83 inch apart. While the Savage .17 did not repeat its sub-half-minute performance, I've no doubt that, with some trigger work, it would deliver tight groups consistently. So would its synthetic-stocked counterpart, the 93 R17FV. It was handicapped by the most recalcitrant trigger in the test battery.

Edging the Savage 93 R17GV slightly with 0.9 averages, the Ruger 77/17 RM and Marlin 17VS joined the Cooper and Anschutz as sub-minute rifles. The Marlin's creepy trigger is manageable because the movement is both smooth and consistent. Letoff comes at lower pressure than with the Savage 93s. A hard but relatively short trigger pull on the Ruger challenged me, but a consistent tendency to shoot into 0.75-inch told me this rifle was inherently accurate. The Ruger's 1.2-inch group included four shots inside 0.4 inch. I might have helped the other shot out. The Ruger is a handsome rifle and nicely finished, though a trifle muzzle-light. Its nine-round magazine proved a convenience; so too the Marlin's seven-shot box. Truly, .17s are more about shooting than they are carrying. Any shooter who doesn't fall for this snappy cartridge, with its endearing crack and nonexistent recoil, needs to take up shuffleboard.

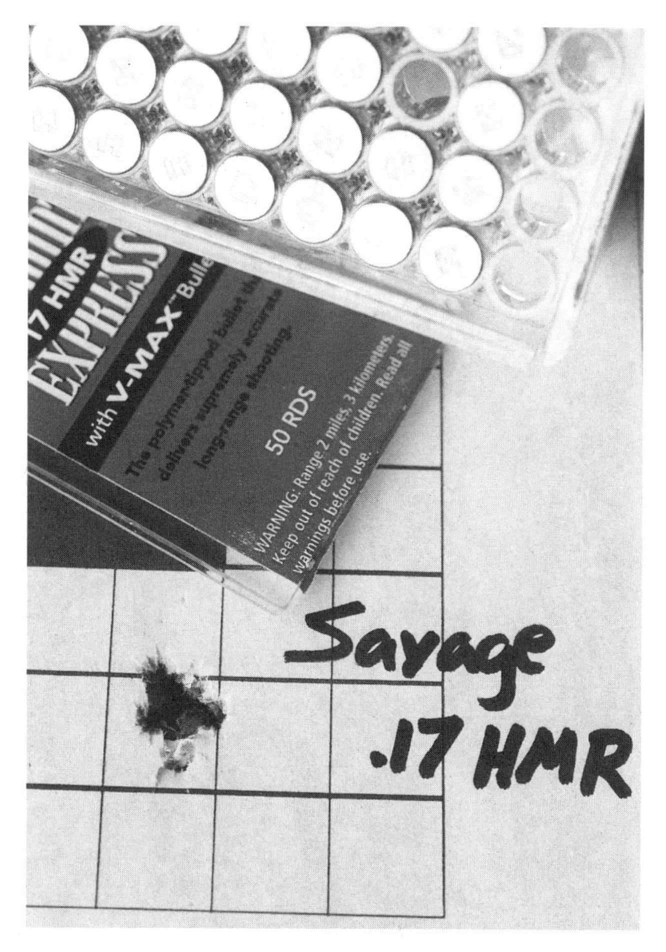

A one-hole, five-shot group at a hundred steps is tough to punch with a .17, but the author's Savage 93 did it.

With a 1.4-inch average, the H&R break-action single-shot yielded good accuracy despite vertical stringing. The heavy barrel promised better. I was pleasantly surprised by the trigger pull. Compact and comfortable in the hand, this rifle also balances well. And it's the least expensive of the lot—a great choice for the back window of the pickup. I like the way it kicks empties into the next township. It's easy to load.

Marlin's bolt-action rifles in .17 deliver excellent accuracy at a bargain price.

The other single-shot rifle, Savage's 30 R17, is fashioned after the Stevens Favorite. The octagon barrel and Spartan walnut stock are both appealing. Alas, this rifle suffers from a heavy trigger, and the liability is greater because the barrel is so light. No matter how hard I scrunched the forend into the rest, I could see the reticle move as the trigger re-

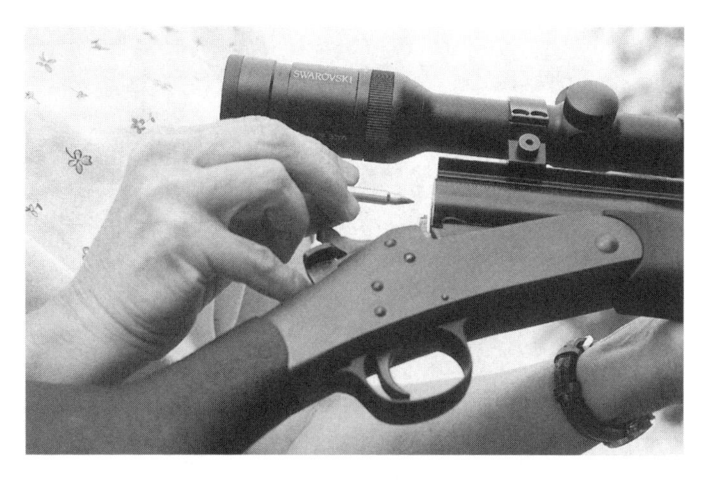

Almost every gunmaker chambering for the .22 WMR has barreled to .17. This is an H&R rifle.

luctantly cried "Uncle!" under my white knuckle. Loading was difficult under the low-mounted scope. While a more sensitive trigger would no doubt shrink groups, this rifle would look and handle best with a tang sight. Sure, you'd lose precision. But some rifles just don't go well with glass. The Savage 30 R17 is a delight to handle.

The same is true of the Chipmunk. Pick it up, and you'll think you're grasping a Daisy Red Ryder. It's so light that even compact scopes affect the balance. Chipmunk's makers wisely offer a receiver sight for this fine little rifle. At the risk of sounding like a stuck record, I'll register a trigger complaint. When the weight of pull exceeds the weight of the rifle, you can expect some movement during letoff. I got plenty, as the group sizes indicate. There was also an annoying, inconsistent hitch in the trigger travel. While some would argue that a rifle for young shooters should have a "safe" trigger, my view differs. A trigger is a firing device, not a handle. The sooner shooters learn that, the better.

Triggers with a rough, hard pull make hitting difficult, just as a dull ax impedes your progress splitting wood. Beginning shooters would be better served with triggers that help them gain confidence in their shooting and encourage them to keep their fingers off until ready

Fashioned from the .22 WMR, the .17 HMR fits WMR actions and magazines.

to fire. Anyway, the Chipmunk in both .22 and .17 serves a need so far not addressed by other makers, and it's a solid rifle. Accuracy is probably better than I managed here.

My pick of these rifles is the Cooper. On a budget, I'd choose the Marlin. I'd scope either with a 6x or lightweight 3–9x in low mounts.

While the .17 has more reach than a .22 Long Rifle, it's no paragon at extreme range. Shooters who've used it on ground squirrels report that the heavier, slower bullet of the .22 WMR seems deadlier on long shots, although they acknowledge that the .17 delivers better accuracy. To get first-hand experience with the .17 on game, I grabbed a Savage 93 and headed into rockchuck territory. No luck—well, I did manage to avoid a rattlesnake up close, which is pretty good luck, even when the 'chucks win.

My second day out, Anschutz in hand, I fared better. A husky marmot took a 17-grain bullet through the ribs and shuffled off a few feet before dying. There was no exit hole. A smaller rockchuck, hit center in the chest, expired after some convulsive kicks. The bullet left low in the sternum after expanding. Damage was extensive, but more what you'd expect from a .22 hollowpoint than from a .222. I shot both animals at modest ranges, offhand. The third 'chuck, high on a boulder, sprinted at my shot. I fired again as it paused near a hole but couldn't anchor the rodent. Blood sign on the rocks indicated a paunch hit. Poor shooting. Though I'm convinced a .22–250 would have turned this rockchuck inside out, mine was the blame for its suffering.

I decided to quit hunting for the day. The .17 can be deadly, but it's good to remember that high speed always comes at the expense of bullet weight. In this case, the bullet is *very* light. Penetration won't

The .17 HMR likes to shoot groups approaching a half minute of angle.

match that of .22 Long Rifle bullets, and even when expansion is complete, damage is limited by the .17's low mass. Incidentally, tests at close range on water-filled milk jugs showed a violence on impact equal to that of .22 WMR hollowpoints. The .17 bullets came apart inside; exit holes were tiny, from shrapnel only.

I lacked the ammunition to conduct extensive tests in wind, but I did fire a Savage 93 in light (6- to 8-mph) four o'clock breezes at two hundred yards. Drift amounted to about six inches, a little less than I'd expected. The bullets dropped four to five inches (with a zero of +1½ inches at 100 yards). It was heartening to see groups hold together. For capable wind-dopers, the .17 HMR is a two-hundred-yard squirrel cartridge. As this is written, a new 20-grain .17 HMR load is slated to join Hornady's line, at roughly 100 fps below the speed of the 17-grain offerings. It should deliver better performance in a breeze.

If you own a .22 rimfire rifle, you don't need a .17. But there's no doubt it will boost your reach. Not only will it more successfully defy wind and gravity, odds are this sprite will print tighter clusters on target than you ever got with your .22. And it gets there right away.

Perhaps the .17's most endearing trait is its shootability. No recoil. And a set of soft earplugs is barely necessary outdoors. You'll want to keep loading up. People at AcuSport, an Ohio distributor that handles Anschutz rimfire rifles and HMR loads, say the .17 gave all rimfire sales a boost and generated an extraordinary surge in ammunition sales. Indeed, the pipeline took some time filling. It's now pretty clear that those who dismissed the tiny .17 as a sideshow were wrong in a big way.

AN AUTOLOADING .17

When Remington announced its Model 597 in 1997, the rifle was just another .22 autoloader. Oh, the Remington people didn't say that—they pointed out the dual steel guide rails, the Teflon-coated/nickel-plated bolt, sear, and hammer. The 597 does feature a staggered-stack magazine for greater capacity and an adjustable rear sight. There's even a last-shot hold-open latch to show when the follower is empty. OK, so

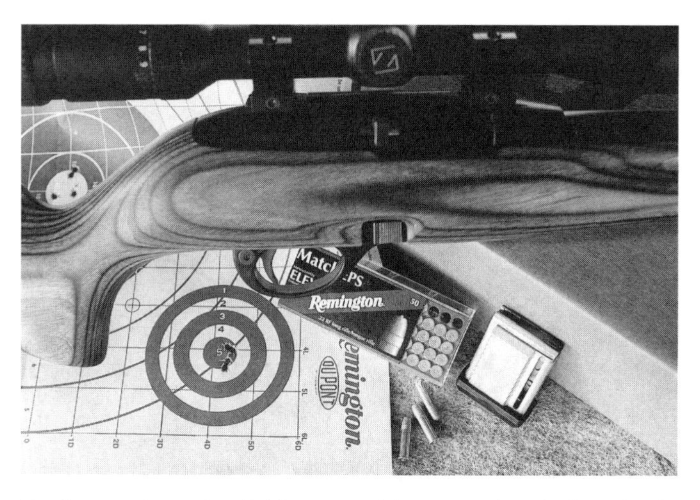

Remington chose the highly successful 597 as the platform for its .17 autoloader.

all this makes it a little extraordinary. And the Remington people are quick to add that 597s appear in .22 WMR as well as .22 Long Rifle. Not much competition in *that* category.

The 597 has since been offered in seven configurations, with standard and heavy barrels, synthetic and laminated stocks, and blue (chrome-moly) and stainless steel. Now there's another version: a synthetic-stocked, chrome-moly Model 597 in .17 HMR. Since its introduction a year ago, the .17 Hornady Magnum rimfire has delighted shooters with its light recoil, mild report, sizzling speed, and astounding accuracy. In those trials I ran with ten of the first .17 rifles, the round delivered minute-of-angle accuracy from four of them. That's at a hundred yards, by the way, and the average of five 5-shot groups. Three groups miked under half an inch; the best was a one-holer, very hard to accomplish with a bullet this small.

So it's about time for a .17 autoloader. Because the .17 HMR cartridge is simply the .22 WMR necked down, any rifle that handles the .22 Magnum can handle .17s. With bolt guns, you need only rebarrel to have a functioning .17. But blowback autoloaders aren't quite that easy to convert. Remington has successfully adapted the 597, cataloging a

John Trull, firearms product manager at Remington, examines a polymer-stocked 597 in .17.

six-pound rifle with a ten-inch, button-rifled barrel. Twist rate: 1-in-9. The compact detachable box magazine holds eight rounds. And to be sure you're using ammo from green boxes, Remington began loading its own .17 HMR cartridges. The first rifle manufacturer to join Hornady in this enterprise, Remington chose the same 17-grain polymer-tipped bullet.

My sample 597 functioned without a hitch. The trigger pull ranked above average in the arena of autoloading rimfires—less takeup and less grit. Thank the coated sear, according to Remington. Sure, it has a heavy pull. In a quest to make guns lawsuit-proof, manufacturers have all but disabled them. The 597's crossbolt safety must be "activated" with a special L-shaped screwdriver (supplied) before it can be used. Thereafter the tool is unnecessary and can be shelved unless you have reason to again render the rifle inoperable.

I scoped the test rifle with a 3–9x40 Cabela's in Talley rings fashioned for grooved receivers. The rifle cycled flawlessly and shot accurately. My first three bullets at twenty-five yards went into one hole. The first five-shot group at a hundred yards measured 1¼ inches. The trigger moved this lightweight rifle during letoff; better accuracy may well be possible. This is bolt-gun precision in a compact, affordable rifle with an indestructible stock and fast firepower at your fingertip.

MANUFACTURERS CURRENTLY PRODUCING RIFLES AND PISTOLS IN .17 HMR

J.G. Anschutz Gmbh & Company KG
P.O. Box 1128
D-89001 Ulm, Germany
www.anschuetz-sport.com
Distributed in the U.S. by AcuSport Corporation, One Hunter Place, Bellefontaine, OH 43311; 1-800-543-3150

Cooper Firearms of Montana, Inc.
P.O. Box 114
Stevensville, MT 59870
www.cooperfirearms.com
406-777-0373

H&R1871, LLC
60 Industrial Rowe
Gardner, MA 01440
www.hr1871.com
978-632-9393

Marlin Firearms Company
100 Kenna Drive
P.O. Box 248
North Haven, CT 06473–0905
www.marlinfirearms.com
203-239-5621

Remington Arms
P.O. Box 700
870 Remington Drive
Madison, NC 27025

Rogue Rifle Company, Inc.
1140 36th Street North, Suite B
Lewiston, ID 83501
www.chipmunkrifle.com
208-743-4355

Savage Arms
118 Mountain Road
Suffield, CT 06078
www.savagearms.com
1-800-235-1821

Sturm, Ruger, & Company, Inc.
411 Sunapee Street
Department LK
Newport, NH 03773
www.ruger.com
1-888-317-6887

Thompson/Center Arms Company, Inc.
P.O. Box 5002
Rochester, NH 03867
www.tcarms.com
603-332-2394

Chapter 10

THE SECRET

What delivers the muzzle velocity of a .22 WMR yet makes less noise and shoots flatter? What offers minute-of-angle accuracy at half the price of .17 HMR ammo and weighs less? What could be so closely guarded in development but so universal in its appeal that nine firearms manufacturers signed nondisclosure agreements for an introductory peek?

I didn't know. In fact, the cloak of secrecy lay so heavy that I didn't even have the above clues.

"You'll fly out next Thursday."

"Where?" I asked.

An awkward pause on the line. "We'd rather not say."

I started to tell him that ticketing a flight without a destination would be problematic. "We'll be in touch," he snapped, and rang off.

The airfield of choice came on another call. "Have you made plans for Lincoln?"

I assumed it wasn't a code word. "No."

"Better do that." Nothing at all on who or what lay beyond Baggage Claim.

It costs a lot to fly three days after ticketing, so to make the trip worthwhile, I started phoning people I knew in Nebraska.

"Who contacted you?" Steve Johnson was suspicious.

"Rather not say," I rasped. "Have you made arrangements?"

It was five below zero when the jet touched down, and just as frigid the next morning when I drove to Grand Island. The door was locked. A stern fellow peered critically through the glass, then withdrew the bolt and ushered me down a long hall to a small conference room.

"This is it," said Steve. He slid a sheaf of papers across the table . . .

The company is older than I am. In the 1960s I was awed by men like Joyce Hornady, who had forged an industry from the post-war boom in handloading. Later, I'd seat Spire Point bullets from bright red boxes with a fifteen-dollar Herter press heavy enough to anchor a destroyer. I suffered through the math to understand "secant ogive" in Hornady's loading manual. The company eventually offered tools for handloaders, then got into the ammunition business. It boldly introduced cartridges with modest sales projections: the .450 Marlin, .480 Ruger, .458 Lott. Hornady Light Magnum and Heavy Magnum loads add horsepower to traditional hunting cartridges—under established pressure lids. A 1995 refocusing effort, plus substantial R&D investment, paid off over the next seven years; Hornady's business doubled.

In 2001, the firm introduced the .17 Hornady Magnum Rimfire on a necked-down .22 WMR case. Its 17-grain, .172-diameter, polymer-tipped bullet travels 2,550 fps—600 fps faster than the .22 WMR can drive its blunt 40-grain hollowpoint. Accuracy is outstanding. Even modestly priced sporting rifles have delivered sub-m.o.a. averages for five 5-shot strings at 100 yards. Eight of the first ten rifles I shot in tests gave me averages of less than 1.75 inches. A Savage 93 actually printed a one-hole 0.35-inch cluster at 100 yards.

HMR rifle and ammunition sales remained brisk long after the initial run on ammo depleted stocks below Hornady's capacity to supply bullets. Because hunters found the heavier .22 Magnum bullet more reliable on rockchucks and other sturdy small game, Hornady followed up with a hollowpoint load for shooters seeking more penetration. The 20-grain spitzer mushrooms like a big game bullet.

But this wasn't about the HMR at all. I thumbed through the papers Steve had given me. "Another .17?"

Steve shifted in his seat. "And then some." He handed me a sample cartridge. The tiny bottleneck case was about 0.1 inch longer than that of a .22 Long Rifle. Same as a CCI Stinger, according to Steve: 0.694. At 0.975, cartridge length matched the Long Rifle and Stinger. So it would fit the mechanisms of ordinary .22s. It would function in self-loaders, and shoot flatter than any .22 rimfire ammunition—even the hypervelocity rounds that became popular after the Stinger debuted in 1977. Even the longer .22 WMR.

"It's called the .17 Mach 2," said Wayne Holt, who had just joined us. "Dave Emary designed it, right on the heels of the HMR. But while both rounds came from our lab, we've agreed to leave our name off the final packaging." He added that Eley and ATK (Federal) were also tooling up to load the new round. "The CCI plant will load ours, because it has the necessary plate equipment." All the ammunition, he confirmed, would feature Hornady's 17-grain V-Max bullet, though the 10 million bullets ordered by Eley would be fitted with blue polycarbonate tips. Hornady has patented the Mach 2's design and trademarked the name.

As soon as Hornady informed the industry of its new rimfire, nine U.S. firearms manufacturers lined up to chamber the .17 Mach 2: Marlin, North American Arms, Remington, Ruger, Savage, Smith & Wesson, Taurus, Thompson/Center, and USRAC (the current label for Winchester). Because Browning and USRAC are in the same family, I wasn't surprised to spot a Buckmark pistol in the handful of prototype guns in Hornady's lab. Eley had been in touch with Anschutz and CZ, two European firms well known for accurate rimfire rifles.

"The playing field will broaden when we get ammo in the pipeline," Wayne smiled. "We're not scheduled to ship until September, 2004. We want enough on our docks to provide a steady supply to the retailer, once shooters start buying."

The .17 Mach 2 was still new when this book went to press. In fact, the description here even precedes any mention of the cartridge in

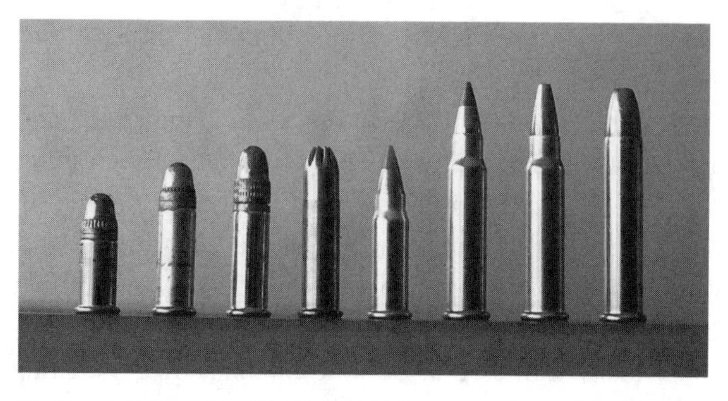

Rimfires left to right: .22 Short, .22 Long, .22 Long Rifle, .22 Shot Cartridge, .17 Mach 2, .17 HMR with V-Max bullet, .17 HMR with hollowpoint bullet, .22 WMR.

gun periodicals. If .17 HMR sales are any indication, Hornady is already up to its elbows in bullets for the Mach 2. "During 2003, our customers bought 146 million rounds of HMR," Wayne told me. "And that's long after the backlog of orders had been filled." The price for .17 magnum ammo has fluctuated wildly, from less than eight dollars per box of fifty to more than eighteen dollars. The suggested retail price for the .17 Mach 2 will be about eight dollars. Shooters should expect to pay five or six dollars a box, half the average price for HMR loads.

Despite its modest cost, tooling up to produce rimfire ammunition is expensive. "We have to bank on huge sales volumes to make the effort," Wayne pointed out. "The .17 HMR was delayed before release because we weren't sure we could quickly sell 5 million rounds. That was the smallest batch of primed cases we could order from CCI. Then we had to buy plates that would load 1,200 cartridges at a time. And, of course, produce 5 million tiny, jacketed, polymer-tipped bullets to very close tolerances. That post-introduction market shortfall of 12 million rounds was almost good news!"

Engineering and production costs are one reason that relatively few smallbore rimfire rounds have followed the .22 Short, by far the oldest rimfire still made. A review might be helpful:

Steve Johnson fires a T/C Contender G2 rifle, one of the prototype guns used in developing the .17 Mach 2.

Introduced in 1857 by Horace Smith and Daniel Wesson for their First Model revolver, the Short was then loaded with a 29-grain bullet and 4 grains of black powder. In 1871 the .22 Long appeared, with the same bullet but 5 grains of powder in a longer case. The .22 Long Rifle came sixteen years later, a product of the J. Stevens Arms and Tool Company. It featured a 40-grain bullet atop 5 grains of powder, in the Long's hull. Smokeless powder soon showed the superiority of the Long Rifle cartridge. While many rifles and pistols chambered for the Long Rifle will feed Shorts and Longs, the .22 Long Rifle is now the best seller by a wide margin.

Other rimfire rounds dating to blackpowder days have fared less well. The .22 BB Cap (Bulleted Breech) appeared in 1845 for the Flobert parlor rifle. Initially, this round held only a priming charge and a .22-caliber ball, but U.S. makers later added a pinch of powder and a conical bullet. The BB Cap lived long in relative obscurity, disappearing after World War II. The .22 CB Cap (Conical Bullet) is more potent. An original charge of 1.5 grains of blackpowder was replaced by smokeless in 1920. CCI still sells CB Caps with 29-grain bullets in Short cases. Velocity: 727 fps.

The .22 Extra Long showed up in 1880, with a 40-grain bullet and 6 grains of black powder in a case 0.750 inch long (compared to the 0.595 Long case). It survived with smokeless loadings until 1935.

The .22 WRF (Winchester Rimfire) was more popular. Introduced in 1890 for the Winchester pump rifle of that year, it came with 45-grain flat-nose solids or 40-grain hollowpoint loads in standard and high-speed versions. Remington offered a round-nose bullet and called the cartridge the .22 Remington Special. Like the later .22 WMR, the WRF features a .224 bullet whose shank is gripped by the case. Consequently, the case is larger in diameter than the hulls of the Short, Long, and Long Rifle, whose outside-lubricated bullets are case-diameter at midsection and gripped only at the heel. At 1,450 fps, the high-speed hollowpoint load had a significant edge on the .22 Long Rifle hollowpoints of its day.

No rifles in .22 WRF have been made for decades, though Winchester recently cataloged the cartridges again for owners of vintage rifles. Revival is unlikely for the .22 Winchester Automatic and .22 Remington Automatic, developed for specific rifles shortly after the turn of the last century. They both fired 45-grain bullets at around 1,000 fps.

The most powerful .22 rimfire appeared in 1959. Initially offered in Ruger and Smith & Wesson revolvers, the .22 Winchester Magnum Rimfire launched 40-grain bullets at 1,550 fps. In short order, rifles became available, boosting velocity to a listed 1,910 fps. The 1.05-inch case is the longest of any .22 rimfire. A jacketed bullet gripped at the shank also requires the hull to be larger in diameter than that of a .22 Long Rifle.

In 1970, Remington tried to upstage the .22 WMR with a 5mm (.20-caliber) rimfire. The case was almost as long; 38-grain hollowpoints sped downrange at 2,100 fps. But the 5mm Remington never caught on and is no longer loaded. The .17 Aguila, a Long Rifle–length rimfire that kicks a 20-grain .177 bullet out at 1,850 fps, is the only round close in design to the Mach 2. Not yet chambered in production rifles, it's gaining a following after a failed attempt several years ago.

Prior to the .17 HMR, the most successful high-performance rimfires have been those Long Rifle–length cartridges loaded with lightweight bullets (32 to 36 grains) reaching velocities of 1,400 to 1,650 fps.

But that's not even close to 2,100 fps. And the hyperspeed .22s still arc like rainbows to distant targets. In comparison, the .17 Mach 2 is a laser. And lest you think a superlight bullet won't "carry" at long range, here's a chart with Hornady's lab data:

cartridge	muzzle	50 yds	100 yds	150 yds	200 yds
.17 HMR (17-gr. V-Max)					
speed (fps)	2,550	2,212	1,902	1,621	1,380
energy (ft-lbs)	245	185	136	99	72
arc (inches)	−1.3	0.1	0.0	−2.6	−8.0
.17 Mach 2 (17-gr. V-Max)					
speed (fps)	2,100	1,799	1,530	1,304	1,134
energy (ft-lbs)	166	122	88	64	49
arc (inches)	−1.3	0.7	0.0	−4.4	−14.0
.22 WMR (40-gr. solid)					
speed (fps)	1,910	1,600	1,330	1,140	-
energy (ft-lbs)	324	225	155	115	-
arc (inches)	−1.3	.07	0.0	−5.2	-
.22 LR HV (40-gr. solid)					
speed (fps)	1,260	1,100	1,020	940	-
energy (ft-lbs)	140	110	90	80	-
arc (inches)	−1.3	2.7	0.0	−10.8	-

OK, so the .17s shoot flat. What about wind drift? Those minuscule bullets look as if they'd yield to the prop wash from a hummingbird. Well, not quite. The math shows that a 10-mph wind blows a Mach 2 bullet about 4½ inches off course at 100 yards—an inch *less* than the same breeze moves a high-speed .22 Long Rifle solid that's nearly twice as heavy. On lazy June days, the .17 Mach 2 delivers prairie dog precision to 150 yards. At that distance, you'll be testing your shooting ability, no matter what the conditions. I'll have fun snaking the tiny V-Max spitzers through wind to paper targets far away,

Minute-of-angle accuracy from carbines like this Marlin 795 would make anyone smile. Dave Emary, who developed the .17 Mach 2, is very pleased with the results.

but I'll keep my shots at game close enough to ensure center hits and 90 ft-lbs. of energy. It seems the humane thing to do.

"Help yourself," Steve said as he brought out a handful of prototype rifles barreled to .17 Mach 2.

Shooting in a 100-yard tunnel when the prairie wind outside is driving the chill factor to 13 degrees below zero is more fun than should be legal. The only drawback: Errant shots can't be blamed on conditions. I'd have preferred to drill my first groups with an Anschutz or Cooper rifle, the most accurate in my tests with the .17 HMR. Alas, the only .17 Mach 2 rifles available were a Marlin 795 autoloading carbine and two T/C

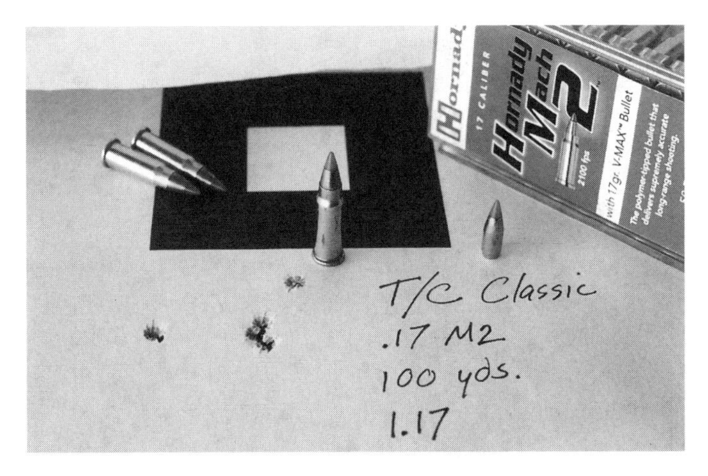

Even autoloaders shoot the .17 Mach 2 well. Thompson/Center's Classic fed it flawlessly and put all five of these bullets inside 1.25 inches.

rifles: a classic autoloader and a G2. The Marlin had an 18-inch barrel and, incongruously, a Leupold Vari-X III 3.5–10x40 scope. The T/C rifles, with 22- and 23-inch barrels respectively, wore 2.5–7x sights bearing T/C labels. Triggers had an off-the-shelf feel, to put it charitably.

I shouldn't have fretted. While good shot execution took all the concentration and muscle control I could muster, the resulting groups brought a grin. I hadn't expected a sub-minute five-shot group from the Contender, or one that miked 1.17 from the T/C autoloader. It's been a long time since I've shot into 1.06 at 100 yards with any rimfire autoloader, let alone an inexpensive carbine like the Marlin. Matching those groups with a .22 would be a real challenge. Few sporting guns would make the grade, and then only if you fed them competition-quality ammo.

I also fired a Browning Buckmark pistol chambered for the .17 Mach 2, convinced that its stiff ten-inch barrel would perform. But my hand couldn't provide the consistent support needed for tight groups.

Incidentally, rifling twist for the .17 Mach 2 is 1–9, same as for the HMR. "That's in rifles," said Dave Emary. "Because short barrels trim velocity, a sharper twist, say 1–7½, works better in pistols."

Marlin's 795 autoloading carbine liked the Mach 2. The author fired this tight group at 100 yards.

What about terminal performance? The beauty of a ballistics lab is that great slabs of gelatin lie all about, quivering with anticipation. We propped one up twenty-five yards from the G2's muzzle. At the shot, the gelatin barely shook. The wound channel was nine inches long, the expansion cavity beginning at the one-inch mark. About the size and shape of a lemon, it ended just beyond three inches. From there, a thin tunnel led to the remainder of core and jacket. Hairline streaks radiating from the tunnel showed the tracks of jacket fragments. The core-jacket lump at the end of the channel weighed 9.5 grains. All the bullet fragments that could be handily extracted amounted to 12.9 grains.

"Rarely, we get more," said Steve. "If a bullet tumbles, to travel heel-first, there's less break-up."

While Hornady is very content with the Mach 2's V-Max bullet, it is not—as of this writing—committed to a powder charge. "We still have to tune the time-pressure curve so the ammo functions in autoloaders," Dave Emary told me. "Early loads moved the breechblock on some rifles before pressure had dropped, so we got a few bulged cases. It's not a problem, just a matter of finding the right propellant."

The 17-grain .172-diameter V-Max bullet exits a .17 Mach 2 rifle at 2,100 fps. It opens violently in ballistic gelatin, leaving only fragments in the channel.

He explained that there are about as many rimfire powders as centerfire powders. Small differences in burning rate can make a big difference in small, thin hulls and rifles operating on blow-back. "We'll stay with ball powders from St. Marks," he said.

Like the .17 HMR, the Mach 2 is a hunting cartridge, ideal for fox and gray squirrels, prairie dogs, cottontails, and jackrabbits, even some furbearers. The bullet's tendency to disintegrate should make it a favorite of trappers for dispatching animals with valuable pelts.

It's unlikely the .17 Mach 2 will unseat the .22 Long Rifle as the top-selling rimfire round. A 115-year dynasty in the ammunition field is exceedingly rare. But compared to the various rimfires that have appeared since 1887, the Mach 2 certainly earns top marks. Accurate, flat-shooting, effective on game all out of proportion to its size, and almost without recoil, it is adaptable to virtually every rifle and handgun chambered for Long Rifle ammunition. You might not share my view that this is one of the most significant cartridges since short belted magnums appeared in the 1950s, but we'll all hear a lot more about it before we can decide who's right.

Part 3

The Makers

Chapter 11

BROWNING GENESIS

While John Browning has earned his share of plaudits as America's most prolific gun designer, he didn't come by them easily. His roots show more adversity than privilege. John's father, Jonathan, was born to Edmund and Sarah Browning near Brushy Fork in Sumner County, Tennessee, where the newlyweds established a farm in the late 1700s. It was a harsh time: eighty-three local settlers were killed by Indians between 1787 and 1793.

None of the Browning children had a formal education. Still, they were encouraged to learn. Jonathan showed an early interest in guns, and at the age of thirteen he accepted a broken flintlock rifle as payment for work on a neighboring farm. A nearby blacksmith helped Jonathan fix the gun in exchange for help at the smithy. When the rifle was put right again, Jonathan sold it for four dollars—to its original owner! Then he continued to work for the blacksmith.

By the time he was thirty-five, Jonathan had invented a "slide rifle" with a rectangular bar that moved side to side through a slot in the frame. The bar had chamber cavities (usually five); a thumb lever advanced it to line up a new chamber cavity after the charge in an adjacent cavity had been fired. The hammer swung up from underneath. Had cartridge firearms not appeared soon after, Jonathan Browning's reliable slide gun would no doubt have become more popular.

In 1842 Jonathan and his family set up shop in Nauvoo, Illinois. He joined the Mormon faith and, at the direction of Brigham Young,

Current Browning .22s—lever-action and autoloader—derive from the genius of John Browning.

stayed behind when the westward migration began, to supply Young's pioneers with slide rifles. On July 24, 1847, the Mormons, thinned by time and hardship to 143 people, reached Salt Lake City. Five years later Jonathan Browning and family settled in nearby Ogden.

In 1862 Jonathan built a tannery. John Moses Browning, one of Jonathan's twenty-two children, was then seven years old and capable of riding the harnessed horse that plodded in a circle to operate the machinery. It was no place for a youngster with an active mind. John often fell asleep, and would then fall off. His mother rescued him by insisting he attend school. John went to school until he was fifteen, at which point the schoolmaster told him. "No sense coming back. You know as much as I do."

John was only ten when he built his first gun, a flintlock made from a scrapped musket barrel and a board he shaped with a hatchet. He fashioned a crude metal pan and screwed it to the board, stuffed the barrel with a heavy charge of powder and rough shot, and then heated a small batch of coke on the forge. He scooped the coke into a perforated can and called to his younger brother Matt: "Let's go huntin'!"

John's gun had no lock. The coke provided fire, but to keep it burning the youngsters had to keep pumping air to it. Matt traipsed behind John, swinging the perforated can on a long string. When at last they found some dusting prairie chickens, John aimed and Matt lit a long splinter, then inserted it through the touch-hole. The charge went off with a roar, and John found himself on the ground under a cloud of smoke.

In 1878 John turned twenty-three. With no drafting tools, he sketched a single-shot cartridge rifle. With no milling machine, he hand-forged the parts, then trimmed them with file and chisel. A foot-lathe his father had brought by oxcart from Missouri helped finish the gun, whose massive parts and simple construction suited it perfectly to the frontier. John filed for his first patent May 12, 1879. Shortly thereafter his father died. Now John needed to build and sell guns to support two households. Matt's help with gun repair freed John to do some drafting. They were eventually joined by brothers Ed, Sam, and George.

In 1883 Winchester salesman Andrew McAusland came across a used Browning single-shot rifle and delivered it to Winchester president Thomas G. Bennett. Bennett had never heard of John Browning, but the design and construction of this gun impressed him, and the serial number (463) told him he needed to know more. At that time Winchester had a stranglehold on the lever-rifle market, but lever-actions wouldn't handle the popular .45-70 cartridge. This rifle would. If John Browning sold his single-shot to Winchester, reasoned Bennett, Winchester would lose a competitor and fill a big gap in its product line.

Bennett lost no time in traveling to Ogden to see what was billed as the biggest gun store between Omaha and the Pacific. He found half a dozen young men, barely out of their teens, bustling about in a shop smaller than a livery. But Bennett was no fool. He met with John Browning and came straight to the point: "How much will you take for your rifle?" One rifle? No, the rifle. All rights.

"Ten thousand dollars," said John coolly, as if bartering over moccasins. It was an enormous sum.

"Eight thousand, plus jobbing grants." Browning agreed. Bennett then wrote a check for one thousand dollars, promising the rest later.

This elegant custom rifle was built on the Browning dropping-block action design, circa 1883.

Each man signed a short note of obligation. Less than six hours after he'd arrived in Ogden, Bennett was on a train for the six-day ride back to New Haven.

Thomas Bennett recognized John's genius and immediately engaged him for other work. During their twenty-year association, Winchester bought forty-four of John Browning's patents, apparently for his asking price but with no royalties. Ten were manufactured as Winchester guns. Bennett, who was Oliver Winchester's son-in-law, paid willingly for designs he couldn't use, just to keep them from the hands of competitors.

Typically, John would deliver new prototypes on his infrequent trips to New Haven, opening the brown paper wrap with a flourish and explaining each gun to eager salesmen. One early hit was the Model 1890 .22 pump rifle, which John proposed by mailing sketches to Winchester engineers. Nobody at the company liked the idea. John built the gun anyway, shipping it to New Haven with a note: "You said it wouldn't work, but it seems to shoot pretty fair for me." It was the first of several popular rimfire designs to originate from Ogden and sell from New Haven.

When John Browning built rifles, .22 rimfires were typically very trim, like this falling-block.

About this time, Bennett asked Browning for a lever-action gun to replace the Model 1873. He wanted something like the Model 1886 but smaller, for short cartridges.

"If you can get a prototype to me in three months, it's worth ten thousand dollars," said Bennett. "Make it two months and I'll give you fifteen thousand."

John Browning sat silently for a couple of minutes. Then, looking Bennett in the eye, he replied, "The price is twenty thousand if I can deliver it in thirty days. If I'm late, you get it free."

Incredulous, Bennett agreed. Within two weeks John and his brothers had built a prototype for what would become the Winchester Model 92. It arrived in New Haven before deadline, and John got a check for twenty grand.

Successful lever- and slide-action designs left John an itch for a tougher assignment. He allegedly found it at a local shooting match, where the grass in front of a prone marksman was flattened by muzzle blast. Why not harness that energy? thought John. At home he strapped a '73 Winchester to a board, then placed a wooden block a quarter inch from the muzzle. The block's center was drilled out to allow passage of the bullet, so any movement of the block had to come from escaping powder gas.

At the shot, the block flew violently into the shop wall.

By 1900 John Browning was working on a recoil-driven gun. In both ensuing World Wars, and in Korea, every U.S. machine gun—land, sea, and air—would be of Browning design.

Three of every four guns carried by American sportsmen in the days before World War I were Brownings, manufactured and marketed under the Winchester label. John's last contribution to New Haven came as a result of Thomas Bennett's request for an inexpensive rifle to compete with the Belgian Flobert. John had already designed five guns like that. He sent all of them to Bennett, who purchased the lot and put the latest in Winchester's catalog as the Model 1900, a four-pound bolt-action that listed for five dollars and promptly buried the Flobert. Winchester eventually sold nearly 1.5 million copies of the Model 1900.

Ironically, the close relationship between Winchester's president and John Browning would be destroyed by one gun so good that when Browning offered it, Bennett said no. Sharp but conservative, Bennett had seen Winchester prosper as John filled holes in its line. Browning, brilliant but independent, thrived on new frontiers. The clash came over a shotgun completed as a prototype in March 1899.

Bennett was in no hurry to accept John's revolutionary new gun. For one thing, John was asking for royalties in addition to a fat fee up front, not a single cash payment as had been the custom. Secondly, the autoloading design was an unproven departure from traditional thinking. Even if it worked as John said, would American shooters buy it? The gun, costly to build, would have to be priced high. Also, if this autoloader did succeed, it would put the skids under the popular '97.

John said later: "I'll bet Bennett would have given a hundred thousand dollars to have been rid of that gun. He and Winchester were doing just fine with levers and pumps. But if he didn't buy it, he knew I'd take the design to a competitor." He did just that, traveling with

The autoloading shotgun John Browning offered to Winchester caused a rift in their long and productive relationship.

Matt to Ilion, New York. On January 8, 1902, as they waited at Remington, company president Marcellus Hartley died of a heart attack. Reluctantly, the brothers booked passage to Belgium, where they got a warm welcome at Fabrique Nationale de Guerre (FN).

FN agreed to build the self-loading shotgun, and John stayed there three months to oversee start-up. By autumn of 1903, a shipment of ten thousand guns was on its way to Schoverling, Daly, and Gales in New York. Even John Browning must have been surprised when the entire lot sold within a year.

After John's death in 1926, FN continued producing Auto-5 and Superposed shotguns, adding autoloading pistols, rimfire rifles, and bolt-action centerfire rifles. In the early 1970s inflation put Superposed shotguns beyond the reach of most people, so Miroku Firearms Manufacturing Company of Tokyo started making Browning's alternative shotgun, the Citori. When FN retooled, Browning moved the manufacture of all but the Superposed, a 9mm pistol, and parts for its BAR sporting rifle to Japan. Bolt rifles built on Mauser and Sako actions were replaced by the Japanese BBR, which later became the A-bolt. Browning subsequently introduced two pistols built in Utah.

A modern rendition of the Browning 1885 "Low Wall," this rifle is bored to .22 Hornet.

The Browning .22 Automatic rifle, with bottom ejection and tube magazine in the buttstock, was to the Remington 241 (introduced in 1935) what the Auto-5 shotgun was to the Remington Model 11. FN built Browning's self-loading .22s from 1965 to 1972, when Miroku

This Browning .22 pistol comes late in a long line of handguns that includes the 1911 government-issue .45.

took over production. The Browning BAR-22, with a traditional under-barrel magazine and side ejection, came along in 1977, remaining in the line for nine years. Longer lived is the BL-22, a lever-action announced in 1970 and still available. The Browning T-Bolt, an ingenious and nicely configured straight-pull bolt rifle, arrived in 1966 and was made by FN until 1974. A short run of these rifles appeared during the late 1980s. Currently, Browning fields an array of autoloading Buckmark .22 pistols and a rifle based on that mechanism.

Fabrique Nationale bought Browning in 1977, but left Browning headquarters in Morgan, Utah (actually, just outside a town called Mountain Green). Other corporate repositionings followed. Now the company that owns Browning also has U.S. Repeating Arms, maker of Winchester rifles. So John Browning and Winchester's Thomas Bennett did indeed share a common destiny.

Chapter 12

COOPER—AN ORIGINAL

He's a rifle enthusiast. You can tell that right away. Dan Cooper talks guns with a fluid ease; matter-of-fact, but with enough energy to show you he's still interested. Dan won't brook boredom. If he didn't get a charge out of building fine rifles, he probably wouldn't.

"I've explored other options," he says, leaning back in an ordinary, cluttered office under a not-so-ordinary mule deer mount. "It's a Montana deer," he digresses, reading my mind. Then he bounces right back to where he'd been. "I studied at Purdue, then went west to Lewis and Clark College out of Portland. Thought I wanted to work in foreign affairs. Law agreed with me for awhile, but I got my fill fast," he says, grinning. "Entrepreneurs don't do law. I left school and mowed lawns and started walking. From Mexico to the Bering Strait. That took longer than I thought it would."

For a couple of years, 1980 and '81, Dan and a friend hiked the spine of North America, south to north. He ended up in Deese Lake, British Columbia, where he built cabins until work ran out. "I came back to Oregon and landed a job at Kimber after mowing Jack Warne's lawn. I couldn't do much physically because I'd hurt myself logging. Jack put me to work as an inspector. In '83 I went back to Canada to finish the walk. That northernmost section was tough: bad weather, no trails, rugged terrain, little access to civilization. And bears. But in 1985 I got to the Strait. It's not a good idea to let things go unfinished."

That philosophy probably impressed people at the Institute of Arctic Biology. He worked for them at a remote University of Alaska field station until 1988. "I got back on with Kimber, to shepherd the Government .22 project and the All-American Match target rifle. The shop had moved to Clackamas by then." But the firm soon floundered. The big game rifle—Model 89—sucked money. When Kimber changed hands, many people were laid off. Dan went to work as a delivery boy for a construction company.

"See?" he laughs. "Always upwardly mobile. I could have had a law office."

But he was not long idle. He and Linda Williams, Rita Eller, Jeff Lufbourough, and Steve Little joined forces to "do what Kimber should have done." Dan sold his 1949 Lincoln and Honda motorcycle to come up with a legitimate set of drawings for a new rifle action. "That was in 1990. We went on the road, looking for a spot with some economic development money. We incorporated in Mollala, Oregon, late that year; then I drove to South Dakota to visit Tom Houghton at H-S Precision. He had a great shop. But he also had a lot more money than I did."

On the way back, Dan slept under his truck near Helena, Montana, where a friend, who happened to be the state's assistant Attorney General, pointed him to the Department of Economic Development. "I brought my partners out, and they liked Montana too."

They decided to move Cooper Arms to Stevensville, in Montana's Bitterroot Valley. "The first Cooper rifle was assembled in a garage near Bell Crossing south of town. The action design borrowed heavily from the work of my favorite gunmakers: P. O. Ackley, Len Brownell, Pete Grisel, Darwin Hensley. And yes, the Warne Kimbers left their mark."

During the next four years, Cooper Arms would move to four new locations in the valley. In 1994 Dan and his partners bought the place just north of Stevensville that's still headquarters. "It's almost like home now," he deadpans. "I've slept here so much."

The 7,000-square-foot plant houses woodworking, metalsmithing, and assembly cells, and Dan's office. "We employ twenty-two people and ship around two hundred rifles in a good month. We still use the old Bridgeport mill that we started with. But we've made the rifles better. We even turn a profit once in a while."

Cooper's first rifles were Model 36s—single-shot, three-lug rimfire target guns similar to the Kimbers that Dan had helped develop. "The 36 cost two thousand dollars to build and sold for six hundred. We made seventy-five or so before we figured out that it's best to cover your costs. We were pretty naïve."

Ever looking for ways to promote his rifles, Dan decided to present one of the first 36s to the governor. "We had Stan Stevens ready to

The elegant Cooper (right) is a full-size rifle, dwarfing the Chipmunk.

accept the gun at a ceremony at the capitol," Dan recalls. "But I had to get it in the building first. I asked my friends at the Department of Economic Development if anyone would mind me toting a rifle up the capitol steps. 'No problem,' they said. 'This is Montana.' Well, by the time I got to the door I was in cuffs, a policeman on each arm."

Cooper Arms used up parts from the Model 36 on silhouette rifles that "shot great." Then Dan concocted an American version of the .22 Velo-Dog loaded by Fiocchi. "We called it the Cooper Centerfire Magnum. The .22 was followed by a .17. They both used small-rifle primers. Cute cartridges, and much more accurate than a .22 WMR. We contracted for brass in-state at first, then went to Utah, then to Fiocchi." Worth the trouble? Dan smiles—probably the way he smiled when someone first asked him if walking the Continental Divide was worth the trouble.

The CCM cartridges were indeed interesting rounds. Operating at between 45,000 and 50,000 psi, the .17 (engineered by Mike Hill) would drive a 20-grain bullet at 3,600 fps. The rifle became known as the Cooper Model 38. Cooper's enterprise would grow as new models, rimfire and centerfire, were added. In 1991, at age thirty-seven, Dan married. "Diane is another reason I've settled down a bit," he says. "She and my two stepsons."

In my tour of the plant, I learn that Cooper uses mostly Claro in its elegant stocks. "Double X and Triple X fancy," explains Lenny Standish, who adds that the company also stocks rifles in English and French walnut, myrtle, maple, and other woods on order. "We checker the wood 22 lines per inch for the high-grade guns, 18 or 20 on standard-grade versions. We use an oil-based final finish, for that warm, classic look."

Cooper's general manager, Dan Pickett, takes me to the metal shop, where Wilson hand-lapped, button-rifled barrels are mated to Cooper receivers. "We use CNCs for most of our primary milling operations," he says. "But a lot of final work is still done with old-fashioned equipment." Matte-finished steel gets bead blasted with 220-grit and then 400-grit abrasive. For a shinier product, the shop winds up with 500-grit.

Randy Craft, who started with Cooper at age nineteen as the firm's fourth employee, is busy hand-stoning the extraction surface on a

Rifle blanks being laid out at the Cooper factory in Montana.

bolt. "We like to think we build rifles by hand," he laughs. "And honestly, that's almost true." Randy is not only a machinist but one of the design team here. Some of his ideas have proven real winners.

"Early on," says Dan Cooper, back in his office, "Randy and my nephew Jason tried to convince me they could sell an accurate .223 single-shot. I told them they were full of prunes. Heck, they were both just out of high school!" But Dan humored them. "If you can put one together, I'll try to dredge up some interest. That's what I told 'em. Then one afternoon they came back from the range with a target that had three shots in one hole, dead center. I sent one to Ronan Sport, a retail shop up the road. The proprietor phoned me and said to send five a week until he told me to stop."

Cooper Arms formally introduced itself to the industry at the 1994 SHOT Show. Dan had made a new Model 21 .223 Varmint Extreme for Bob Milek. Sadly, Milek died before he could take delivery. The rifle went to Bob Petersen, of Petersen Publishing. The 21 became Cooper's top seller, surpassed only in 2001 by the Model 57, a rimfire repeater stout enough to handle the .22 Hornet as well. I bought one the first year they were available in .17 HMR. The sporter-weight rifle averaged 0.9 inch for five 5-shot groups at a hundred yards. Its classic stock, beautifully sculpted, finished, and fitted to the metal, makes this rifle a standout even when it's not tossing bullets downrange.

A Model 22, trotted out in 1994, accommodated cartridges based on the .22-250 and .308.

Asked how the business is running, Dan chuckles. "I don't hear much from my employees. They're here because they like to make guns. If they have a problem, they solve it. I'm lucky to have a crew as concerned about turning out high-quality rifles as I am." He tells me that "good help is what makes Cooper Arms a success."

Despite its modest size and rural setting, Cooper Arms can turn out fine work in short order. "We can machine a receiver in thirty minutes, complete a rifle in a week," Dan says. "In October 1992, we had a chance to build a special rifle for President Bush—if it could be ready in three days. Hoo boy! But we went to work. I had to borrow a stock from a friend. I drove all night to make the presentation in Billings. The President gave me a ride to the airport and said the cartridge—a .17 CCM—was just what he needed for turkeys on his Texas ranch. He called us later to thank us for the rifle, then sent it back so we could mount a scope and package up some handloaded ammo." But the job wasn't quite done. One Sunday evening, long after the scoped rifle and ammunition had been shipped, the phone rang. It was President Bush. "He wanted me to send more cartridges. White House Marines had evidently shot up the five hundred rounds I'd delivered."

Dan Cooper's rifles are still in demand, not only by dignitaries who like to shoot, but by ordinary riflemen who demand exceptional accuracy. The Cooper guarantees seem almost unreasonable: 0.25-inch five-shot groups at fifty yards for rimfire rifles, 0.5-inch five-shot groups at one hundred yards for centerfires. "Nobody else I know makes those claims for off-the-shelf rifles," says Dan. "Then again, we Montanans can be fussy. A rifle's not finished until it's shooting well. And we do like to finish what we start."

Chapter 13

COMEBACK AT KIMBER

Among the most highly regarded .22s currently produced is the Kimber 22. The Kimber company got its start in Australia, where founder Jack Warne was born in a place called Kimba-Abo (meaning bush fire). Jack's Aussie company was once CCI's largest customer, buying .22 blanks for nail guns. Joining CCI, Jack quickly ascended the corporate ladder and helped organize what became the Blount Group, with RCBS and other companies. After retirement, Jack became restless and formed Kimber with son Greg. They patterned their new .22 rifle after a bolt-action Winchester. According to Jack, the Winchester's magazine was the starting point, because designing a reliable, easy-loading rimfire magazine is surprisingly difficult.

"What became the Model 82 was first presented to the industry on a VIP rockchuck hunt near the Speer/CCI plant at Lewiston, Idaho," says current Kimber marketing chief Dwight Van Brunt. "Legend has it that Jim Carmichael and Arlen Chaney and Jack Slack examined a prototype 82 during a noon break. All agreed that the metal looked good. None liked the wood, because the quality of material and workmanship had been set by a target retail price. Carmichael spoke his mind and said that the world didn't need another cheap .22. It needed, instead, a replacement for the lovely Winchester 52 Sporter, then twenty years defunct."

Dwight Van Brunt, Kimber's vice president of marketing, checks a target before a prairie dog shoot.

Jack Warne enlisted the help of crack stockmaker Len Brownell. The resulting design was much more appealing, though slightly European in profile. Duane Wiebe refined the shape. Conservative and classic, the Model 82 got a tepid response at its first SHOT Show. But orders soon followed. By the time Greg (previously an accountant for Black & Decker) had moved to Kimber's front office, both collectors and shooters were snapping up the sleek .22s.

Nearly as petite was a rifle designed for the .17s, .222, and .223: the Model 84. The first of them came with a .400 or better test target looped through the trigger guard. The subsequent Kimber 89 BGR (Big Game Rifle) looked like a Winchester M70 and chambered standard hunting rounds like the .30-06. In those days (the 1980s) Dan Cooper, who later founded Cooper Arms, ramrodded Kimber sales. Talented Oregon gunmaker Darwin Hensley worked for awhile at Kimber, then Butch Weyand ran the stock shop.

Kimber's fortunes faded during the 1980s. The Model 89 didn't live up to expectations, and the Warnes were forced to sell controlling interest in the company to a wealthy Oregon lumberman. Concerns over the spotted owl were then beginning to affect logging operations. Suddenly, the new owner ran into financial troubles. In 1989 Chapter 7 proceedings left Jack and Greg Warne with use of the Kimber name.

Greg gathered up the machinery and, three years later, staged a comeback, even leasing the same space in Clackamas for headquarters. Shortly, 82B rifles (there was no 82A) were being boxed and shipped.

Enter Les Edelman, then president of a huge sporting goods wholesaling firm. Les had not only the marketing infrastructure to sell Kimbers, he had vision. Eventually he bought controlling interest in Kimber, augmenting its manufacture of rifles with the importation and sale of Daewoo firearms. There was also an assembly line to "sporterize" surplus M96 and M98 Mauser rifles. Les speculated on the flourishing demand for handguns with a new, high-quality pistol after the 1911 Colt design and followed up at the 1995 SHOT Show with a prototype.

World speed-shooting champion Chip McCormick arrived to explain to doubtful listeners the myriad advantages of this new pistol. It had the attributes of custom 1911s at a much lower price. Lukewarm response from dealers didn't deter Les, who bought a factory in

Steve Cox bears down with a short-barreled Kimber 22 SVT (Short Varmint Target).

Tom Gresham examines a Kimber 22, built along classic lines with carefully checkered walnut.

Yonkers, New York, projecting a run of five thousand pistols. His projection proved conservative; now Kimber makes 44,000 Model 1911-style pistols annually. Initial demand was so strong that many handguns sold for more than the $550 retail price.

In 1998, Les and his sales team—rifle enthusiasts Dwight Van Brunt and Ryan Busse—got back into the rifle business with a rimfire designed by Nehemiah Sirkis. They called it the Kimber 22. About then, a new Model 770 centerfire rifle came together in Kimber's shop. Designed by Jack Warne and Pete Grisel, the 770 died in prototype stage.

It was followed by the 84M, proportioned for .308-class cartridges. While the 84M continues to evolve, so does the Kimber 22. It has a full-length Mauser extractor for controlled-round feeding, and an eccentric receiver, whereby the barrel is offset so the bolt itself can function as does the firing mechanism of a centerfire. The striker is shorter and more tightly fitted than that in most rimfire rifles, and travels a shorter distance. Improvements in stock design and finish followed.

The Kimber 22 is really the first Kimber assembled with all in-house parts, and it's still boxed with a .400 group.

"The driving philosophy behind Kimber rifles and pistols is custom quality at an affordable price," says Dwight Van Brunt. "We ensure quality by doing virtually all the work ourselves, and we hold costs down with direct-to-dealer distribution. There's no wholesaler or rep commission to pass on to customers."

Variations of the Kimber 22 include a short, heavy-barreled rifle I find ideal for rimfire silhouette shooting and an elegant sporting rifle with select walnut. Kimber's vibrant health may be due largely to its pistol sales, but the company is obviously re-committing to its original mission of building a .22 sporter to rival the Winchester 52. Some shooters would say the Kimber is the better rifle.

Chapter 14

MARLIN AND ITS MARVELOUS 39

Some rifles just seem right. Somehow the proportions of wood and steel, the marriage of profile and function, are perfect. Not even the men who design such rifles could tell you why they came out the way they did, why a product engineered to make money becomes instead an icon. They'd be at a loss to explain the happy accident in the bowels of a sooty factory with no artistic purpose.

If a rifle with siren-like good looks proves reliable and accurate, and feels right to the ill-proportioned masses hoisting it at hardware stores, you can bet it will last awhile. Give it a few decades in catalogs, and it can carry a company.

There aren't many such rifles. Among centerfires, Winchester Models 94 and 70 come to mind—and they've changed enough over the years that early versions command a hefty premium on the used market. Marlin's 336 has been around as long as the Winchester 70, and has changed less. It gets my vote. So do a couple of rifles that didn't make it through the twentieth century: Savage's spool-fed Model 99 and the Mannlicher-Schoenauer carbine.

Only one rimfire rifle has the looks, lift, and longevity to earn the plaudits given our best-known big game guns. It's the Marlin 39. And no other rimfire even comes close.

In production since 1922, when it replaced the Model 97, the Marlin 39 has the longest run of any .22 rifle still being made. And

The Marlin 39 is a superb .22 rimfire.

it's still as fetching to the eye and hand as when the first one left the factory.

John Mahlon Marlin didn't set out to build a legendary rifle. At eighteen, he just wanted to be a good machinist. That was in 1853, when, as an apprentice, he agreed to work for no wages for six months. His pay, when he finally did get it, came at a rate of $1.50—per week. A year later, he'd earned a raise to $2.50.

During the 1860s, John fashioned small pistols. Then he built Ballard rifles. They sold better than an under-hammer lever-action repeating rifle he designed, which was prone to feeding failures.

John's first successful lever-action was a side-loading, top-ejecting rifle incorporating ideas from H. F. Wheeler, Andrew Burgess, and E. A. F. Toepperwein. Introduced in 1881, but not named the Model 1881 until seven years later, the rifle featured a twenty-eight-inch octagon barrel in .45-70 or .40-60. It cost thirty-two bucks, if you didn't want the set trigger. A lightweight version with twenty-four-inch barrel and slimmed receiver came later. It weighed 8½ pounds, two pounds less than the original. New chamberings included the .32-40, .38-55, and .45-85 Marlin. Late models were drilled for folding tang sights. Hailed by some as the first successful big-bore lever-action repeater, the 1881 had a couple of weaknesses. One was top ejection, eliminated on the Marlin 1889 rifle. The other was a flawed carrier that often produced jams at the rear of the magazine. A more reliable split carrier appeared in rifles after 1884.

In 1888, John Marlin began offering a Hepburn-designed lever gun chambered for the short-action .32-20, .38-40, and .44-40. A side-loading, top-ejecting rifle, it weighed just 6½ pounds with 24-inch barrel and retailed for $19.50. For a dollar a barrel inch, you could get a 26- or 28-inch barrel. Rifles with the longest magazines held sixteen cartridges.

L. L. Hepburn's next effort would establish Marlin as a major armsmaker. The Model 1889 came out in September of that year. Like the 1888, it fired .32-20, .38-40, and .44-40 cartridges and locked with a square bolt sliding up vertical rails in the frame. But it had a solid

The Marlin 882 is a rimfire workhorse, ideal for the cab rack of a pickup.

receiver top. Even with iron sights, side ejection made sense: you didn't have cases flying through your line of sight. The 1889, available with 15- to 30-inch barrels, listed for eighteen dollars. Select walnut added six dollars to the price, checkering twelve dollars. A rear catch held the lever tight to the grip during carry. This lever lock was eliminated on subsequent rifles.

Marlin's first rimfire was, by most accounts, the company's fourth rifle. Like its predecessors, the 1891 was a lever-action designed by L. L. Hepburn. Its bolt locked in the manner of the Model 1888, under a solid-top receiver. A side-loading model was followed by three tube-loading versions, one chambered in .32 rimfire. Changing the firing pin allowed for use of centerfire .32 Long Rifle ammunition (introduced in 1875 and using 13 grains of FFFg to launch an 80-grain bullet at about 850 fps). I'm told the .32 S&W Long and .32 Long Colt also could be used in the 1891—or sized so they would chamber. Marlin recommended the .32 to farmers for small game and to kill hogs and steers, emphasizing that the cartridges were cheaper than .32-20s and could be used safely in tighter quarters.

Marlin's early rifles featured fine engraving. This 1893 wears a petite but practical receiver sight.

The six-pound Model 1891 had a take-down screw on the right-hand side of the receiver, a feature destined to remain on Marlin lever-action .22s for more than a century. It was included early on because .22 rimfire ammo in those days was outside-lubricated with grease that melted when the rifle got hot and could quickly gum up the mechanism. Remember, too, that .22 rimfires began as blackpowder cartridges that left a lot more fuel residue than modern rounds. Frequent cleaning was important, and Marlin made it easy. A bonus of take-down rifles was from-the-breech swabbing of the bore.

During its twenty-five-year production run, the Model 1891 earned fame as the choice of "Little Miss Sure Shot," Annie Oakley. All but a handful of the 18,643 rifles were built in the first five years of production. The Model 1891 was followed in 1895 by the Model 1892 Marlin, which was similar but wore a superior trigger without a lever-operated safety. Both rifles came standard with twenty-four-inch round or octagon barrels and straight-grip stocks. Each retailed for eighteen dollars. List price of the Model 1892 later dropped as low as $13.25. A few more than 40,000 Model 92s were built during an eleven-year production run. Three out of four were .22s.

In the mid-1890s, Marlin turned its attention to centerfire rifles, announcing Models 1893, 1894, and 1895. In 1897, the firm trotted out an improved Model 1892, with tapered, twenty-four-inch round or octagon barrel. Its rubber buttpad replaced one of steel, and the takedown screw was larger than on the 1892. The standard Model 1897 came with case-hardened receiver (an option on the '92) and straight-grip stock. You could special-order a longer barrel, steel buttplate, and, beginning in 1899, a sixteen-inch magazine. A Bicycle Rifle version had a sixteen-inch barrel and full-length magazine (capacity: 16 Short, 12 Long, 10 Long Rifle). A leatherbound canvas case could be strapped to a bicycle, bringing the total cost to just under seventeen dollars. The Bicycle Rifle is rare; only 216 are confirmed as shipped.

In 1905 the Model 1897 became the Model 97, though no substantive design changes occurred. At that time, about 38,500 rifles had been produced—roughly half of the 81,000 eventually manufactured (though post-1905 records do not confirm totals). In 1916, production of Model 97s probably ceased, as Marlin's company was acquired by a

Built on the 39 frame, this Marlin 1897 offers cosmetic differences.

syndicate that used the facilities to manufacture machine guns. After World War I, John Moran formed the New Marlin Firearms Corporation. Its first catalog appeared in 1922 and featured a new lever-action .22 rifle called the Model 39. The 1892 and 97 rifles were absent.

Looking much like its predecessors, the Model 39 had a take-down receiver and a full-length tube magazine that held 25 Short, 20 Long, or 18 Long Rifle cartridges under a 24-inch octagon barrel. Its solid-top receiver was case-hardened. The pistol-grip walnut stock wore a rubber or hard-fiber buttpad. Rocky Mountain rear and ivory bead front sights were standard. Catalogs touted the 39 as "the choice of expert shooters for hunting small game such as rabbits, squirrels, crows, foxes, etc., and for target shooting up to 200 yards." In every significant way, the 39 was the same rifle as the pistol-grip Model 97. Incidentally, the very first 39s had "Marlin-Rockwell" stamped on the barrel. They're very rare. In the 1930s, a new, improved ejector came along for the 39, courtesy of Gus Swebilius. In 1936, the rifle was renamed the 39A.

Early rifles had a flawed bolt that would crack when used with high-speed ammunition. A better bolt was installed in 1932, and the serial numbers given an "HS" prefix. Introduced at a price of $28.40, the Model 39 became more affordable as the Great Depression settled in. When the improved 39 appeared, it listed for only $25. About then a silver bead replaced the ivory. By 1939 the rifle was selling for $29.75.

The 39A featured a round barrel. At 6½ pounds, it was 12 ounces heavier than the catalog weight of the first 39, due in part to the longer, thicker forend. A flat grip bottom and rounded lever soon replaced the S-shaped grip heel and square-topped lever of earlier rifles. The flat buttplate of the first version gave way to a ribbed buttplate with a curved surface.

Marlin produced no Model 39s during the war years, 1942–1944. When the rifles again went into production in 1945, they had blued, not case-colored receivers, which were drilled and tapped for receiver sights. The bead front sight was put on a ramp and given a sight hood.

In 1953 Marlin introduced the 39A Mountie, with a twenty-inch barrel and straight grip. A full-length magazine held 20 Short, 15 Long, or 14 Long Rifle cartridges. Rifle weight was trimmed to six pounds. Not long thereafter, white-line spacers were added to the buttplate and grip cap. The 1954 debut of Marlin's Micro-Groove button rifling marked the end of five- and six-groove Ballard-style rifling in Model 39 rifles. The sixteen multiple shallow grooves reduced bullet deformation. By 1956, Marlin had added Micro-Groove rifling to all its barrels. But while it delivers good accuracy, especially in smaller bores, there's no indication that this rifling form will consistently out-shoot other types.

During the mid-fifties, Marlin began drilling and tapping M39 receivers destined for sale by Sears. As scope use became more common, the 39 and all other popular .22 rifles were either grooved or drilled.

The Mountie and the standard Golden 39A became the first Marlin commemorative lever-action .22s, selling for the eye-popping price of a hundred dollars when they were announced in 1960. Only five hundred each of these chrome-plated, hand-checkered rifles were built. They get lots of collector attention now. Just a year later Marlin brought out the 39A-DL, a blued-steel rifle with hand checkering and a gray squirrel carving on the buttstock. It wore a leather sling and retailed for a hundred dollars. Just over three thousand 39A-DLs were built between 1961 and 1963, when production ceased.

Another rare 39 is the carbine, a slimmed-down Mountie with ⅔ magazine introduced in 1963 and dropped four years later. About 12,140 left the shipping docks. This fast-handling .22 is the lightest of the Model 39s, at 5¼ pounds. Several commemorative versions of the 39A and 39A Mountie followed in the 1970s, including the Centennial, the Century Limited, and the Article II.

In 1971 the 39D appeared, its pistol-grip stock reminiscent of the standard 39A rifle, but its twenty-inch barrel with full-length magazine and slim forend was more like the Mountie. The 39D forend had a barrel band instead of a steel cap. In 1973, after a yearlong absence, the Model 39D again appeared in the catalog, this time without white buttplate and grip spacers. Meanwhile, a series of changes had been made to the open sights.

Marlin bolt-action rimfires come in .22 LR, .22 WMR, and .17 HMR.

In 1983 Marlin assembled its 2-millionth Model 39. To celebrate the longevity of this rifle, the firm commissioned a special rifle, later donating the highly engraved piece for auction at the 1984 SHOT Show to raise funds for the National Shooting Sports Foundation's educational programs in five thousand schools.

Marlin added a crossbolt, hammer-block safety to the Model 39 in 1988, redesignating it and the Mountie the Models 39AS and 39MS. Swivel studs came standard on the new models, which in most other ways remained unchanged. The actions were still made of six steel forgings; assemblers fitted the wood as carefully as it had been fitted in pre-Depression days. A short-barreled version of the 39 debuted in 1988. The 16½-inch barrel and full-length magazine, the straight-grip stock and a take-down carrying case gave the 39TDS the look of the 1897 Bicycle Rifle.

The 39 went through more changes during the 1990s. After the turn of the century, it emerged as a 6½-pound rifle with pistol grip and hand-filling forend (both checkered). The 24-inch barrel supports a full-length magazine. There's a rubber buttpad, swivel studs, adjustable semi-buckhorn rear sight, and ramp front. The sandblasted receiver top is drilled and tapped, and each rifle comes with an offset hammer spur for scope use.

A companion to the 39 is the modern 1897 Cowboy, built on the same action but with a twenty-four-inch octagon barrel and traditional Marble sights. The straight-grip stock and short, slim forend are checkered. Marlin has successfully courted the favor of Cowboy Action shooters; this rimfire complements the 1894, 1895, and 336 Cowboy centerfire line (which, incidentally, feature deep-cut Ballard-type rifling).

Every so often, any honest reporter feels a twinge of guilt saying only good things about a product. But in all candor, I don't feel bad at all about beating the drum for Marlin's 39. First, this rifle is less a product than an institution. The history comes at no extra charge. Second, even a numbskull with no appreciation of history will like this rifle. It

The incomparable Marlin 39 has been produced in a variety of forms since 1922, such as this TDS carbine.

has the look and feel marksmen covet but can't explain. Heck, even people who know nothing about rifles fall for the 39. Its lean, lever-action lines evoke the spirit of times past, in a West still wild, where saddles carried rifles and men demanded much of them.

On the other hand, there's a delicacy to the profile, an almost aquiline look to the lever, a daintiness about the receiver that tells you the rifle was designed around the .22 rimfire, not just chambered for it. Saddle gun or squirrel rifle? A little of both. But the fit of wood to steel, the slick, solid cycling of the bolt, and the jolt to your pulse as the sights tug your eye to the target make the 39 something more than just another .22.

What it is, exactly, I can't say. But a rifleman without one has missed something.

Chapter 15

REMINGTON, OUR FIRST GUNMAKER

It was 1816. Jethro Wood of Cayuga County, New York, had yet to invent the first all-metal plow, and Eliphalet Remington II was going on twenty-three. "Lite" and his wife Abigail lived in his father's stone house on Staley Creek in Litchfield, four miles from German Flatts and the Mohawk River. A wooden flume carried creek water to a paddlewheel, powering the elder Remington's forge, where Lite fashioned his first gun.

Pumping the bellows, Lite heated the rod he had chosen for his barrel to a glow, hammered it until it was half an inch square in cross section, then wound it around an iron mandrel. The mandrel was not quite as big in diameter as the finished bore, in this case .45 caliber. Next, he heated the barrel white-hot, sprinkled it with Borax and sand, and, holding one end in his tongs, pounded the other vigorously on the stone floor to seat the coils. When the tube had cooled, Lite checked it for straightness and hammered out the curves. Then he ground eight flats because most barrels in that day were octagonal.

After several days of work, Lite's barrel still was not rifled. Young Remington then traveled to Utica, a growing town of 1,200, where some say that Morgan James cut the grooves. But at least one historian argues that James, well known for his barrel work, was not operating a shop at the time and that Remington's job was done by someone else. The price, then, might also be questioned. But four double reales—a dollar in country currency—was a fair price for two days' work at a time when mill hands made two hundred dollars a year.

At the home forge, Remington bored a touch-hole and forged a breech plug and lock parts, finishing them with a file. He brazed the priming pan to the lockplate and finished all metal parts with hazel-brown, a preservative of uric acid and iron oxide. The walnut stock, shaped with drawknife and chisel, was smoothed with sandstone, then

Eliphalet Remington, whose original gun-building effort in 1816 fueled an industry.

sealed with beeswax. Lite assembled his rifle with hand-wrought screws and pins.

Not long afterward, Remington took his rifle to a local match and placed second. Other shooters were impressed; the match winner wanted a Remington rifle. How much would it cost and when could he have it?

"Ten dollars," Lite said, "and you'll have it in ten days."

Remington's work soon became widely known, due largely to a need for finished rifles on the frontier. The Staley Creek foundry could hardly meet demand. Then, on October 26, 1825, the Erie Canal was completed, cutting the cost of moving a ton of goods from New York to Buffalo from one hundred dollars down to twelve. These were compelling reasons to build a new facility closer to port. In January 1828, Lite purchased a hundred acres on the Mohawk. It included most of what is now Ilion's business district. Remington Arms still occupies that site today.

Remington's production capacity doubled when his first factory building was completed in 1832. The Schenectady and Utica Railroad enabled Lite to travel and for customers to visit more easily. Remington's son Philo was soon helping the business with fresh ideas. Instead of straightening rifle barrels with a plumb line, the popular method then, Philo used the shadow of a window bar in the bore. The principle is still in use. Philo also installed steel facings on trip hammers, for closer manufacturing tolerances. The Remingtons employed a drill to bore a small-caliber hole through four feet of bar stock. Result: barrels without seams.

On August 12, 1841, Lite's wife, Abigail, and their daughter, Maria, hitched a spirited horse to the carriage for a drive. On the road that had taken Lite's father in a wagon accident thirteen years earlier, Maria opened her parasol. It cracked like a shot and the horse lunged, galloping out of control across a stream. The carriage was smashed to splinters against a great oak and Abigail was instantly killed.

Though his wife's death profoundly affected Lite Remington, his company continued to prosper. In 1845 impending war with Mexico prompted the government to contract for more rifles. Shopping for

This early Remington facility made guns for pioneers.

plant machinery, Remington visited Chicopee Falls, Massachusetts. The N. P. Ames Company, renowned for its cutlery, had failed on an experimental breechloading carbine designed by William Jenks. Remington acquired the Ames gun business and the services of Jenks, who kept plugging his rifles for military service. Finally, in 1858, U.S. Ordnance came to its senses. The Jenks lock was modified by J. H. Merrill of Remington to feed cardboard cartridges coated with beeswax and tallow. After immersion for one minute, and a day's drying, the gun passed muster. A year later William Jenks was brushed from the top of a hay wagon as it entered a barn on his Washington-area farm. The injuries were fatal.

Remington entered the handgun market in 1849 with an improved Beals revolver. Shortly afterward, Joseph Rider, who later helped develop the rolling block rifle, came to Remington with a new revolver design. Remington paid him twelve brace of revolvers and four hundred acres in Ohio for partial rights. Rider built the first double-action revolver in 1859 and engineered ladies' or "muff" guns that launched a BB with a percussion cap.

When Harper's Ferry fell, the U.S. War Department lost half its arsenal. Remington immediately expanded his Ilion plant to accommodate what would amount to nearly $30 million in gun orders from the army and navy. Anticipations of a brief Civil War were dashed when Stonewall Jackson's brigade routed the Union Army at Bull Run on July 2, 1861. A month later Lite was bedridden with what doctors called "inflammation of the bowels." It might have been appendicitis; perhaps it had something to with the strain of wartime production at the Remington plant. On August 12, 1861, Eliphalet Remington II, age seventy, died.

The Remington factory stopped for the funeral of its founder in Ilion's cemetery. Then it resumed production under the direction of his sons Philo, Samuel, and Eliphalet III. By 1864, a flood of ammunition contracts prompted the construction of five new buildings. Before they reached capacity, however, the war ended. On April 10, 1865, Lee surrendered, and workers at Ilion sat by silent, mortgaged machinery, wondering about the future.

Fortunately, Remington had diversified. In 1864 the foundry across the Erie Canal had been equipped to produce industrial machinery. In 1865 a separate joint stock company, the Agricultural Works, was formed. Remington's Joseph Rider also pursued a breechloading rifle for sportsmen. A strong, simple gun, the Rolling Block used a rotating breech lock to seal a cartridge in the chamber. The hammer hit a striker in this block, firing the round. In one test, a 50-caliber Rolling Block was loaded with 40 balls and 750 grains of powder, the charge filling 36 inches of a 40-inch barrel. Upon firing, "nothing extraordinary occurred." Almost foolproof in operation, this mechanism was also quick to load. A practiced shooter could fire an amazing seventeen rounds a minute.

In 1874 Remington engineer L. L. Hepburn began work on a target rifle for long-range matches like those the Irish had won at Wimbledon. The Irish had challenged "any American team" through an ad in the *New York Herald*. The team would comprise six men, who would shoot three rounds of fifteen shots, one round each at 800, 900, and

1,000 yards. A fledgling National Rifle Association and the cities of New York and Brooklyn put up five thousand dollars each to construct a range for the match on Long Island's Creed's Farm. It would be called Creedmoor. The State of New York bought the land. Remington's new target rifle, a .44-90 shooting 550-grain conical bullets, came off the line in March. In September a favored Irish team with muzzleloaders bowed to the Americans and their Remington and Sharps breechloaders.

Remington's Agricultural Works lost much of its profitability as new Midwest firms competed with lower shipping costs. One of its innovations, the Remington typewriter, came too early for the market. Anemic sales forced Philo to put the typewriter business on the block. Remington executive Henry Benedict bought it for $186,000. Later, it would be valued at that many millions.

By 1886 Remington was reduced to paying its contractors (many of whom had grown rich) with script redeemable in goods at Ilion stores. Later that year creditors forced bankruptcy proceedings. In March 1888 Marcellus Hartley, founder of Union Metallic Cartridge Company (U.M.C.), joined Winchester's Thomas Bennett to pay $200,000 for Remington's property, stock, and reputation.

Hartley, sickly as a child, was a prodigy in business. As a young man in 1854 he entered a venture with J. Rutsen Schuyler and Malcolm Graham that would become the biggest sporting goods distributor in the country. During the Civil War, Hartley was asked by President Lincoln to procure guns for the Union Army. Bucking Southern sympathizers in banks, gun factories, and shipping firms, he tied up firearms production in England and on the Continent, undercutting Confederate offers. By war's end Hartley, age thirty-seven, was looking for new challenges.

He decided there was opportunity in the new self-contained rimfire cartridges made for the Spencer rifle by the Crittenden and Tribbals Manufacturing Company of South Coventry, Connecticut. He bought that plant and another in Springfield, Massachusetts. He moved all cartridge operations to Bridgeport, Connecticut, and in

The Union Metallic Cartridge Company broadened Remington's financial base and, eventually, its product line.

August 1867, incorporated Union Metallic Cartridge Company. It was quick to adopt a new cartridge developed by Colonel Hiram Berdan of Berdan Sharpshooter fame. Instead of having the priming compound blown into a folded rim, it held a percussion cap in a pocket in the center of the case head. Two flash holes, on either side of a fixed anvil, admitted the spark. This was the first practical centerfire design, superior in some ways to the Boxer cartridge developed in England at about the same time.

U.M.C. made cartridges for all kinds of handheld guns, and by 1900 it offered 15,000 different loads, from BB caps to 10-gauge shotshells and big-bore rifle cartridges. With Remington Arms under his control, Marcellus Hartley invited bright young inventors to Ilion. In 1892 Arthur Savage came to work on a lever-action gun with a spool magazine. Hartley's business savvy put him on the boards of railroads and banks and insurance companies. He founded the International Banking Corporation and in 1896 engineered the sale of a floundering *New York Times* to a publisher from Chattanooga named Adolph Ochs.

In January 1902, Marcellus Hartley stopped to see a doctor because of indigestion. Declared "sound as a dollar," the seventy-five-year-old Hartley went immediately to a board meeting of the American Surety Company. He collapsed there and died. His grandson, Marcellus Hartley

Dodge, would complete his studies at Columbia and, at just twenty-one, become president of M. Hartley and Company, successor to Schuyler, Hartley, and Graham.

In 1907 J. D. Pedersen, a Danish contemporary of Browning, developed Remington's first slide-action shotgun, the Model 10. The Model 12 .22 rimfire pump came along in 1909 and a centerfire Model 14 in 1912.

Marcy Dodge realized that Winchester ammunition was sought by people owning Winchester guns. Changing Remington's company name to include U.M.C. was not popular with the old guard at U.M.C., which was then generating thirty times the revenue of Remington's plant. But Dodge did it anyway, and in 1912 bought the last of the family stock to become sole owner of Remington-U.M.C.

The new company garnered publicity when it helped sponsor Annie Oakley's trick-shooting exhibitions (Oakley's husband, Frank Butler, later became a Remington salesman) and fielded several shooting teams. The firm designed its Model 24 .22 autoloader for Italian General Pisano, who could hit rimfire cases tossed in the air. But the carefree days of glass balls and applause were cut short in 1914 at Sarajevo, when an assassin's bullet killed Archduke Ferdinand. War fears brought arms contracts to Remington from France and Great Britain. Ilion's payroll increased tenfold in 1917, to 15,000. To further boost production, Dodge and other magnates formed a separate Remington Company of Delaware, leasing a locomotive factory at Eddystone, Pennsylvania.

During the course of the First World War, Remington built 69 percent of the rifles shipped to American forces, including the .30-06 Enfields suggested by company engineers as a substitute for Springfields.

At war's end, Remington-U.M.C. closed three plants but found capacity still far above peacetime needs. Deleting U.M.C. from its name, Remington delved into cutlery, cash registers, and other enterprises, while growing its market share in sporting arms and ammunition. One day in 1922, fifty-one carloads of shotshells and rifle cartridges—more than 27 million rounds—were shipped from Bridgeport. In 1926, Remington cataloged the first noncorrosive priming made in the U.S. It contained no potassium chlorate. Lead styphnate, made by DuPont, replaced the corrosive element. Remington awarded prizes to W. A. Robins of Jonesboro, Louisiana, and Nelson Starr of Goshen, Indiana, for independently suggesting "Kleanbore" as the market name.

When the stock market fell in 1929, Remington was badly shaken. By 1932 the firm was losing $1 million a year. To rescue the company, Marcy Dodge offered controlling interest in Remington to E. I. DuPont de Nemours & Company, a firm that had long supplied Remington with powder. During the 1930s, Remington bought the Peters Cartridge Company, a rival company founded in 1887 by Baptist preacher Gersham Peters. Soon after, it acquired the Parker Gun Company, originally started in 1832 by Charles Parker to make a coffee grinder. The first Parker shotgun came in 1868. Remington manufactured Parkers until the 1940s. In 1933 Remington bought the Chamberlain Trap and Target Company, maker of "Blue Rock" targets and Leggitt "Ideal" traps.

Remington's first bolt-action rimfire was the Model 33, designed in 1931 by Crawford C. Loomis, who during that period had his hand in developing many Remington products. Targeted at the boys' rifle market, the single-shot 33 carried a low price tag, even for the period: just five dollars at introduction. It was ready to catalog just five months after Loomis began work on the project. Featuring a 24-inch barrel and a one-piece walnut stock, the rifle wore a cocking knob at the rear of the bolt. This knob had to be pulled to a catch by hand each time before firing. Remington made improvements in 1932 and 1933, including a longer stock with finger grooves, a simpler and better-finished bolt, and a slimmer trigger. Available in smoothbore and target versions, the Model 33 lasted only through 1935.

Crawford Loomis also designed the company's first repeating bolt gun, the tube-fed Model 34. Starting the project in October 1931, just three months after the 33's debut, he finished in July 1932. It, too, was available as a target rifle. And like the 33, the 34 was replaced in 1936.

Near the end of the Depression, Remington planned a family of rimfires with interchangeable parts. The core of the 500 series would be an inexpensive receiver of seamless steel tubing. DuPont's Ray Crittenden is credited with bringing that project to fruition with a bevy of new .22s: The 510, 511, and 512 were all bolt rifles (single-shot and

In 2003, Remington reentered the market in high-quality bolt-action rimfires with its 504.

with box and tubular magazines), introduced in 1939. The 513S and 513T were box-fed bolt-actions of higher grade. The 550 was a self-loader; the only one on the market at the time that could digest mixed loads of Short, Long, and Long Rifle cartridges. It was the last of that initial series, appearing in 1941. Remington has continued the tradition of designating its .22 rifles with a three-digit number beginning with a five.

Prompted by a recovering economy, Remington designed several new sporting guns during the 1930s: the slide-action 141 centerfire and autoloading 241 rimfire in 1935, the autoloading 81 centerfire and slide-action 121 rimfire in 1936, and the 37 rimfire target rifle a year later.

Just twenty-five years after the Great War had inflamed Europe, another erupted. Ilion's work force burgeoned from 900 to 9,000. The pace of ammunition manufacture was even more hectic. With the Western Cartridge Company, Remington expanded Frankfort Arsenal. A new factory at Lake City employed 21,000 workers and at capacity produced 8.9

Remington's autoloading Nylon 66 was among the first success stories for synthetic stocks.

million cartridges daily. Another factory grew at Salt Lake City, Utah. Overall, Remington expanded its operations by 2,000 percent.

Remington changed its sporting-gun line after World War II, designing new models to take advantage of modern materials and manufacturing techniques. The "family of guns" marketing concept hatched in the 1950s entailed the use of common receivers, trigger assemblies, and other parts in guns of different design. Using its ties to DuPont, Remington pioneered synthetic stocks. Its "Nylon 66" .22 went public in 1959, followed by other rifles and the "Zytel"-stocked XP-100 pistol.

The firm has also developed innovative ammunition, adding the respected Eley name to its rimfire line and engineering rimless magnum rounds. Like other companies, it has had losers—the 5mm rimfire and a small family of electronically ignited centerfire cartridges, for example. But the number of bloopers from Remington has been astonishingly small.

Today, Remington is diversifying, adding its name to outdoor clothes and accessories. It must adapt to a public that did not grow up on a frontier and, in large measure, sees little use for firearms of any kind. But the company's long history of successful adaptation puts it on competitive footing. New product lines from "Big Green" show that Remington is as nimble as ever.

Chapter 16

RUGER: A GENIUS FOR GUNS

William Batterman Ruger, founder and Chairman Emeritus of Sturm, Ruger & Company, died at his home July 6, 2002, at age eighty-six. He was a rarity, a twentieth-century pioneer.

Born June 21, 1916, in Brooklyn, New York, Bill discovered his passion for guns when his father, attorney Adolph Ruger, gave him a rifle at twelve years of age. He often accompanied his father on duck shoots to eastern Long Island. One day afield, he met a man with a .30-06. The blast of that rifle was intoxicating to the young gun enthusiast. Soon he and a pal, Bill Lett, had anted up $9.75 for a surplus .30-40 Krag. Later, Ruger practiced riflery on a high school shooting team, then designed a light machine gun—and built a prototype.

At prep school in Salisbury, Connecticut, Bill had to keep his machine gun and the rest of his gun collection off campus. He spent weekends and holidays in Brooklyn machine shops, learning about fabricating things from metal.

As a student at the University of North Carolina, Chapel Hill, he converted an empty room into a machine shop. There he fashioned an autoloading rifle from a Savage Model 99 lever-action. In 1938 he came up with initial designs for what eventually became a machine gun. He finished the technical drawings on his in-laws' dining-room table. Army Ordnance officials liked the result, and Ruger was on his way as a full-time gun designer. Over the next fifty-three years, he helped invent and patent dozens of sporting rifles, pistols, and shotguns.

Bill Ruger wedded Mary Thompson in 1939 and immediately looked for a job designing guns. Nobody wanted him. He approached Army Ordnance with plans for another new machine gun. The Army turned him down. With money running short, Bill accepted a job at Springfield Armory. The $130 monthly check kept him there for a year. Eventually, though, claustrophobia set in. The Rugers moved to North Carolina, where Bill renewed his efforts to develop a better machine gun. Offered an improved version, Winchester, Remington, and Smith & Wesson demurred—but several job tenders followed. Ruger went to work instead for Auto Ordnance, which made Thompson submachine guns. The company liked Ruger's design; however, the end of World War II killed government interest in new ordnance.

Bill Ruger stayed with Auto Ordnance for three happy years, earning $100 a week at the design table. There he met Doug Hammond, who broached the idea of building guns from sheet metal to trim production costs. Ruger concluded that modern factory machinery could hold acceptable tolerances, and that parts could be made to fit easily and interchangeably, yet closely enough for a solid feel, positive functioning, and good accuracy. Short years later the first Ruger autoloading pistol proved him right.

" . . . There's really only one gun company in America," Bill Ruger told me once during my visit to his New Hampshire facility. He said it as if he were recommending the chowder over the sandwiches at a local cafe. No swagger: You want the straight scoop, don't you?

Ruger's first dive into the waters of free enterprise had him gasping for air in no time. The product—carpenters' tools—cost too much to make. Lesson: No matter how good the item, it must also be a bargain. The Ruger Corporation, hard on the heels of World War II, expired quicker than had Italy.

In 1948 Bill Ruger got a boost. Alex Sturm, a graduate of the Yale Art School, had no interest in carpenters' tools, but he did have

$50,000 to invest. And he collected guns. Ever the opportunist, Bill was all too willing to take the small grubstake offered him for the manufacture of a pistol he'd designed. The .22 autoloader featured a revolutionary idea. Instead of incurring the expense of machining a frame, Ruger had fashioned it and most other major components from sheet steel. This gun must have generated some snickers from the cognoscenti, but at $37.50, it was substantially less expensive than its competition. Ruger had managed to make his gun look good and shoot reliably, too. A 1949 review by the NRA's technical staff (including Major Julian Hatcher, Ruger's mentor) helped promote the pistol. An avalanche of orders followed.

The quick rooting of Bill Ruger's new gun company was marred by the death of Alex Sturm, who was not yet thirty. To commemorate his partner, Bill had the Ruger "red eagle" emblem (in fact, the likeness of a griffin) changed to black. Red emblems remain in some company literature, but not on Ruger guns.

Bill was not just a shooter; he studied guns. Their history and function, changes in metallurgy and marketing—all were interesting. Ruger had started collecting in his teens. Those first Luger and Colt pistols, Sharps and Springfield rifles whetted an appetite that remained. But knowing what came before did not satisfy Bill Ruger.

In 1952 plans for a tip-up revolver were discarded in favor of a solid-frame, single-action .22 patterned after Colt's famous Single Action Army revolver. Announced in 1953, this gun gathered a huge following. Like Ruger's autoloader, it was affordable. But instead of sheet steel, it featured an investment-cast frame—a solid casting held to fine tolerances and smooth finish by what is commonly called the "lost wax" process. This technique uses wax templates as cores for parts molds. Each part (receiver, in this case) is cast in a mold that has been formed around a template, which has been melted out. The mold's interior is thus wax-smooth. Final machining is either eliminated or reduced, cutting production time and expense.

The Ruger Single Six sustained a few early modifications, one of the most brilliant being the addition of an auxiliary cylinder in .22

With interchangeable cylinders, Ruger's Single Six allows you shoot both .22 Long Rifle and .22 WMR cartridges.

Winchester Magnum Rimfire. More than 250,000 of these guns have been sold.

Bill was always quick to build on success, and in 1955 he brought to market a centerfire version of the Single Six. The Blackhawk revolver, initially chambered in .357 Magnum, would eventually be offered in .41 and .44 Magnum, .30 Carbine, and .45 Long Colt. In 1959 the .44 Magnum Super Blackhawk appeared, with an unfluted cylinder and a square-backed trigger guard. That year a trim single-action .22 revolver called the Bearcat also made headlines. It had a brass frame, fixed sights, and lightweight four-inch barrel. Eventually it was discontinued, along with the Hawkeye, a single-shot pistol that looked like a single-action revolver. The Hawkeye was chambered for the .256 Winchester cartridge, a bit anemic for big game and not as appealing to varminters as Remington's .221 Fireball in the XP-100 pistol. Ruger later announced the Fireball as a Hawkeye chambering, but no guns were produced for that round.

In 1961 Ruger began building rifles, starting with a chunky .44 Magnum Carbine designed for the whitetail woods. The six-pound autoloader with an 18-inch barrel and factory-fitted peep sight certainly

Ruger's 10/22 is easily the most customized rimfire rifle ever made.

made sense for close-cover big game hunting, but eventually the company dropped it. As I recall, the first retail sticker on this delightful little gun was only $108.

But the Carbine's design didn't die. In 1964 Ruger announced a look-alike, the 10/22 rimfire rifle, with a clever ten-round rotary magazine that fit flush in the action well of the stock. This gun has now become one of the most popular .22 rifles ever. A cottage industry in custom accessories and services has grown up around the 10/22.

By 1968 Bill Ruger had become well known for his innovative thinking. All of his guns were truly fresh designs, with internal features that made each model better than its competition. In some cases there was no competition, because Ruger wasn't afraid to try something nobody else would—like build a single-shot hunting rifle. The last centerfire of this type had been designed by John Browning when Teddy Roosevelt was in his twenties. The Ruger Number One, introduced in 1968 at a list price of $265, got a lukewarm reception.

Fashioned after the British Farquharson action, but trimmer, it had strength, good looks, a crisp trigger, and an ingenious quarter-rib that accepted Ruger's scope rings. But it lacked a bolt handle and magazine, defining features of contemporary hunting rifles. The Number One has since gained a loyal, if limited, following among hunters serious enough to make their first shots count. Available in six styles, in chamberings from .218 Bee to .458 Winchester, it has even generated competition, the true mark of success.

In 1969, a year after announcing the Number One, Ruger brought out its bolt-action Model 77. If a single-shot seemed a lonely venture, this bolt gun faced even greater risk in a field dominated by Winchester's Model 70 and Remington's 700. Sending a new rifle into the ring with these heavyweights, Bill Ruger showed not only confidence in his product, but a willingness to gamble. The 77's investment-cast receiver kept costs down. Its conservative-style stock appeared at the height of a revolution against garish angular stock designs. Its great range of chamberings and sensible barrel choices gave it wide appeal. The integral Ruger bases and machined-steel rings provided with each rifle made scope mounting a snap. A Mauser claw extractor helped both reliability and appearance, though it did not provide controlled-round feeding. In short order, Ruger's 77 muscled aside the giants for a slice of market share. An understudy rifle, the 77/22 rimfire, followed in 1983.

Consistent with his pioneering bent, Bill Ruger next designed a cap-and-ball revolver, a fifteen-shot, double-action autoloading pistol, and an over/under shotgun with no visible action pins. His Mini-14 car-

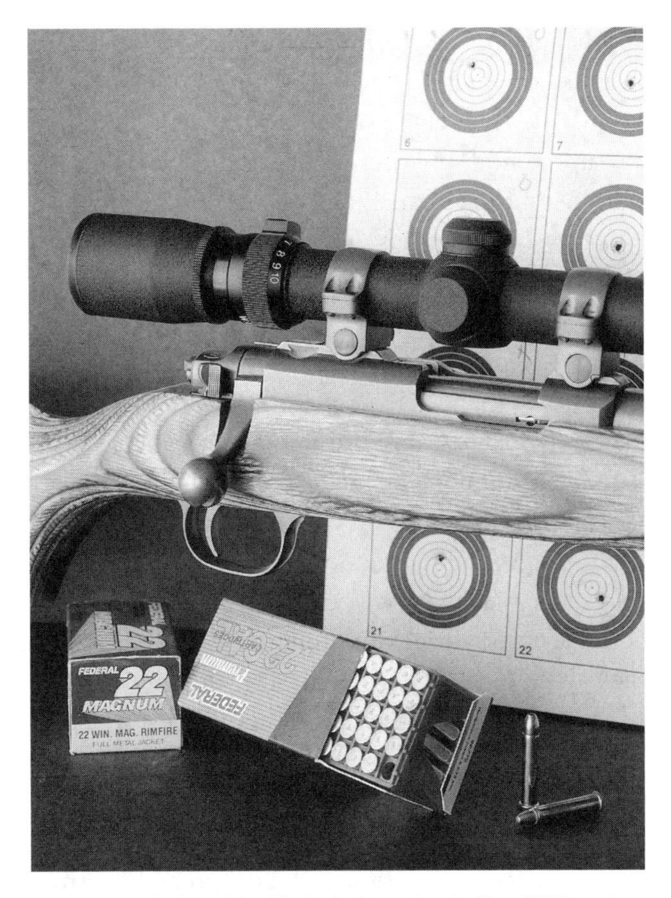

Accurate, and with a big-rifle feel, the 77/22 in LR or WMR versions will sharpen your shooting before deer hunting.

bine in .223 and 7.62x39 has become a popular self-loader. It's also used by law enforcement agencies, as are the firm's double-action revolvers, which come in various frame sizes. The .44 Magnum Redhawk is among the best-selling hunting handguns. The Super Redhawk, with extended frame and integral scope mounts, is even better. Since then (1987), Sturm, Ruger & Company has expanded its line of firearms mainly by cataloging many variations of basic and proven models.

Debt-free and with assets of about $100 million, the company headquarters remained for years in Southport, Connecticut, where Bill

Ruger's first manufacturing enterprise struggled in 1946, and where the first Ruger guns were built. Now the corporate offices are in Prescott, Arizona. Newport, New Hampshire's factory, now the biggest Ruger plant, grew up around an investment casting operation called Pine Tree Casting. Most Ruger frames and receivers originate here, as do all but the longest revolver barrels, which come from the outside source that supplies Ruger rifle barrels. Shotgun barrels are forged in-house. Ruger button-rifles its long barrels, but short pistol barrels are broached.

The company operates its own wood shop next to the Pine Tree Casting plant, where it fashions rifle and shotgun stocks from American walnut. European walnut is standard on some guns. Ruger lists synthetic stocks for most models. These are supplied by outside vendors, as are revolver grips. Assembly is done in-house. Afterward, the guns are proofed on a range that also serves the company's armorer program, offered to police agencies. Roughly 4 million bullets fly down Ruger's test tunnels each year.

When not involved in firearms design, Ruger collected antique firearms and early Western American art. And automobiles. His garages held more than thirty antique and modern vehicles, including Bentleys, Rolls-Royces, Bugattis, Stutzes, and a lovely 1913 Mercer Raceabout. In 1970 Ruger commissioned the design and construction of a sports tourer he dubbed the Ruger Special. It was based on a 1929 Bentley 4½-liter.

Bill Ruger's philanthropy supported several charities and the Buffalo Bill Historical Center in Cody, Wyoming, where he served as a trustee for fifteen years. His son, William B. Ruger, runs the firearms business now. (Son James Thompson "Tom" Ruger and wife Mary Thompson Ruger died before Bill.) The company has to date produced well over 20 million firearms for hunting, target shooting, self-defense, and tactical use.

Chapter 17

ARTHUR SAVAGE'S BRILLIANT IDEA

Most of the guns developed before 1900 are obsolete. Some should not be. The Savage 99 lasted into the 1990s, and was dropped not because it needed improvement but because production costs were on the rise.

Like many of his predecessors, Arthur William Savage used this one successful gun design to found a company that would later manufacture a variety of firearms. Born June 13, 1857 in Kingston, Jamaica, young Savage went to school in England and the United States. His father was England's Special Commissioner to the British West Indies, and he made sure Arthur was well schooled. But the boy had an adventurous streak, and immediately after college sailed for Australia, where he found work on a cattle ranch. Arthur also found a wife, Annie Bryant, and started a family. Eventually the Savages would have four sons and four daughters. An astute businessman, Arthur quickly built a stake in cattle. At the end of his eleven-year stay in Australia, he was said to own the biggest ranch on the continent.

The Outback had given him fortune and thrills (Aborigines reportedly captured and held him for months), but Savage itched for new frontiers. Back in Jamaica, he bought a coffee plantation, tinkered with machinery, and pursued an interest in firearms and explosives. With another inventor, he developed the Savage-Halpine torpedo. It got good reviews from the U.S. Navy, but no contract. Later this torpedo was sold to the Brazilian government.

In 1892, when Savage was just thirty-five, he finished the blueprint for a new repeating rifle. It was a hammerless lever-action—a daring design, given analyses that blamed the failure of the 1878 Sharps-Borchardt on its lack of a visible hammer. Arthur submitted his

Arthur Savage's lever-action launched his company after vying for military service with the Krag.

rifle for testing at the 1892 ordnance trials on Governor's Island, New York. It was beaten by the Krag-Jorgensen, which became the official U.S. infantry rifle. Turning to sportsmen, Savage redesigned his gun, altering the lever to accommodate three fingers. He developed a new cartridge for the rifle and in 1894 formed the Savage Arms Company in Utica, New York.

Savage's first commercial rifle was called the Model 1895. It had a rear-locking bolt that abutted a thick steel web machined into the tail of a streamlined receiver milled from a solid forging. Side ejection kept cases out of the line of sight and would later prove a requisite for scope use. Savage's action was much less vulnerable to dust, water, and debris than were contemporary Winchester lever guns. The 1895 also featured a coil mainspring—the first of its kind on a commercial lever-action—and a through-bolt to join buttstock and receiver. But the best part of this gun was its magazine, a spring-loaded brass spool housed in the receiver. No magazine was simpler, smoother in operation, or better protected. It didn't change rifle balance as it emptied, because the weight was always between your hands. Most importantly, pointed bullets were safe to use in the Model 95 because the cartridges did not rest primer-to-bullet tip. So you could use bullets with greater reach.

Arthur Savage's new cartridge, designed expressly for this rifle, drove a 190-grain bullet at around 1,900 fps. It was called the .303 Savage, though bullet diameter was .308, not .311 as it was for the .303 Lee-Enfield. A longer, heavier bullet gave Savage's .303 an edge over the .30-30. Hunter testimonials attested to its power.

E. E. Jones of Townsend, Montana, bet all comers fifty dollars that he could "shoot through a grizzly endwise" with his Model 1895; E. T. Ezekiel of Wood Island, Alaska, claimed to have killed a whale with his .303. A frugal marksman in British Columbia used his first box of twenty cartridges to take eighteen big game animals, including grizzly bears.

Other chamberings followed as the Model 1895 became the Model 1899. Charles Newton developed for Savage a .250 that drove an 87-grain bullet 3,000 fps, an attention-getting speed in those days.

A marvelous big game rifle, Savage's hammerless Model 99 survived for nearly a century.

Newton also designed the Savage .22 High-Power, or "Imp." Featuring a 70-grain .228 bullet at 2,700 fps, the High-Power quickly—and surprisingly—chalked up a long list of kills on game as big as lions and moose.

During nearly a century at market, the Savage 99 was listed in thirty-one versions and fourteen chamberings—not including a take-down model that came with a .410 shotgun barrel. The action has stayed essentially the same, though its safety went from the lever to the tang hump in 1961, and four years later the lovely spool magazine was replaced by a cheaper detachable box.

Arthur Savage no doubt relished the early success of this gun, but he was too much a pioneer to put his feet up. And he knew that his company would grow only if it diversified. In 1903 Savage announced a slide-action .22 called, predictably, the Model 1903. Short runs of slightly modified 1903s were called the Models 1909 and 1914. A take-down .22 pump came in 1925, to be replaced four years later by the Model 29. Savage entered the bolt-action market with Models 1904 and 1905, single-shot .22s. In 1912 the company introduced an autoloading .22, a box-fed take-down rifle that lasted only four years. The

Model 19 NRA, a box-fed bolt-action, did better, remaining in the company line until 1937. Of the 50,000 Model 19s produced, about 6,000 were used to train U.S. military forces.

To smooth its post-war landing and strengthen its competitive position, Savage introduced a new rifle, the centerfire Model 1920. This gun featured a Mauser-type action and a checkered stock with schnable forend. Available in .250-3000 and .300 Savage, the M1920 didn't prove as popular as the 99. It was dropped in 1926. Two years later its successor, the Model 40, appeared. It and the deluxe Model 45 lasted until 1940.

Post-war diversification prompted Savage to buy the J. Stevens Arms and Tool Company of Chicopee Falls, Massachusetts. This solid firm was founded by Joshua Stevens, who had started a gun business about the time Arthur Savage was starting grade school. Stevens had shrewdly chosen a path no one else had trod. Winchester, Marlin, and Remington had already established a formidable block of competition in the repeating-rifle market. Smith & Wesson had challenged Colt for a share of revolver sales. Parker and Lefever made fine shotguns. Joshua Stevens developed inexpensive guns for farm and frontier, and target rifles for the serious marksman. He was the first American to forge a hinge-action shotgun barrel and lug in one piece.

To make his guns more marketable, Stevens hired famous barrelmaker Harry Pope. Pope checked the quality of Stevens's barrels, and his name gave the company credibility among target shooters. Like Mr. Savage, Stevens saw in diversity a hedge against market fluctuation. His company developed several useful cartridges. The .22 Long Rifle, arguably the most useful of all time, debuted in 1887. The .25 Stevens rimfire appeared in a single-shot falling-block rifle called the Ideal. A successor, the Favorite, came in .22, .25, and .32 rimfire. These relatively inexpensive guns comprised the plinking and hunting section of a line of rifles that included the Walnut Hill, a target-style .22 claimed by many in that day to be the finest of its kind.

Joshua Stevens died in 1907 at the age of ninety-two. Two years after his death the firm started making a 12-gauge repeating shotgun

Savage revived the popular Stevens Favorite design in this trim single-shot: .22, .22 WMR, and .17.

under a Browning patent, and in 1913 it introduced the first American-built .410 shotgun. After Savage purchased the J. Stevens Arms and Tool Company in 1920, more shotguns were added to the catalog. In 1929 Savage bought the A.H. Fox Gun Company of Philadelphia. "Savage-Stevens-Fox" on company literature told shooters not only of a broad product line, but of long experience in gunmaking.

In 1930 Savage further expanded by purchasing the Davis-Warner Arms Company. A year later it bought the Crescent Firearms Company. Despite the Depression, Savage designed and marketed many new guns during the thirties: The Models 19L and 19M, built between 1933 and 1942, added various barrel and sight options to the .22 rimfire Model 19 NRA. A Model 19H was available in .22 Hornet. The Model 3 single-shot .22 and its magazine-equipped variations came along in the mid-thirties, as did a Model 10 .22 target rifle. Model 6 and 7 autoloading .22s followed in 1938 and 1939. Savage introduced its Model 220 single-shot hinge-action shotgun in 1938, and a Model 420 boxlock over/under.

During the Second World War Savage manufactured 2.5 million submachine guns, aircraft machine guns, and infantry rifles. Between

Arthur Savage built an arms company that's still a major producer of .22 rimfire rifles.

1941 and 1943 production lines operated around the clock every day, and the payroll jumped tenfold, to 13,000. There were no strikes, no missed deadlines. But as in 1919, peace brought new challenges. In 1946 the Savage Arms Company closed its Utica operation, consolidating gun production at Chicopee Falls. By 1950 Savage was marketing several new guns, including the Model 340 centerfire bolt-action rifle. Designed to offer utility at little expense, the 340 came in .22 Hornet, .222 Remington, and .30-30. The .223 Remington was added later. This homely but serviceable gun stayed in the Savage line for thirty-five years.

In 1950 Savage announced its Model 24, an over/under combination gun in .22/.410. This model has proven so popular that it is still carried, and other chamberings have been added. The 24 was followed in 1958 by the Savage Model 110, a bolt-action rifle developed for serious big game hunters and priced to compete with Remington's 721 and 722. The 110 and subsequent 111 and 112 rifles are still offered in several chamberings and configurations, including heavy-barrel, tactical, and synthetic-stock variations.

From 1960 to 1968 Savage cataloged its Model 101 pistol, the only handgun it has made since 1917. The 101 looked like a single-action revolver, but in fact held only one .22 rimfire cartridge. The year

The author shoots the Savage 30G in .17 HMR.

it was dropped Savage started selling an Italian-made over/under shotgun, the Model 440. It lasted only a couple of seasons, but a successor, the Finnish Valmet 330, stayed from 1969 through 1980. Savage tried marketing autoloading .22 rifles again in 1969, with its Models 60, 88, and 90. These were actually variations of the same gun; they expired quickly.

In 1960 Savage moved to its present site, a modern facility in Westfield, Massachusetts, where in 1963 it was bought by the American Hardware Corporation. Savage Arms Company became Savage Industries, a subsidiary of the Emhart Corporation, a conglomerate that relinquished ownership in 1980. Changes in the ownership and operation of Savage Arms since then have left corporate offices in Suffield, Connecticut. A bolt-action Striker centerfire pistol for long-range shooting ranks among the most innovative Savage guns of late, along with a muzzleloader advertised for use with smokeless powder. Savage's line of hunting rifles no longer includes the great Model 99, but a dizzying assortment of bolt-action rifles offer fine value and the performance to stay competitive with Remington, Ruger, and Winchester. The .22 rimfire stable has been augmented with rifles chambered in .17 HMR. "Accuracy at an affordable price" could well be the slogan.

In his later years, Arthur Savage indulged his own curiosity. He invested in a citrus plantation and a tire enterprise, and even went prospecting for oil. He became Superintendent of the Street Railway in Utica. He died in 1941, at age eighty-four. A gun designer who spent his first years punching cattle, he could not have imagined what would come from his first lever-action prototype. But he surely would have approved.

Chapter 18

WINCHESTER: THE UNLIKELY COMPANY

Winchester's early successes were almost all due to fortuitous timing and the efforts of people who never worked for Winchester Repeating Arms. Walter Hunt was building on the work of other inventors when he came up with his lever-action "Volitional Repeater" in 1848. Its conical "rocket ball" held a powder charge in a hollow base covered with a cork cap perforated in the center and sealed with paper. Spark from priming pellets fed by a pill-lock mechanism shot through the paper, igniting the charge. The failure-prone mechanism was nonetheless a marvelous application of what had been discovered at that time about repeating mechanisms, breech loading, priming fulminates, and bullets. Hunt's rifle was, by all contemporary measures, quite an invention. Its tubular magazine was a landmark development.

Hunt sold his repeater to George Arrowsmith, a New York entrepreneur who hired Lewis Jennings to improve it. Arrowsmith then marketed the rifle to fellow New Yorker Courtland Palmer. The Robbins and Lawrence Arms Company of Windsor, Vermont contracted to build five thousand rifles for Palmer. The mechanism proved hard to make and unreliable, and many guns were sold as single-shots. Horace Smith and Benjamin Tyler Henry worked together on improvements.

The limited partnership of Smith & Wesson resulted when Daniel B. Wesson joined the project. While Henry was not named in the two subsequent patents, he influenced the design of both rifle and ammunition. The cartridge described in these patents had a metallic case tapering outward near its base (almost like a rim, but not folded). Priming mixture was spread all over the inside of the cartridge head, then a metal disc was placed on it, to confine it and act as an anvil. A hit anywhere on the head would detonate the primer, so this round served as both rimfire and centerfire.

Unfortunately for Smith & Wesson, the machinery of their day could not economically produce this cartridge. Undaunted, the partners unearthed Hunt's rocket ball and reworked it, incorporating a fulminate-of-mercury primer in a glass cup in the bullet's cavity. The cup rested on an iron anvil; a cork base wad sealed the propellant (first fulminate, in later cartridges 6½ grains of blackpowder). Smith and his crew found the cork debris caused malfunctions, and the primer often misfired because the cork cushioned the striker. The solution was a copper base cap, later changed to brass. A brass anvil replaced the iron one.

In June 1855, forty New England businessmen pooled funds to form the Volcanic Repeating Arms Company. Among these financiers was Oliver F. Winchester, a forty-five-year-old shirt merchant, who became Volcanic's director. A month later they bought out Smith, Wesson, and Palmer. Smith & Wesson received $65,000 cash in three installments, plus 2,800 shares of stock. They were also paid for their Norwich, Connecticut plant machinery.

The first Volcanic guns came off the line in February 1856. The ammunition, adequate for traditional handgun uses, lacked the power shooters expected even of muzzleloading rifles. But even vigorous demand could not have sustained the firm. Creditors forced it into receivership in February 1857. On March 15, Oliver Winchester purchased, for just under $40,000, all assets. The price was barely enough to cover claims against the corporation, so stockholders got nothing.

Despite this setback, Winchester saw a bright future for the lever-action repeater. In April 1857, he reorganized Volcanic Repeating

Arms into the New Haven Arms Company. In June 1859 the factory was moved to No. 9 Artizan Street in New Haven, where Winchester fretted over the Volcanic bullet. Skinny and light, it had a shallow base cavity that limited the powder charge and velocity. But B. Tyler Henry had already begun adapting the Volcanic rifle to metallic rimfire cartridges. He was rewarded in 1860 with U.S. patent 30,446. It covered a lever-action rimfire repeating rifle with a fifteen-round tubular magazine and a two-pronged firing pin that came down on both sides of the rim of a chambered case.

The Henry's cartridge featured a .44-caliber, 216-grain pointed bullet atop 26 grains of blackpowder, for a muzzle velocity of about 1,025 fps. Anemic by modern standards, the .44 Henry rimfires developed ten times the muzzle energy of the old Volcanic bullets. Grease grooves filled with tallow helped prevent leading and improved accuracy. No patents were taken out on Henry's rimfire cartridges, headstamped "H" in his honor. (He may have been unaware of the efforts of Smith & Wesson that culminated in .22 rimfire cartridges in January 1858.) Henry began engineering his .44 rounds in the fall of that year. His rifle and its ammunition debuted in 1860, just in time to prop up a

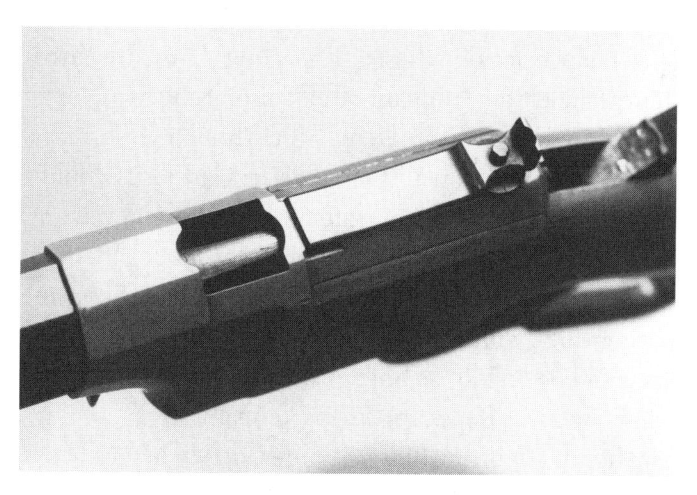

The Henry rifle borrowed heavily from Walter Hunt's Volcanic, the gun that spawned an institution at Winchester Repeating Arms.

nearly bankrupt New Haven Repeating Arms. Without Tyler Henry and the Civil War, Winchester and company would have perished.

Oliver Winchester's appeal to the U.S. government for military adoption of the Henry repeater made it appear fearsome indeed. But even when President Lincoln overrode Ordnance objections to breech-loading rifles, Winchester faced a problem. The seven-shot Spencer lever-action rifle, designed by Christopher Spencer in 1860, was sturdy, reliable, and destined to become the most popular breechloader in the war.

The Henry's major fault was its under-barrel magazine tube, weakened by a full-length slot. Dents rendered the follower unreliable, and debris worked its way into the slot. But the Henry held fifteen rounds to the Spencer's seven, and one motion of the lever would both reload and cock the gun, while the Spencer required a separate cocking motion. Many soldiers bought the Henry with their own money, with the understanding that the government would furnish ammunition. The rifle's greatest accolade came from the Confederates: "Give us anything but your damned Yankee rifle that can be loaded on Sunday and fired all week."

In 1865 Oliver Winchester changed his firm's name to the Henry Repeating Arms Company. A year later the legislature approved a second name change to Winchester Repeating Arms. By this time, B. Tyler Henry had left the company, and Nelson King was shop foreman. In 1866 King redesigned the Henry rifle's troublesome magazine by adding a spring-loaded port in the receiver. Cartridges could then be more easily loaded. This change, with a wooden forend, gave Winchester a new rifle. Like the Henry, the Winchester Model 1866 was chambered for .44 Pointed and .44 Flat rimfire cartridges. Sportsmen were soon paying fifty dollars for Winchester 66s—when war-surplus Spencers could be had for as little as seven bucks. In 1868 Winchester acquired the Spencer Repeating Rifle Company.

Winchester got his first foreign order for Model 66s when Benito Juarez, the Mexican leader opposing Emperor Maximillian, ordered 1,000 rifles and 500,000 rounds of ammunition. In 1870 Winchester

Generations of hunters have carried Winchesters. The company predates the .22 Long Rifle.

struck more foreign deals. The Bridgeport plant was dismantled and a new one built at the corner of Munson and Canal Streets in New Haven. Canal Street later became Winchester Avenue.

In 1870 Thomas Gray Bennett, a Yale graduate, began work at Winchester. Bennett later served as vice president, then president; and he became Oliver Winchester's son-in-law. Bennett's work was crucial to the design of the Winchester Model 1873, an improvement on the

Model 1866 and the firm's first centerfire rifle. This gun was chambered for the .44 WCF or .44-40, which launched a 200-grain bullet with 28 grains of blackpowder. At a muzzle velocity of 1,300 fps, this bullet generated nearly 30 percent more energy than the .44 Henry, and over twelve times the energy of the old Volcanic bullet. The brass frame of the 1866 was dropped in favor of forged iron on the '73. The iron in turn was replaced with steel in 1884.

About 19,552 Model 1873s in .22 rimfire were produced between 1884 and 1904. This Winchester was, in fact, the first American .22 rimfire repeating rifle. The first Model 73 rimfires were take-downs, but solid frames proved superior. Model 1873 parts were manufactured until 1919, though a few rifles were put together as late as 1925. Incidentally, the 1873 was the first lever-action Winchester to be called by its model number. So popular and distinctive was the 1866 that everyone knew it as simply "the Winchester."

New Haven's next winner, the Model 1876, was a big Model 1873. A new .45-75 Winchester round, with its 350-grain bullet, doubled the energy of the .44 WCF. The 1876 was for many years the official rifle of the Royal Canadian Mounted Police. Winchester dropped the rifle in 1897.

Winchester's Model 1883 Hotchkiss was the first U.S. bolt rifle to bottle high pressures. Invented by B. B. Hotchkiss, an American living in Paris, this gun had a tubular magazine in its buttstock and raised Oliver Winchester's hopes for a military contract. But the first batch of Winchester-Hotchkiss rifles showed flaws in workmanship, and soldiers disliked the unfamiliar action.

Still, the 1880s were boom years for Winchester. Its market position for both rifles and ammunition was strengthened by the company's ability to design one for the other and follow advertising with sure supply. In 1888 the firm teamed up with Marcellus Hartley's Union Metallic Cartridge Company to buy Remington Arms. Because of the Sherman Anti-Trust Act, that marriage was brief.

Winchester announced its first breechloading shotguns in 1880. The imported double-barrels lasted only three years due to stiff tariffs.

Rich Freudenberg aims a Model 62, an updated version of the pump-action Winchester 1890.

Winchester then built a lever-action shotgun on a design supplied by John Browning in 1886. First cataloged in 1888, this was the fourth repeating shotgun made in the U.S.—behind designs by Colt, Roper, and Spencer. But it was the first successful repeating smoothbore.

Seeking stronger actions to handle more powerful cartridges, Thomas Bennett had traveled to Ogden in 1883 to negotiate with the Browning brothers on a single-shot rifle. While there, he examined a sketch of a new lever-action mechanism. Bennett secured the rights to both rifle designs for a total of eight thousand dollars. One would become the Model 1885 single-shot (High Wall), the other the Model 1886 lever-action. A rich haul indeed, but only a taste of what was to come. Browning would sell Winchester the plans for more than forty mechanisms that spawned seven important rifles and three shotguns.

By 1890 gun design in the United States had eclipsed the development of cartridges. Blackpowder was essentially the same mixture the Chinese had used in the fourteenth century. Developments in Europe, however, would soon make it obsolete. Following the work of the Swiss chemist Schoenbein and the Italian Sobero, who discovered nitrocellulose and nitroglycerin, Vielle, a Frenchman, found in 1885 that dissolving nitrocellulose in ether produced a stable colloid that could be dried and used as propellant. The compound became single-base smokeless powder. Alfred Nobel and Frederick Able later added nitroglycerin to get double-base smokeless.

Winchester didn't catalog smokeless ammunition until 1893, when it advertised shotshells with new "nitro" propellant. Within a year the company was offering seventeen smokeless centerfire cartridges. Ammunition fueled much of Winchester's growth in the early days of the automobile. By 1914, the company was loading 175 smokeless cartridges. Though it served handloaders, Winchester called the handloading of smokeless cartridges "impractical."

Between the advent of smokeless powder and the start of World War I, Winchester developed some of its most famous guns: the Model 1890 .22 rimfire pump rifle and Model 1897 pump shotgun, as well as Models 1892 and 1894 lever-action rifles. The Model 1903 autoloading .22 was the first successful self-loader produced in quantity in the United States. The Model 12 pump shotgun became one of the most popular smoothbores ever.

Winchester pioneered the use of nickel steel barrels in centerfire rifles in the Model 94, an instant hit. The 92, chambered for shorter, less potent rounds like the .44-40, was advertised it as "the rifle that helped Peary reach the North Pole."

The twentieth century brought new men to Winchester. Thomas Bennett's split with John Browning was a blow, but in Thomas Crossly Johnson the company found another gifted gun designer. Johnson specialized in autoloading mechanisms, developing the recoil-operated Winchester Self-Loading Rifles, Models 03, 05, 07, and 10. Johnson engineered Winchester's first autoloading shotgun, a recoil-operated, hammerless, five-shot repeater designated the Model 11. He had to work around the Browning patents, which he had actually helped write.

During the First World War, Winchester supplied more than 50,000 Browning Automatic Rifles, plus thousands of short-barreled Model 97 shotguns for trench fighting. Each shell had six .34-caliber

The 9422M is a slick-feeding rimfire saddle gun.

pellets. They proved so devastating that the German government protested, warning that any American carrying a shotgun when captured would be shot. Other contracts called for 44 million .303 British cartridges and 400,000 Enfield rifles for the British government, plus 9 million .44 WCF rounds for the British Home Guard's Winchester 92 rifles and 50 million .22 Long Rifle cartridges, also for England. Winchester's plant had doubled in size, to 3.25 million square feet. During hostilities, 17,549 people worked there. But long-term price contracts didn't cover steeply rising labor costs. At war's end, with demand on a slide, these oversights crippled Winchester.

In 1920 Thomas Bennett and other patriarchs reorganized the firm. The Winchester Repeating Arms Company made guns and ammunition, while its sister firm, the Winchester Company, manufactured cutlery, gas refrigerators, skates, flashlights, fishing gear, hand tools, washing machines, baseball bats, skis, batteries, paints, and household brushes. This diversification failed to reduce debt; ironically, the gun division prospered.

For some time after Armistice Day, Winchester gun designers had almost no budget. Still, they came up with two fine rifles: the Model 52 bolt-action rimfire in 1919 and the Model 54 centerfire in 1924. The 54 was Winchester's first successful bolt-action centerfire rifle, though the company had tried to enter that field for thirty years. The .45-70 Hotchkiss was discontinued in 1900; the Lee Straight Pull lasted from 1897 to 1903.

Engineers working on the 54 focused on the 1903 Springfield. It had the Springfield's coned breech and an ejector by Newton. The Mauser-style bolt wore a beefy extractor and safety. The stock was patterned after the popular Sedgely sporters of that period. A nickel steel barrel on a cyanide-hardened receiver bottled pressures from the new .270 WCF cartridge, whose 130-grain bullet at 3,000 fps awed hunters used to .30-30s.

When the Depression hit, Winchester was too weak to stand. In February 1929 the old organization was dissolved, and the Winchester Repeating Arms Company of Delaware took its place. The company went bankrupt in 1931, the year the Model 21 shotgun would come to market. In December of that year, Winchester was acquired by the Western Cartridge Company. Western acquired the company for $3 million cash and $4.8 million (par value) of Western stock. The company entered the Depression under Franklin Olin's son, John, who had a keen interest in firearms. In the next decade twenty-three new Winchester guns would appear.

The decision to replace the Model 54 with another rifle was prompted largely by a desire for a better centerfire target gun. Since its introduction in 1919, the Model 52 rimfire rifle had steadily built an unassailable record on smallbore ranges, and Winchester wanted centerfire laurels to match. In 1937, the Model 70 debuted.

The first M70s, cataloged at $61.25, came in nine chamberings. Seven more were added in the 1950s and early '60s before a drastic reconfiguration in 1964. Several cartridges fell along the way, and Winchester made some 70s in chamberings special-ordered by customers. "The rifleman's rifle," Winchester's Model 70 gave the company a much-needed post-Depression boost.

Winchester's 52 target rifle has won truckloads of medals.

In 1936 the M1 Garand rifle became the main infantry weapon for U.S. armed forces. The first New Haven–built Garands were delivered a year before Pearl Harbor. In 1940 Winchester also developed a lightweight carbine. In preliminary work, Winchester designer David "Carbine" Williams used a new short-stroke piston to operate the action, later scaled down to accept the .30 Carbine cartridge.

The Second World War fueled huge production jumps at Winchester-Western. Total wartime output: 1.45 million guns and more than 15 billion rounds of ammunition. After the war, John Olin's ammunition firm concentrated on developing sporting ammunition. Ball powders came in 1946, Baby Magnum shotshells in 1954, the .22 Winchester Magnum Rimfire round in 1959, and a compression-formed shotshell in 1964.

In August 1954, Olin was swallowed by the huge Mattheson Chemical Corporation. Ten years later Winchester guns were redesigned to take advantage of cheaper materials and manufacturing processes. Sound on paper, the change triggered a colossal revolt in the marketplace. Pre-64 Winchesters suddenly commanded premiums on the used-gun market. The company scrambled to correct its blunder. In relatively

The Winchester factory employed more than 20,000 workers during World War II.

short order it was offering guns with the traditional features shooters wanted, but without the hand finishing that had become prohibitively expensive. When Olin-Mattheson sold the Winchester Sporting Arms business in July 1981, the new company, U.S. Repeating Arms, continued improving its products, contracting some shotguns from Japan.

In 1984 USRAC filed for Chapter 11. In 1987 five investors bought the company. Among them was Fabrique Nationale (FN), a Belgian firm that also owns Browning. FN is itself owned by Société Générale, which controls 70 percent of Belgium's gross national product. Early in 1991 a French conglomerate bought FN and, with it, USRAC. These days, you'll likely hear "use-rack" in talk about guns of New Haven lineage. But they're still Winchesters to shooters who value history.

PART 4

To Shoot a Rimfire

Chapter 19

REAL GUNSTOCKS

If you're old enough to remember the manual typewriter, you probably recall the real gunstock. It was walnut. It looked warm and felt like part of a real rifle.

Sadly, real gunstocks have diminished, driven from the market by rising prices for walnut. When I was a lad, you could buy a fancy American walnut stock blank for twenty-five bucks. I paid $7.50 for the plain but semi-inletted blank that went on my first deer rifle. Now even American walnut has become too costly for ordinary rifles. Birch and other cheap hardwoods are replacing it, especially on .22s. The problem with walnut is that you can't make it. You have to grow it. Growing walnut takes a lot longer than growing tomatoes, so we're inletting wood from trees that may have been around before the V-8 engine, before metallic cartridges, even before the Declaration of Independence. Don't figure on cutting gunstocks from trees you're planting now.

In a cruel twist of circumstance, the people who discovered walnut had no guns to put it on. That was back in the thirteenth century, when Marco Polo allegedly brought walnuts from their native Persia to Italy. Nuts and seedlings eventually found their way to England, then to France and other parts of Europe. The scientific name for the species is *Juglans regia*, or "royal walnut." Though grain structure and color varies, *J. regia* is the same worldwide. Common names denote location, not genetic differences. English walnut is *J. regia*; so is French. The tree eventually wound up in California, to be adopted as

Anschutz rifles are still stocked in European walnut, but they don't come cheap.

"California English." Typically, California English wood grown from nuts has a tawny background with black streaking and less "marble-cake" than England's version. Classic French is often red or orange. Most of the Circassian walnut I've seen runs heavy to black. It's named after a region in the northwest Caucasus, on the Black Sea.

"These days the best *regia* walnut comes from Turkey and Morocco," the late Don Allen told me in an interview not long before his untimely death. Don knew more about walnut than anyone else I could name. Before establishing Dakota Arms, he built rifle stocks while finishing a career as a commercial pilot. His passion was fine wood, and he traveled all over the world to get it. Currently, Dakota processes about a thousand stock blanks a year. Its .22 rimfire rifles wear wood as lovely as that seen on most custom-built centerfires. "The best Turkish walnut is superb," Don said. "Unfortunately, it's being sawed into dollars at an unsustainable rate." He predicted that current reserves would be depleted before 2010. "We think some of the trees being cut in Turkey are three hundred to four hundred years old. Age adds color and figure to wood. But old trees soon become scarce."

As supplies of suitable walnut continue to dwindle, laminated and synthetic stocks have become more prevalent.

Claro walnut, *J. hindsii*, was discovered around 1840, in California. Decidedly red, and with more open grain than English walnut, Claro was crossed with English to produce ornamental Bastogne walnut. The nuts from these shade trees are infertile, but fast growth and dense grain have made Bastogne a favorite of stockmakers. It checkers more cleanly than Claro and withstands heavy recoil. The best of Bastogne has beautiful color and figure. Sadly, this walnut is almost gone, the limited supply diminishing fast under unrelenting demand. As with *J. regia*, the most desirable Bastogne comes from trees at least 150 years old.

American, or black, walnut (*J. nigra*), has been the mainstay of our firearms industry since the first "Kentucky" rifles were forged in Pennsylvania. This relatively open-pored wood is warm brown in color, with just enough black to justify the name. It can be as plain as a power pole or richly patterned, depending on the tree's age and locale, and the location and type of cut. Quarter-sawn walnut has the striping most of us are used to; the saw runs across growth rings. Plane-sawn walnut shows wide color bands because the saw runs tangent to growth rings. Either cut can yield a sturdy, handsome stock, but quarter-sawn walnut is most in demand.

Walnut must be dried before it is worked. Don Allen explained: "Immediately after a blank is cut, free water starts to escape. Think of a soaked sponge dripping. If the water leaves too fast, the wood surface can crack and check, and eventually crust, inhibiting movement of bound water from the core. Structural damage may result." Don explains that a kiln helps throttle the release of free water. "Most drying damage occurs in the first weeks after cutting a blank. Moisture content will then stabilize at about 20 percent, after which time the blank can be air-dried or kiln-dried without damage." He adds that you don't need a special environment to air-dry wood that's been properly brought to 20 percent moisture. "Just avoid extremes of temperature and humidity. Weigh the blank periodically. When the stock no longer loses weight, it's dry enough to work." Stockmakers may turn the blank to profile at this point and let it dry another six months before inletting.

In France, walnut growers used to steam logs before cutting them into slabs or flitches. Steaming colored the sap, turning it from white to amber. It also wiped out resident insects.

Dakota rifles are renowned for their fine walnut. Don told me that Dakota's wood room is one of the few places in the country where you can handle high-grade walnut. "Less than five percent of all walnut passes muster as fancy or exhibition-grade," he said. "Without a market for standard-grade wood, large mills can't afford to deal in fancy walnut." Dakota Arms has established a milling operation in New Zealand, still a source for dense, figured walnut.

Don was always on the lookout for good wood. He bought one of the largest Bastogne trees in the world. Very old, the lone tree towered over a surrounding prune orchard. Its trunk measured twelve feet in diameter, and the canopy spanned over 150 feet. Thirty feet above the ground some branches were twenty feet in circumference. "It was a real find," said Don, "And quite a commitment! First we had to limb it, then trench around the stump. We didn't cut the tree down as you might fall a spruce. Instead, we cut all the roots and pushed it over. Wood deeper than a foot underground is too soft for gunstocks, though the buttwood usually delivers the best color. Figure can reach high in the tree. In this case fiddleback ran all the way to the small limbs."

The author (left) with Jim Morey and the late Don Allen (gunmaker, walnut guru, and founder of Dakota Arms).

That light-colored walnut is commonly assumed to be worthless, according to Don. "Truth is, many walnut trees contain no dark wood, and the white core is hardly distinguishable. Knowledgeable buyers know that the best colors lie next to the core or sap pillar, so they don't mind a little white trim in their blanks."

Sections of tree go to the mill, where they're sawn into blanks three inches thick. "The big Bastogne gave us 4,700 blanks," chuckled Don. "More importantly, we got some of the finest figure I've ever seen."

Handsome walnut is of no value if it breaks. "Layout" is an important first step in stockmaking. The grain on a quarter-sawn walnut blank should run roughly parallel with the top of the grip, when viewed from the side. That way, you'll get maximum strength through the grip, while reducing the tendency of the forend to bend. Viewed from the top, the grain should run parallel to the bore, to prevent side pressure on the barrel. Many costly rifles have stocks with highly figured butts and plain forends. Figure in the butt doesn't affect accuracy, but up front the knots and crotches that make for interesting patterns can twist the forend. Though figured wood may be dense, it is not as strong or stable as straight-grained wood.

Browning appropriately keeps walnut on its lever-action .22s.

Glass bedding strengthens wood but does not eliminate warpage. My own preference is for glass or epoxy in the recoil lug mortise, both to prevent splitting through the magazine well and to give the metal firm and unchanging contact with the stock. With glass compound at the bottom of the mortise, you can tighten the front guard screw securely without compressing the wood. Glass displaced into the first inch or so of barrel channel and under the receiver broadens the metal's platform. You may want to put a smaller bedding patch under the tang to ensure it has a solid base of support. Aluminum pillars around the guard screws serve the same purpose, giving you solid contact from bottom metal to receiver.

The best custom rifle stockers dismiss glass as a fix for shoddy inletting. They pride themselves in skin-tight fit of wood to metal, maintaining that a properly bedded stock won't split at the web or grip. While that's true for most rifles, the brutal kick of some modern magnums tests not just inletting but the integrity of the walnut. That's why you'll see crossbolts reinforcing wood stocks on "safari" rifles. Pins fore and aft of the magazine well appeared on Winchester M70s when stocks began to give way under the pounding of the .458 Magnum. Of course, restocking a .22 rimfire, you needn't fret over recoil putting the tang through your zygomatic arch if the stock isn't perfectly inletted. But the fit of recoil-bearing surfaces to the wood and the mating of wood to metal in the bedding area affect both looks and accuracy.

Whoever came up with checkering deserves a free elk hunt in Arizona. Not only does checkering help you grip the stock; it can be an elegant finishing touch. The finer the checkering, the more demanding the work, because each diamond must be the same size as all the other diamonds and properly "pointed up." Checkering can be as fine

Beautifully finished and checkered, this Cooper in .17 HMR wears a fine piece of walnut.

as 32 lines per inch (lpi), though such small diamonds are more decorative than functional. You'll get better purchase with crisply checkered panels cut 22 to 26 lines per inch. I like 24-lpi checkering, but it's hard to find on production-class rifles. Expect from 18 (coarse) to 22 lpi.

Though electric cutters have taken the place of traditional tools for hand checkering, most factory stocks are now checkered on machines. They're remarkably good at keeping diamonds uniform, borders clean. If you want intricate panels or wraparound checkering at the grip, better see a good stocker—after a trip to the bank. Oddly enough, *fleur-de-lis* patterns that typically draw the most admiration are easier to cut than point patterns. That's because the *fleur-de-lis* is a fill-in job. You scribe a border, then simply cut grooves to it. (In a point pattern, the border is part of the checkering, not simply a frame.) If you're off a tad on a fill-in effort, the border will still be right, and only close inspection will show an error. Get the cutter angle a tad off in a point pattern, and the mistake follows you to completion. A full-wrap point pattern on a grip is for experts only. So too ribbons inside patterns.

Among the most skilled contemporary stockers is Gary Goudy of Dayton, Washington. His ribbons are fine as fly line, uniform and unbroken by overruns. I can't tell you how he does that, because I don't know.

Checkering is best done after finishing; otherwise, finish gums up in the trenches. To finish fresh-cut panels, I use a toothbrush, which is also handy for cleaning the checkering. Dip the brush in boiled linseed oil and scrub vigorously.

By the way, boiled linseed oil (raw linseed oil will not dry) is the traditional finish for walnut stocks. It's still a good choice, albeit tedious to apply. After sanding, wet-sand with 600-grit paper to raise whiskers in the wood, polish off dust, and rub in oil until it gets hot under your hand. When you're tired, wipe off excess oil with a clean rag and set the stock aside to dry, preferably where conditions match Death Valley in July. When the stock is *really* dry, repeat the process, building up microscopically thin films of boiled linseed oil over several weeks. Open-grained wood takes longer to fill. To polish out trapped dust, use a slurry of rottenstone in oil, then wipe off the excess.

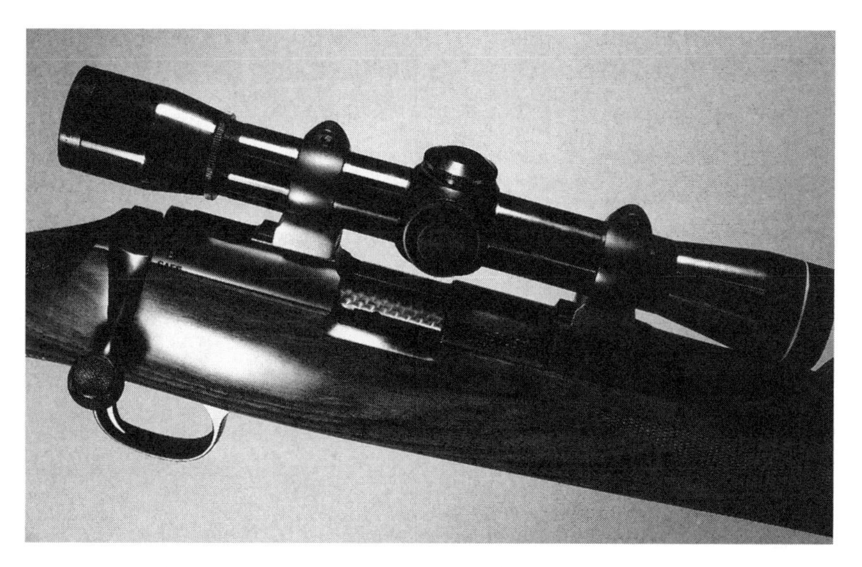

This gorgeous Winchester 52 Sporter, custom-built by Len Brownell, features a stock in superb French walnut.

One advantage of boiled linseed oil finish is its easy maintenance. Because the oil has soaked into the wood, scratches wipe away with an oily cloth. Dings can be steamed out with a flatiron over a wet washcloth. Then use the rottenstone slurry to smooth and blend. Boiled linseed oil can be used with stain, but by itself often brings out the most pleasing look. It is not a waterproof finish; however, it does repel water adequately for most elk hunting.

Polymers, such as those used on bowling pins, deliver more durable finish, but the look is neither warm nor natural. Polymers do excel as sealants, and have largely supplanted the traditional spar varnish I used thirty-five years ago on my first gunstocks.

If you want a sturdy, lightweight, weatherproof riflestock, buy one of Kevlar. But if you crave one with personality, walnut is your only choice. Really.

Chapter 20

BETTER SIGHTS, BETTER SHOTS

When you buy a scope, you buy a sight picture. Though people who sell scopes may talk about them as if they added functional or aesthetic value to the rifle, they don't. A rifle works just fine without a scope. And while the profile of a scoped rifle can be attractive, a rifle with iron sights is sleeker, weighs less, balances better, and is easier to carry. A scope is still an appendage. Rifles made to use with scopes look just like rifles made to use without scopes, except that rifles—even .22 rimfires—increasingly come without sights. The assumption is that everybody uses a scope.

And, in fact, almost everybody does. A scope not only magnifies the target, it puts the target in the same apparent plane as the aiming device, in this case, the reticle. So your eye doesn't have the impossible job of trying to simultaneously focus on open rear sight, front bead, and target. With an aperture rear sight, you need concentrate only on the bead and the target, but that's still a chore. And even a small bead can cover a distant target. A scope's reticle can be plainly visible and as sharp as a tack without obscuring your target.

Because .22 rifles are most commonly used on little targets, any reticle has a huge advantage over a front bead. At relatively low magnification, a scope beats iron sights in delivering sharp, clear target images quickly. At high magnification, it gives you precision you'll never

This Kahles 2–7x scope, parallax-corrected for seventy-five yards, is an ideal sight for a .22.

get with irons, even if they're tailored to the target (as competition sights are).

What you see affects how well you shoot.

You must see the target. You must see the reticle.

But your eye will also be aware of other things about the sight picture. It will notice brightness, for example, and contrast. It will perceive sharpness and the trueness of colors. It will detect unnatural curvature of lines, and image distortion. Of course, it will show you apparent image size, and breadth of field, and eye relief. Plus reticle movement.

All of what your eye takes in helps form your sight picture. Expecting the most powerful or costly scope to give you the best performance is like buying an automobile using engine displacement or sticker price as the sole criterion. If you want a *hunting* scope, look to other measures.

Though you'll want better optics for your .22 than the dim, tinny ¾-inch scopes commonly stuck on rimfire receivers in my youth, it's hard to justify scopes that cost as much as a divorce. A scope, after all, is

Leupold Vari-X III scopes, popular with big game hunters, also excel on .22 rifles, like this Kimber.

not a binocular, used to discern detail in tangles of foliage and to sift shades of color from desert or rock wall. A scope is a sight, used only for a brief moment. You paste the reticle on the target and shoot as soon as you can. Until you shoot, and afterward, the scope is worthless.

Which is why I like scopes that are lightweight and compact, with only the features that enhance their utility as sights. Here's my checklist:

A one-inch tube. The current trend toward 30mm tubes is largely without basis. Unless you want extra room for shifting the erector assembly as you move zero out to extreme range, there's no need for a tube bigger than one inch. A few 30mm scopes do have bigger erector lenses than those in one-inch (25.4mm) scopes, and because bigger glass improves the image (lens quality being equal), tubes with oversize erectors have an optical edge. But it won't be nearly as noticeable as the extra weight of the bigger scope. On rimfire rifles, a 30mm tube looks as appropriate as tractor tires on a sports car.

Fully multicoated optics. The first lens coating, used in Germany around 1940, was magnesium fluoride. It reduced the amount of light lost to reflection and refraction at the air-glass surface. Such loss can amount to 4 percent of incident light *at each surface.* In a scope

Light transmission is determined largely by lens coatings. Insist on fully multicoated optics.

with many uncoated lenses (variables have more than fixed-power scopes), total loss can result in a dim picture indeed. "Fully" means that every lens in the scope is coated; multicoating helps by influencing several wavelengths of light individually as they enter and leave each lens.

Lens coating imparts color to the lens. It's not like a surface tint, but seems to issue from the depths of the glass—commonly straw, green, blue, or purple. But you cannot assume, when you see color in the ocular and objective lenses, that all internal lenses are coated. You

This European-style ocular adjusts reticle focus quicker than a fine-threaded bell and lock ring.

must look to the scope's specifications. High-quality coatings certainly help you see better. And, typically, they're applied only to high-quality lenses. Collectively (and loosely), lenses and their coatings are often called "optics" in a scope, though optics more accurately describes a range of instruments using lenses to improve vision. A scope with the best "optics" will cost more than one with mediocre glass and coatings. This may be where you'll want to spend your tax refund.

A bold reticle. If you can't see it, you can't aim with it. It seems to me that most reticles are too fine. They give you precision you don't need and often can't use. If a reticle doesn't cover what you want to hit, it's fine enough. On a small game animal, my target is an imaginary one-inch disk on the forward ribs or skull. Most of the time, my wobble amounts to at least six times the thickness of an ordinary crosswire in a 4x sight. Why should I use a finer wire?

Target shooting calls for another standard, because the rifle is usually steadier, the target much smaller. In the 20x Redfield scope on my .22 match rifle, the crosswire is so slender that I have a hard time covering a bullet hole at fifty yards. It's still thick enough to see easily against the black of the target on a cloudy day. I once peered through a 36x scope with a crosswire so delicate it got lost in the black. To me, that is a useless scope, as is any hunting sight with a reticle that doesn't immediately grab your attention in timber at dusk.

Long eye relief. There are really two measures of eye relief (ER). One is optical—the distance between the ocular lens and your eye at which you perceive the scope's full field of view. The other is physical—the distance between your brow and the rim of the eyepiece when you're looking at a full field. On centerfire rifles, physical ER is as important as optical ER, because it's shorter. If recoil brings the scope 3 inches to the rear and optical ER is 3½, you'll still get bruised if physical ER is 2½.

Among the Lyman Alaskan's endearing qualities was eye relief so generous you could mount it so the ocular lens was forward of the rear-swing safety on an old Model 70. Even if you don't need the safety clearance (you won't on a .22 rifle), four inches of optical eye relief makes for faster, more natural aim. Eye relief that is not critical also makes sense. It enables you to see a full field when your head is a little

Scopes with extended eye relief, like this Nikon, offer greater precision for pistol shooting.

farther forward or a little farther back because of your shooting position. Count on eye relief to shrink as you boost power or increase field of view. (In many variable scopes eye relief at the top of the power range is smaller than at the bottom.)

An adequate field of view. Hunters seem to want powerful scopes now, and field of view has become one of the criteria by which scopes are judged. Expand field of view or increase magnification, and the remaining leg of the "optical triangle," eye relief, must be reduced. Even for .22s, I prefer a scope I can mount well forward—one with *at least* 3½ inches of optical ER. At practical hunting magnifications (to 6x), field is still generous. If you want more power for varminting, you'll get it at the expense of your panorama; on the other hand, when shooting at small targets far away, it's likely you'll take plenty of time from a steady position. You won't need the field required for gunning down sprinting cottontails.

The more you use a scope, the less important field will become, because you'll become skilled at pointing the rifle at what you see. The target will start appearing instantly in the center of your field. Except for shots at running game, you'll need only the center to score.

This scope is set too far back for many shooters. Keep the ocular housing well forward.

Sturdy construction. You must trust what you see. While I've found most claims of scope failure baseless, hunting can be hard on a scope, and you need the confidence engendered by a sturdy sight. You can't test durability without risking damage to the scope, and few makers will replace a scope deliberately hurled to the sidewalk from a third-floor window. To their credit, most companies test their scopes with recoil-simulating machines that deliver the 1,000 Gs they would get on a .375 H&H rifle. But scopes are not designed to fall off mountains.

For a measure of the scope's durability, examine its warranty. Leupold has replaced a lot of scopes that weren't defective, simply to satisfy customers who abused their sights or expected too much of them. The Leupold warranty is now legendary among hunters who specify the gold ring when they want a durable scope. A manufacturer that stands behind its product probably builds a stout product. When through the lens you see the world jarred by your shot, it's helpful to know the bullet will land where the reticle was.

So, what *don't* you want in a hunting scope?

Weight and bulk, for one thing. Not only is extra scope weight a drag to carry; it makes your rifle top-heavy and, on powerful rifles, strains the mount during recoil. A scope with a big front bell is awkward and a poor match for a scabbard. More to the point, weight and bulk don't help you see. Bigger objective glass will make the image brighter in dim light if you're shooting at high magnification, but at 6x or less, it's superfluous. Magnification higher than 6x may show you more wobble than you can control under hunting conditions.

A lightweight rifle can lose its lively feel if you top it with a ponderous scope. In my view, scope and mounts shouldn't account for more than 15 percent of the bare weight of a rifle. For example, the sight for a seven-pound rifle shouldn't weigh more than a pound. The lighter, the better. Alloy mounts lack the cachet of machined steel; however, they're more than stout enough to hold lightweight scopes on rimfire rifles. I prefer mounts that screw to the receiver, but dovetail

In the field, magnification can be overdone. You can shoot only as well as you can see.

mounting is fine if you're using a trim scope. Excess weight on top of the rifle not only adds to your burden, it impairs balance.

Limiting scope weight is easier if you aren't hung up on high magnification. You don't need as much as you might think. In fact, too much power can make shooting difficult. A light breeze that you wouldn't notice while aiming through a 4x scope becomes a problem at 12x because you see not only important reticle movement that must be

Lightweight alloy rings, like these produced by Talley, make sense not only for .22s but also for centerfires.

controlled, but all the little jinks that can't be—the jinks that are present but invisible in a scope of lower power. A reticle that dances the jitterbug makes you nervous, and you waste time trying to calm it. You give up as your muscles give way. Your breath is gone. The reticle is now gyrating wildly. In frustration you jerk the trigger as it flies by the target. You miss. The same can happen if you're winded or chilled or for some other reason can't make your muscles behave. Of course, you may also sacrifice too much field by boosting power, and you'll reduce light transmission at dawn and dusk. Get as much magnification as you can use, but no more.

What you might want but don't need are precise quarter-minute adjustments. On the hunt, you'll not be "grabbing a handful of clicks" to correct for wind, as might a long-range target shooter, or "cranking in" a couple of feet of bullet drop to hit steel rams at five hundred meters. As much as I dislike mushy adjustments, they're not essential in a hunting scope. They don't help you see.

Neither will an adjustable objective—unless, again, you're shooting at very high power. An Ashley Outdoors (AO) scope allows you to "zero out" parallax, the gremlin that causes reticle and target to part ways as you move your eye off the centerline of the scope. Rimfire riflemen shoot mostly at less than a hundred yards, as do hunters with shotguns and muzzleloaders. For this reason all scopes designated for these guns are commonly set to be parallax free at short range; seventy-five yards is the norm, or about half the zero-parallax distance for an ordinary scope for centerfire rifles. If you keep your eye on-axis, however, you needn't fret about parallax at any distance. The other benefit you get in an AO scope is sharper focus at the set distance, but you'll notice that only at high power too—say, 10x or above. By the way, if you choose AO, a turret-mounted dial is handier than the front sleeve.

You don't need a lighted reticle, though in dark places it is easy to find. I like the Aimpoint sight so I won't argue against electronics. But remember that you must see both the reticle and the target. Bright orange dots do you no good if the animal is indistinct. The most reliable lighted reticles are not the red dots that vanish entirely if the power fails; rather, they're the illuminated reticles that give you the black wire as a mechanical fallback. With either, keep power low in dim light. Using more illumination than necessary makes your target harder to see.

A variety of mechanical reticles have gone in and out of favor. The ordinary crosswire, still useful if properly thick, has been supplanted by the plex, with heavy outer bars to catch your eye and thin center wires for precision. I still like dots, but the best size depends on scope magnification. A 3-minute dot is about right for a 4x scope, in my view, a 2-minute dot for a 6x. I like a 4-minute dot on a 2½x sight. The post reticle has never been my favorite, though it's easy to see. Zero with the top of

High magnification is useful if you're target shooting.

the post, not the point of intersection with the horizontal wire. A mil-dot or simple rangefinding reticle like Swarovski's TDA or the Burris Ballistic Plex can help you gauge distance. But it won't help you see or shoot.

The more you shoot, the less you may rely on a scope to help you see. If you hunt where the shots are short, iron sights may work just as well. They let you point your rifle as if it were your finger, so you get on target quickly. They don't encumber the rifle or prevent you from a comfortable "hand-grip" carry. Tang sights deliver the longest sight radius but interfere with your right hand and can come so close to your eye as to be dangerous on hard-kicking rifles. Cocking-piece sights are safer but a bit less precise because they move. Receiver sights like the old Redfield and Williams can't match the sleek lines of newer AO sights that mount on top.

The AO "ghost ring" is a wide-open aperture that shows you most of the northern hemisphere. The front blade, with its white center stripe, is a distant highway. It is not the sight setup for long shooting at little targets. But it's fast in the forest. Remember that only when a reticle or front sight blocks out more of the target than you'd accept as a landing spot for a bullet is the aiming device too coarse. And if you're properly zeroed with a coarse sight, the bullets will land where you want

The author fired these groups, one with iron sights, in competition with a McMillan-barreled Remington 37.

them to even when you don't see where they'll strike when you fire. In iron-sight competition, I cannot see the bull's-eye. All I see is the black round blob comprising several scoring rings. When I center that target, the bullet goes to a middle I cannot see. And that's all right, even with hunting rifles. If the bullet strikes behind the bead or reticle, and the bead or reticle is on the vitals, logic demands only one conclusion.

Scope finishes vary from traditional high-gloss black to matte black and matte silver (to match stainless receivers). Matte finishes bring less attention to you in the woods and, to my eye, look best on all but very shiny rifles. But what's inside the tube is more important than what's outside, because what's inside helps you see.

PRACTICAL SCOPES

The first short, receiver-mounted scopes were engineered for hunting, by and for hunters used to shooting iron sights. Consequently, they had to deliver a big field of view and lots of eye relief, disrupting as little as possible the original lines and balance of the rifle. Bill Weaver's nineteen-dollar Model 330 scope, a 3x brought out in 1930, is commonly acknowledged as the first successful hunting scope for the masses. But Weaver, just twenty-four at the time, followed a number of inventors who paved the way for the 330. As early as 1887, Cummins marketed a "Duplex Telescope Sight." It had achromatic lenses ¾ inch in diameter, and internal adjustments (the first U.S. scope to feature them). You could order magnification of 3x to 18x, in tubes 14 to 18 inches long. Eye relief was generous enough to permit mounting ahead of the receiver on top-ejecting Winchester rifles.

The best-known scopes around the turn of the last century came from the J. Stevens Arms and Tool Company (which in 1887 gave us

A 4x scope like this Bushnell is ideal for most small-game hunting.

the .22 Long Rifle cartridge). It entered the optics field in 1901 with the purchase of Cataract Tool & Optical Company. Legendary barrel-maker H. M. Pope favored a 5x, sixteen-inch Stevens scope, claiming it "enables old men to go on shooting as well as ever, and also enables one to shoot ten or twenty shots at close of day *after* others have been obliged to stop by darkness."

By 1907, Stevens cataloged a number of scopes, including a 3x, ten-inch "Reliable" model that weighed just four ounces. The company's Multiscope, with a power range of 6x to 11x, became the first sight to offer variable power with a sliding erector system. It came with micrometer mounts and cost forty-two dollars.

In 1909, Winchester began marketing scopes. The A5 sold best. Its ¾-inch tube, sixteen inches long, contained adjustable objective and ocular systems. The scope weighed ten ounces and could be ordered with a variety of reticles. At the time, its 5x magnification was considered suitable for fine target work; Winchester also offered 3x and 4x "B" scopes.

The 1930s unleashed a flood of new scopes from Wollensak, Souther, Pechar, and other firms with names shooters today wouldn't recognize. Many of these companies vanished after World War II. One of the most prominent scopes was made by Rudolph Noske. So good

The Aimpoint sight on this Winchester is an excellent sight for fast-moving game.

was this sight that John Amber of *Gun Digest* fame called it "the earliest American-made big game scope." To Elmer Keith, it was "the first good American hunting glass." Available in 2¾x and 4x, the Noske "A" scopes featured ⅞-inch tubes that were nine and ten inches long. With a full six inches of eye relief, they offered fields of thirty-eight and twenty-two feet, respectively. In 1939 they sold for just over fifty dollars.

On the heels of the Noske came the Lyman Alaskan. In the gunsight business since 1878, Lyman bought rights to the Winchester

Scopes on .22s don't have to tolerate recoil, but they still must transmit light and clarify targets.

scope line in 1928, and to Stevens scopes a year later. Modification of the Winchester A5 resulted in the Lyman 5A. The 3x Lyman 438 was patterned after Stevens models. Both new Lyman sights had achromatic lenses by Bausch & Lomb. The Alaskan, introduced in 1937 after other models had appeared, set a standard for hunting scopes. It resembled the Noske with its ⅞-inch tube, 10½ inches long. It had B&L glass and five inches of eye relief with a forty-foot field of view. One-minute internal windage and elevation adjustments were shockproof, even on powerful rifles. Weathertight, lightweight, and slim, the Alaskan would soon prove itself on game fields the world over. During the 1940s it retailed for an even fifty dollars—lots of money when a new Winchester Model 70 listed for under a hundred bucks.

Lyman survived the war, and U.S. snipers used the Alaskan to help win it. Soon thereafter, Wray Hegeman, the Alaskan's designer, was working on its progeny. The 4x Lyman Challenger came out in 1948, the 6x, 8x, and 10x Wolverines in 1953, vanguards in a post-war proliferation of bigger, more powerful scopes.

In this era, alloy tubes would replace steel, and the magnesium fluoride lens coating pioneered by Zeiss engineer A. Smakula in the late 1930s would lead to even more efficient films for brighter scopes. Nitrogen purging would eliminate fogging, and reticles would be engineered

For shots at very small targets, this powerful Weaver T scope with parallax adjustment excels.

to stay in the optical center of the sight. Later, incremental improvements continued to satisfy shooters wanting ever more sophistication.

Perhaps that's why you see so few straight-tube scopes these days. They're just not sophisticated enough. They look plain and old-fashioned. Come to think of it, so am I, but not to the point of rejecting reason. I like the straight, low-power scopes because they work so well on the hunt. Each season, using a variety of new scopes, I'm still impressed by the practicality of the old. Here are some options:

make, model, power x objective diameter	length (in.)	weight (oz.)	field (ft. @ 100 yds.)
BSA Deerhunter, 2.5x20	7.0	7.5	72
Burris Compact, 1x20	8.9	7.0	51
Burris Compact, 4x20	8.4	8.0	24
Burris Fullfield, 1.75–5x20	10.7	10.0	55–20
Burris Fullfield, 2.5x20	10.8	10.0	55
Bushnell Banner, 4x20	11.5	10.0	27
Kahles, 1.1–4x24 (30mm tube)	10.9	14.7	119–35
Leupold Vari-X III, 1.5–5x20	9.3	9.5	66–23
Leupold Vari-X II, 1–4x20	9.2	9.0	75–28
Leupold, 2.5x20	8.0	6.5	40
Pentax Lightseeker, 2.5x25	10.0	9.0	55
Pentax Lightseeker, 0/Vx27 (0–4x)	8.9	10.3	54–15
Pentax Lightseeker, 0x27	8.9	7.9	51
Nikon Monarch UCC, 1.5–4.5x20	10.0	9.3	50–17
Nikon Monarch UCC, 1.5–4.5x20 EER	10.0	9.3	34–11
Schmidt & Bender, 1.25–4x20 (30mm)	11.5	14.3	96–30
Sightron, 2.5x20	10.3	9.0	41
Simmons, 1.5–5x20	9.5	10.8	76–24
Simmons, 2.5x20	7.4	7.0	24
Swarovski, 1.25–4x24 (30mm)	10.6	12.7	98–32
Swift, 1.5–4.5x21	10.9	9.6	69–25
Swift 1x20	7.5	9.6	113
Tasco, 1.75–5x20	10.8	10.7	63–21
Tasco, 1.5–4.5x20	10.3	10.0	73–23
Tasco, 2.5x20	7.5	7.5	72
Weaver V3, 1–3x20	9.1	8.5	87–31
Weaver K2.5, 2.5x20	9.6	7.1	37
Zeiss ZM/Z, 1.25–4x24 (30mm)	11.4	16.7	96–30
Zeiss VM/V, 1.1–4x24 (30mm)	11.8	14.5	108–31

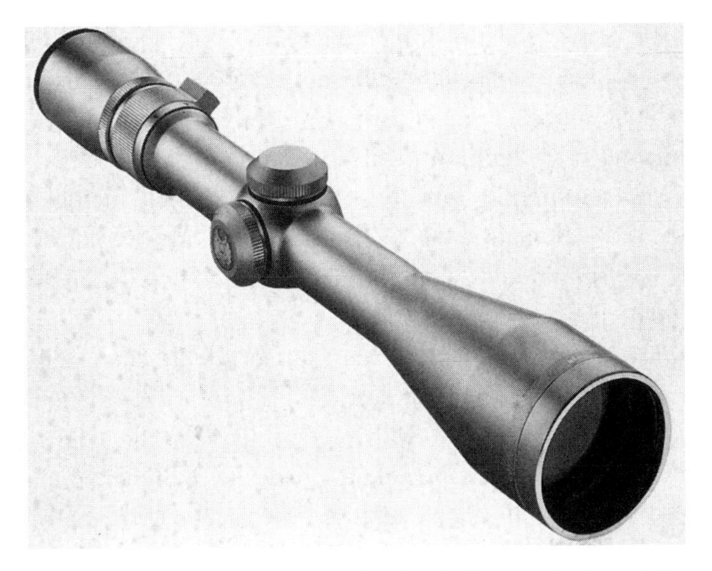

Optical quality and price are directly related, but you don't need the most expensive sight in order to shoot well.

UNTANGLING OPTICS LINGO

Shopping for a new binocular, rifle scope, or spotting scope is easier when you speak the language. When you know what the numbers and acronyms stand for, you'll make a smarter buy. Here's a concise glossary:

Achromatic lens: lens comprising two or more elements that corrects chromatic aberration, or scattering of color by wavelength. The elements work to bring red and blue to a common focal point (also, achromat).

Adjustable objective: ring on the objective housing or dial on the turret of rifle scopes, to correct parallax error and fine-tune target focus at high magnification.

Aperture stop: physical ring that limits the diameter of the light bundle passing through a lens.

Apochromatic lens: lens in which three colors are brought to a common focus by use of three types of glass (also, apochromat or APO).

Achromatic lenses typically bring red and blue colors to the same focal point, while apochromats, correcting for secondary color, also deliver green to that point.

Apparent field: angle subtended by the field of view of the image space of an instrument (as opposed to the true field, defined by the object space). To calculate the apparent field, multiply the power by the true field (a 7x binocular with an 8-degree true field has an apparent field of 56 degrees).

Aspheric: not spherical, a lens surface deliberately altered in shape to reduce spherical aberration.

Center focus: binocular with one center focusing wheel and a "diopter" wheel, usually on the right eyepiece. A CF binocular may have the diopter wheel on the same center spindle as the main focus wheel.

Clear aperture: effective diameter of an objective or front lens, as relates to light transmission (differs from a measure of "objective diameter" that includes the objective bell or housing).

Clicks: graduations in windage and elevation adjustments, typically labeled in minutes of angle (one m.o.a. is approximately 1 inch at 100 yards). An ordinary American hunting scope has ¼-minute clicks.

Collimation: aligning two optical axes so they are parallel, as when zeroing a rifle. A collimator is an optical device; as applied to shooting, it's attached to a rifle's muzzle and called a bore-sighter.

Crown glass: one of two main types of optical glass (the other is flint). BaK4 and BK7 prism glass used in binoculars is crown glass.

Depth of field: distance through which the eye perceives a sharp image when a lens is focused at one range.

ED lens: lens with extra-low dispersion due to a high refractive index, low diffraction. ED is the practical equivalent of APO. The glass can be made with less curvature so it's strong for its weight.

Erector system: series of lenses that right the upside-down image formed by the front or objective lenses.

Exit pupil: measure in millimeters (mm) of the diameter of the shaft of light you see through a lens system when you hold a scope or binocular at arm's length. Exit pupil equals objective (front) lens diameter in mm divided by power. An 8x40 binocular has a 5mm EP. A 4x32 scope has an 8mm EP. Up to 7mm, (a young, healthy eye's limit of dilation) a bigger exit pupil means a brighter image. But in practical terms, a 5mm exit pupil gives you plenty of brightness even in dim shooting light. Old eyes may not dilate much wider, even in total darkness.

Eyepiece: rear lens housing of a scope or binocular barrel, including, on binoculars, a folding rubber cup or pull-out or twist-out section to put your eye the correct distance from the rear or ocular lens.

Eye relief: distance between your eye and the ocular lens at which you get a full field of view. There is a shorter physical eye relief when the lens housing or eyepiece extends beyond the lens.

Field lens: an internal lens, commonly the front lens of an ocular assembly, that receives the image or the aperture of a forward (objective) lens. The field lens can determine an instrument's field of view.

Field of view: width of the "window" you see through a binocular, in feet at 1,000 yards. The higher the power, the smaller the field.

Field stop: aperture inside an optical device. It determines the size and shape of the field.

On the target range with a .22, eye relief and brightness matter little; reticle tracking is important.

Fluorite: optical form of the crystal fluorspar (calcium fluoride). Its low dispersion improves resolution.

Focal plane: a plane at right angles to the axis of a lens. A first-focal-plane reticle in a variable-power scope is located up front. It appears to grow or shrink with changes in magnification. A second-focal-plane reticle stays the same apparent size as you change power. The advantage of the first-plane reticle is that it stays the same size in relation to the target as you change magnification, so you can use the reticle more easily as a rangefinding device. The disadvantage is that a crosswire in front becomes fine when you turn down the power, as you might for fast shots in timber when you actually want a bold reticle. And it becomes coarse as you crank power up, as you might for long shots at small targets, when you actually want a fine reticle.

Fully coated: a scope or binocular in which all air-to-glass lens surfaces are coated with microscopically thin layers of compounds that enhance light transmission. Uncoated lenses can steal up to 4 percent of available light at each surface. Multicoated lenses have at least two layers of brightness-boosting compounds.

Individual focus: binocular with one focus wheel on each barrel, no center wheel.

Magnesium fluoride: first lens coating (discovered in the late 1930s at Zeiss) to boost light transmission.

Magnification: power, or the number of times bigger an image appears than if seen with the naked eye.

Objective lens: front lens, its width noted in millimeters by the second number in binocular descriptions.

Ocular lens: rear lens in the binocular's eyepiece.

Parallax: the apparent shift of a target behind the reticle as you move your eye from the scope's optical axis. Parallax is a function of target range. Images formed by objects at varying distances fall at different points along the scope's axis. Because the reticle does not slide back and forth, it meets a focused image only when the target is at a specific distance. Most hunting scopes are set for zero parallax at 150 yards.

This Kahles 2–7x36x scope is designed specifically for .22s. Here it's on a Remington 504.

Many high-power scopes have parallax adjustment sleeves on the front bell or a third turret dial.

Porro prism: binocular with traditional "dogleg" barrels, named after Ignazio Porro (1801–1875).

Relative brightness: exit pupil squared; a measure of light transmission.

Resolution: the ability of a lens system to show or separate detail. Resolution increases with magnification and objective lens diameter. But the human eye's resolving power of about one minute puts a limit on the effective resolving power of any optical instrument. Resolution is commonly measured on charts that have increasingly finer lines or grids, black on white.

Reticle: aiming device in a rifle scope: a crosswire, dot, post, or other image etched or installed to help you direct a bullet. Range-finding reticles have stadia wires or mil-dots you can use to bracket distant targets.

Roof prism: binocular with straight barrels (as opposed to Porro prism binoculars with dogleg barrels).

True field: size of the field of view in the object space in front of the lens, as opposed to apparent field.

Tube: the housing of a rifle scope, typically of aluminum or steel. Sizes have varied from ¾ inch to 34mm. Most scopes made for the U.S. hunting market have 1-inch tubes. European shooters favor 30mm tubes.

Twilight factor: the square root of power multiplied by objective diameter. TF is a good measure of the resolving power of a binocular in dim light. An 8x40 binocular has a TF of the square root of 320, or 17.9.

Wide angle: binocular whose apparent field of view is 65 degrees or greater (apparent field = true field x power, so a 7x binocular with a true field of 8 degrees would have an apparent field of 56 degrees). Fixed-power rifle scopes with apparent fields of 26 degrees or greater, and variables with 23-degree fields, are also considered wide angle, though the term is usually reserved for binoculars and spotting scopes.

Zero: The zero for a rifle is that range at which a bullet crosses the sightline for the second time, on its trip downward from the apex of its arc. To "zero" or "sight-in" a rifle is to adjust the sight so the bullet strikes the point of aim at a certain distance.

Zoom lens: a lens system of variable focal length but with a fixed focal plane.

Chapter 21

HOW TO SHOOT WITH IRONS

Thirty years ago in Mishawaka, Indiana, I stepped to the firing line for a go at a spot on the U.S. Olympic Team. In the middle of the black scoring area that appeared as a dot at fifty feet was the *real* target, a 10-spot the diameter of a finishing nail surrounded by a 9-ring you could obliterate with a single .22 bullet. Centering the black in the sight, I had to assume my precisely zeroed rifle and its super-accurate ammunition would deliver tens. To reach the final qualifying stage, I'd have to keep a one-hole, sixty-shot group on a spot I couldn't even see. The Anschutz iron sights helped me try to do that.

Later, shooting outdoors, I found iron sights produced scores very close to those I could shoot with my 20x Redfield scope. And I found rabbit and squirrel hunting more fun when using irons on slender .22 rifles.

While competitive riflemen must still master iron sights, you seldom see hunters using irons these days. But some shooting is best done with iron sights, and some people have shot extraordinarily well with them.

Women like Annie Oakley. Men like Ad Topperwein.

Phoebe Ann Moses, born in a log cabin in Darke County, Ohio, in August 1860, had a hard childhood. But subsistence hunting would propel her to fame. She shot her first game, a squirrel, at age eight. Her talent with a rifle led to market hunting. Annie began shooting quail on the wing with her .22, and dominating turkey shoots. Then, at a local match, she beat visiting sharpshooter Frank Butler—who apparently did not know at first that his opponent was a fifteen-year-old girl. A year later they married, and Annie joined Frank's traveling show under the stage name of Annie Oakley. Sioux chief Sitting Bull called her *Watanya cicilia*, or "Little Sure-Shot." When exhibition shooter Captain A. H. Bogardus left Buffalo Bill's Wild West Show, Annie got on

Famous trick shooters performed magic with iron-sighted rifles.

the docket, aiming in a mirror to shoot over her shoulder at glass balls Frank threw in the air.

Petite at a hundred pounds, and sweet-tempered, Annie became an audience favorite. The German crown prince, later to become Kaiser Wilhelm II, asked her to shoot a cigarette from his lips. She obliged, allowing in the wake of World War I that a miss might have changed history. Annie shot coins from Frank's fingers and split playing cards edgewise with bullets. In 1884, using a Stevens .22 at an exhibition in Tiffin, Ohio, she hit 943 glass balls out of 1,000 tossed. She could make one ragged hole in the middle of a playing card, firing twenty-five shots in as many seconds with a repeater. Johnny Baker, another Wild West Show marksman, tried for seventeen years to outshoot Annie Oakley, and never did. "She wouldn't throw a match," he said. "You had to *beat* her, and she wasn't beatable."

Annie used iron sights for exhibition shooting. At age sixty-two, after an automobile accident badly crippled her, she could still hit, with a rifle, every one of twenty-five pennies tossed in the air.

Equally amazing were the stunts of Ad Topperwein, born in 1869 near New Braunfels, Texas. With a .22 Winchester 1890 pump rifle, Ad began shooting aerial targets. He had little use for hunting or paper targets. He replaced the 1890 with a Winchester 1903 autoloader, then with its successor, a Model 63. In 1887, at age eighteen, Ad landed a job as a cartoonist in San Antonio. But he honed his marksmanship during off hours and wound up shooting for a circus.

In 1894, he used a rifle to break 955 of 1,000 clay 2¼-inch disks tossed in the air. Dissatisfied with the score, he repeated twice, shattering 987 and 989. Standard clay shotgun targets proved too easy; he broke 1,500 straight, the first 1,000 from 30 feet, the last 500 from 40. By his late twenties, Ad was also a showman. After firing at a washer tossed aloft, he'd tell onlookers that the bullet went through the middle. Challenged by the audience, Ad would stick a postage stamp over the hole for another toss, and perforate the stamp. He could hit the bullet of an airborne .32-20 cartridge without tearing the brass.

Ad and "Plinky" Topperwein wowed audiences with their feats of marksmanship.

Winchester hired Topperwein when the tall, slim, blue-eyed young man was about twenty-seven. He would shoot for Winchester for fifty-five years. There he met Elizabeth Servaty, who worked in the company's ballistics lab. They married in 1903. To audiences thereafter, she became "Plinky," a fine shot in her own right. In 1916 she blasted 1,952 of 2,000 clay targets with a Model 12 shotgun, and once ran 280 straight.

Ad preferred rifles; and he didn't need a shotgun to hit tough targets. Holding a Model 63 with the ejection port up, he'd fire a cartridge, then swing the rifle up and nail the airborne empty. He could riddle five tossed cans before any hit the ground. He brought his artistic ability to routines where he used up to 450 .22 bullets fired with precision at the headlong rate of a shot a second to draw Indian heads on tin.

Topperwein's exploits sparked competition. Doc Carver (who had no medical background) shot 11 Model 1890 Winchesters over 10 days, 12 hours a day, to break more than 55,000 of 60,000 tossed glass balls, 2½ inches in diameter. The second time, he missed only 650. But

B. A. Bartlett eclipsed Carver's record. Firing 144 hours, he shattered 59,720 of 60,000 balls.

Ad Topperwein responded. In 1907 at the San Antonio Fairgrounds, he uncrated 10 Winchester Model 1903 rifles, 50,000 rounds of .22 ammunition, and 50,000 wooden blocks cut 2¼ square inches. After running out of blocks and ammo, Top got resupplied and resumed shooting. He stopped after 120 hours, 72,500 tosses. He'd missed nine targets. Once he ran 14,500 straight. Ad needed help, after his performance, just to lower his arms. His record stood until after World War II, when Remington salesman Tom Frye began flailing at wood blocks with Nylon 66 autoloaders. Frye missed two of his first 43,725 targets. When he finished with the eye-bugging score of 100,004 out of 100,010, an aging Ad Topperwein wrote to congratulate him. Ad died at age ninety-three, nearly eighteen years after losing Plinky in 1945.

There's a lot of difference between Olympic bull's-eye shooting and popping away at aerial targets. One is deliberate, one instinctive—at least that's how they appear. In truth, both require practiced precision. Though an Anschutz match rifle with Eley Tenex ammo is more accurate than an autoloader firing ordinary .22 solids, both must be expertly manipulated if the shooter is going to succeed. Whether you're looking for a pea-size group or an unbroken string of broken clays, iron sights are up to the task.

The best iron sights for bull's-eye shooting are an aperture (peep) rear and a globe front with an insert that's the equivalent of a scope's reticle. For a long time, my favorite insert was an orange plastic disc with a hole in the middle just big enough to admit a narrow rim of white around the black target. The hole's bevel showed dark, to provide a crisp sight picture. Later I went to a black steel ring (no plastic) because it was recommended by the best shooters.

Still, I shoot as well under most conditions with the orange plastic. It's important that the disc be big enough to allow sufficient light around the target, but not so much light that you're working hard to center it. Some riflemen "shade" with a front aperture, moving it

The trim, simple aperture sight on this Winchester 75 is much more precise than any open sight.

slightly to one side or the other to compensate for wind. This tactic has always given me the willies. I've succeeded at times, but have also blundered by overcorrecting. My eyes weren't (and certainly aren't) sharp enough to shade irons on small targets. I'd rather hold center and dial in the required adjustment on the rear sight.

An aperture sight, like the one on this Marlin 39, is very fast. Use a bigger hole to boost speed.

The sights on my match rifles, ordinary by most standards, have quarter-minute windage and elevation dials and fixed-size apertures. I've used adjustable irises, which allow you to fine-tune aperture size to the light conditions. They're nice but not necessary. If you change front or rear apertures too much, you lose the confidence that comes with familiarity. Experimentation is worthwhile; just be sure you give each option lots of shooting time before you reject it, and make detailed notes. Once you find a sight combo that seems to work, be loyal. You'll fare better than if, after a poor score, you immediately looked for an alternative.

An aperture rear sight is also a good hunting sight, though you'll want a bead or blade rather than a ring up front, for aiming at big, irregularly shaped targets. You'll also want a big aperture in the rear, to make aiming quick and to deliver more light to your eye. On the hunt you may have little time to find the target, and you'll often want to shoot in shadows or failing light. I've taken the aperture out of the sight on my Model 70 .375; now the threaded hole in the sight frame serves as my aperture. It's more precise than it looks, because the human eye automatically centers the front sight in the middle. That's where most of the light is.

The closer the rear sight is to your eye, the longer the sight radius (distance between sights), and the greater the degree of precision you can expect. Also, with your eye close to the aperture, a small hole gives you as much light and field as a big aperture farther away—and the small one further enhances accuracy and depth perception. That's why target rifles for nineteenth-century Schuetzen matches had rear sights mounted on the tang. Winchester and Marlin lever rifles and single-shot hunting rifles were routinely equipped with tang sights before scopes became so popular; now Cowboy Action shooters have rediscovered the value of tang sights.

Cocking-piece sights on bolt rifles have become as rare as crank handles on automobile engines, but they're among my favorite sights because they're close to your eye and compact. The "bolt peep" on Winchester's 71 lever-action rifle has the modest size of a cocking-piece sight, though it's stationed farther forward. You get plenty of precision from either, despite the moving bases. (For hard-kicking rifles like the .348, a tang sight can put the aperture *too* close to your eye.)

My first hunting rifle, a restocked SMLE, had a barrel-mounted open sight: a Williams with a shallow "African" V-notch. It didn't obscure the target as much as semi-buckhorn or even ordinary U- or

Browning's BL-22 would seem overburdened with any scope.

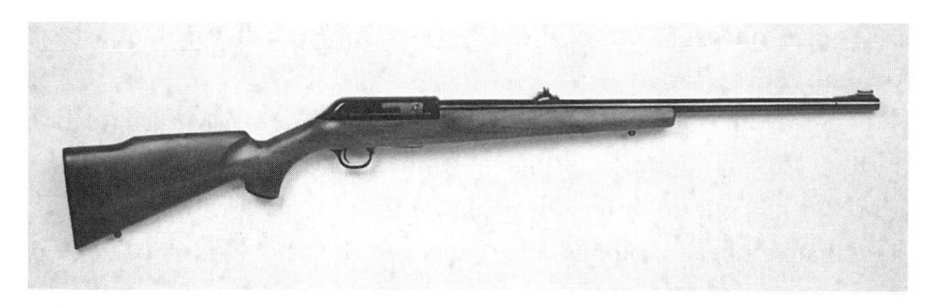

The Thompson/Center's iron sights are just fine for cottontails dashing for cover.

V-notch sights. Consequently, it was faster. I still like the shallow V, with or without an eye-catching white center line. It's a favorite of hunters using double rifles. So is a multiple-leaf option for different yardages. My preference is for one solidly fixed leaf filed to zero. Then there's no choosing the wrong leaf, or having the right one collapse during recoil or rough handling. An open sight is properly a close-range sight. With a single rear notch, you should be able to hold center and count on a lethal hit on big animals out to at least 150 yards. On a .22, this sight should keep you in the kill zone of most small game to seventy-five yards, which is likely as far as you can see small targets clearly behind a bead.

Whether you have an open sight or aperture sight on a hunting rifle, the front sight should be big enough to catch your eye right away. Barrel length affects *apparent* bead size and subtention at the target. There's no perfect bead material or color, either. I prefer ivory, except in snow. Gold works well against a variety of backgrounds. I don't like fluorescent sights because under bright conditions they get fuzzy, with a glow or halo much like that of a street lamp at night. That brightness not only blurs sight edges, it can hide the target. Even metal beads can ruin a sight picture by scattering light. Avoid spherical bead faces; they reflect light off the edge, shifting the bead's apparent position and causing you to miss. A bead should be flat-faced but angled toward the sky to catch light.

Redfield's Sourdough front sight featured a square red insert, angled up. You could employ it as a bead or a post. A black steel post can get lost in timber. It's also designed for a six-o'clock hold—fine for bull's-eyes on paper but obstructive on game and slower than a bead you can slap on target.

Someone is always cooking up new iron sights. My friend Bob Fulton has equipped his Ruger Number One in .411 Hawk with a globe front sight holding a clear plastic insert etched with a crosswire. The rear sight is a modified Krag. At the end of the 27-inch barrel, the flared rear end of the globe sight fits almost perfectly in the aperture of the rear sight. There's a thin ring of daylight around the globe so you can tell instantly if it's out of center. Bob has also built barrel-mounted aperture sights. The rear sight on his Winchester 95 has a platinum-lined ring arcing over the factory notch. "That's the fastest sight I've ever used," he told me. "It's accounted for piles of jackrabbits. We used '06s for bunnies back when I was in the Army because surplus ammo was cheap."

Some innovative sights have gone commercial, like the "Little Blue" peep sight, a dainty folding aperture that screwed to the back of a Redfield scope base as an auxiliary sight.

A few years ago, a tall, rough-hewn Texan named Ashley handed me a Marlin lever rifle with a perforated peg perched on the receiver. Its stem threaded into a small block that dovetailed into a larger base block and moved across it for lateral adjustment. To raise or lower the sight you simply screwed the ring out or in. "How about that, partner?" he bellowed. "Kinda slick, huh?" It was indeed slick. So was the front blade, angled like a Sourdough but all the way to the base, and with a white line down its middle. While I gawked, Ashley warmed to a pig-hunting story, its delivery polished, no doubt, by many repetitions. I could see his long legs leaping cactus, a lever rifle spewing cases as he barreled through the hill-country brush to keep a sprinting porker in that wide-open sight.

Ashley is no longer part of the sight company he started. But XL Sights is up to its Stetson in orders for sights that have now been adapted to bolt rifles, shotguns, and muzzleloaders. They seem to offer the best hunting rear sights these days, though I prefer a Sourdough up

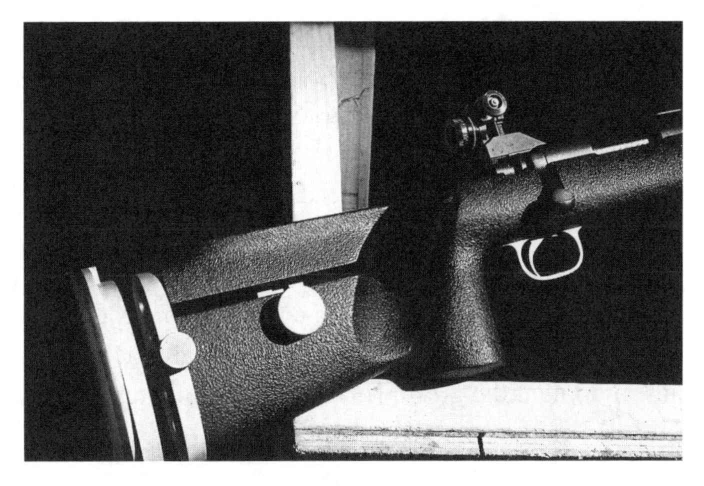

With target-quality iron sights, accomplished riflemen can shoot as well as they would with scopes.

front. The XL's white line does stand out in dark conditions, and against a light background that entire blade is easy to see.

No matter what sight you choose, the key is effectiveness. You'll pick up speed and precision with practice. Here are some things to keep in mind after you zero:

Focus on the front sight. Your eye can't focus at three distances simultaneously, so it's best to get a sharp view of the middle image. That way, you won't have to put two fuzzy images together. The rear sight can be out of focus, and the target not quite as clear as you'd like, and you'll still hit center if the front sight is distinct and in the proper relationship to the other two images.

Remember that every shot is practice, and that the more you shoot the better you'll shoot if you take care with every sight picture and letoff. Sloppy shooting is just practicing bad form. Gifted shooters like Topperwein make disciplined marksmanship look casual. Honestly, good shooting takes focused effort—more with iron sights than with a scope because your eye must do more work.

Finally, keep in mind that most of the world's legendary hunters used iron sights. Jim Corbett, for instance. The famous slayer of man-eating tigers began his career waiting for jungle fowl on the bank of a ravine. Suddenly, he spied movement close by. A leopard! It sprang. Jim fired as the cat sailed over his head and vanished in brush. He reloaded and followed the trail. So confident was he of his rifle and his ability that when he saw the cat's tail ahead, he grabbed it and pulled the dead animal out of a thicket. Such cool, deliberate action up close would save him many times later on, when, at night, he sat alone near tiger baits. Jim killed the great Muktesar man-eating tiger at a range of two yards.

Sometimes scopes just seem superfluous.

Chapter 22

REST THAT RIFLE!

In films, the camera sometimes delivers the view through a sniper's scope, or the field glass of a platoon leader. The reticle or field is always still. No throbbing pulse, no muscle twitch. Ah, Hollywood.

But the rest of us have problems holding both binocular and rifle. That's why we try not to. Better to take a rest on something without heart and muscles and wobbly, slippery joints. A rest gives you sharp images in the binocular because it all but eliminates the blur of motion. It can help you shoot better in two ways. First, it keeps the crosswire from gyrating off-target. You have less movement to fret about, which enables you to focus on trigger squeeze and other fundamentals. Rather than having to wait out wide swings in the reticle, or try to sift uncontrollable hops and dips from primary movements, you can relax. A few tremors won't make any difference if you're aiming for the forward slats on a woodchuck. They won't deny you a zero, either, if you're shooting groups from a bona fide bench.

Second, the rest and gravity, together with the rifle's mass, hold the sight where it needs to be.

Now, you might think the first and second benefits of a rest are the same. They're not. What you perceive in your sight affects your shooting. If you delay a shot because the sight isn't still, or try to catch the target by jerking the trigger as the reticle dives to center, you'll miss. Tired muscles can't control the rifle; yanking the trigger moves it. The only way to hit consistently is to relax into the shot and deliver it with

Some rimfire matches are now shot from benchrests.

proper form—while somehow keeping the rifle pointed at the target. Two tasks.

A rest is essential when you're zeroing a rifle. You don't want to adjust the sight to correct for an error in hold, or for a rifle's dip or bounce as you pull the trigger. So you employ a rest. Sandbags will do, but a mechanical rest with a padded platform lets you position the rifle without effort. If the rest brings the sights onto the target, you will have adjusted its natural point of aim—the direction the rifle "wants" to point. On the bench and in the field, if you can arrange the rifle's support (a rest or your body) so the sights spend more time on the target than off, you've improved your odds for a hit.

Your best shooting will come when the rifle doesn't need encouragement to point where you want the bullet to go. Getting there with your body means adjusting your position, from the ground up. A mechanical rest gives you fingertip control on knobs that tune your sight picture. Many rests have leveling devices and adjustable toe supports. Some, like the Bench Master and Cabela's Elite, feature a strap that arrests the butt during recoil. I like the rest from Target Shooting, too. It's solid and lightweight and can be used on tables (or pickup hoods) with-

A rest builds confidence in beginners, allowing them to concentrate on sight alignment and trigger squeeze.

out marring the surface. Thick felt padding protects the rifle, and the butt rest is adjustable for angle.

But aren't sandbags much cheaper? Yes, and they'll work just fine—if you have enough of them and take care to arrange them so your rifle points naturally at the target without your interference. A pile of sandbags not so structured leaves you too much work. If you must hold the rifle on target, you are putting some human error into the shot. Also, sandbags can shift and settle between shots, especially when you're pounding away with a powerful rifle. Fine accuracy depends upon consistency in details. To be fair, I've shot some good groups over sandbags, and if you fill them with granulated plastic, they're easy to transport afield for zero checks on a hunt. One of my amigos stuffs a mule-ear bag with plastic pellets and straps it atop his spotting scope. Guiding hunters, he can offer an instant rest for a client simply by turning the scope sideways on its tripod.

You'd think a commercial rest, or even sandbags on a bench, would ensure tiny groups. Not so. You can still shoot poorly from a rest. Jerking the trigger can move a rifle as easily as if you were holding it aloft with your left hand. Aim through the corner of the scope, and you

Sandbags will suffice as a rest. Just make sure bag contact is the same for each shot.

can introduce parallax error. Put your hands in different places, or exert variable pressure on the rifle, shot to shot, and groups will open up.

One of the most common mistakes shooters make when using a commercial rest is helping it. You can't make an automobile go faster by opening the door to push against the road with one foot. And you can't make a rest work better by helping it support the rifle. Get your left hand off! The only assist worth considering is a squeeze of the rear sandbag to tweak elevation. (Rifles that recoil so violently as to jump free of rests can use a tug from your hand, straight down from below the forend.) Some rests let you trip lightweight triggers without holding the stock with your right hand. Better to grasp the wrist as you might without a rest. You'll control recoil this way and duplicate pressures that affect the rifle when you're firing at game.

Whether at the bench or in the field, do not touch the barrel with your left hand or allow it to touch a hard surface. On any hard rest, pad the forend with your hand to cushion the rifle's bounce during recoil. Vibrations from the striker's fall and primer detonation begin traveling through the rifle before you feel the kick. They can bump your rifle be-

You'll gain a lot of stability by resting the buttstock as well as the forend on sandbags and other stationary objects.

fore the bullet leaves the barrel. Padding is especially important when steadying a rifle against a vertical rest. The muzzle is now pressured to move laterally instead of up, and without your fleshy palm as cushion, point of impact can shift.

The influence of pressure changes on the forend is easy to see if you shoot a rifle with a tight sling and then again from the same position without one. After zeroing from a hard rest at the bench, try some groups with a sling (if you use one afield), or shoot offhand. (Weak support can also result in low groups.) Remember that lightweight hunting rifles are more susceptible to forend pressure changes than are target and varmint guns with their greater mass. Find out before the season where your rifle shoots when supported, as you'll likely be holding it on the hunt.

In the field, almost any rest is better than no rest at all. A tree might not be exactly where you want it, or have a branch in the right place. And a rock is often too low. But if you keep your eye open for rests, and engineer your shooting to take advantage of them, you'll shoot better. When still-hunting, time your pauses to take advantage of nearby rests. When on stand, make sure you have a rest for each shooting lane. Spend as much time as you can within reach of rifle support.

In the field, an improvised rest is much better than no rest at all.

Some areas don't have sturdy trees, while the brush can obscure targets from sitting and kneeling positions, let alone prone. That's where shooting sticks come in. Use them with a .22 when the woodchucks are in deep clover, or the cottontails stop for a look back on the far side of a fencerow. Sticks are immensely popular in Africa, in the endless thorn that hides kudu and gemsbok, eland and waterbuck, and countless smaller antelopes, as well as Cape buffalo.

Once, after hunting seven days, my trackers and I caught up with a fine eland bull. At sixty yards, I rose from a crouch for what I knew would be a quick shot, and my only one. The eland was shielded except for its head and neck and a window of shoulder. Offhand, I might have made the shot, but I was breathing hard. Grabbing the tracker's tripod of long shooting sticks at the binding, I settled the Kimber on my fist as I came above the thorn, firing when my crosswire found the window. The eland dropped.

Pronghorn hunters in the western U.S. have taken increasingly to bipods, like the popular Harris model that allows you to rock the rifle slightly to compensate for uneven ground. But small-game hunters with .22s can also use bipods to advantage. In fact, one aftermarket stock for the Ruger 10/22 comes with an integral bipod. I've not been enchanted with those that telescope out for use in higher shooting positions. Perhaps I need more practice with them.

This aftermarket stock for the Ruger 10/22 has a folding bipod—rudimentary but effective.

You'll often be tempted to shoot too quickly at game from a rest. Your breathing and pulse can still move a rifle braced against a tree or laid across a rock, especially if the support cradles only one end of the stock. A rifle with the toe unsupported can seesaw up and down. You'll get a three-to-nine-o'clock swing in a rifle held against the curve of an upright sapling. It's usually worth the time to find a rest that supports the rifle both fore and aft. Bracing your body against something solid is as good—sometimes better—than pressing the buttstock against it. Seeking additional support can help you even if you don't find it. Your breathing has a chance to subside as you look, and you can calm yourself. A careless or hurried poke at game is ill-advised, rest or no rest.

A low, steady position with a sling can make any rest more effective. I carry a Brownell's Latigo sling on my rifle, because in thirty-five years of hunting, I've never found a better shooting aid. It's not just a carrying strap; it has a shooting loop that's adjustable independent of overall length. With the loop above my left triceps and tight to the forend swivel, the rear of the sling hangs loose. The tension pulls the rifle straight into me, relieving my left hand of the rifle's weight and transferring it to the larger muscles of my left shoulder. There's no sideways tug on the butt, no pull from my triceps coaxing the butt from my shoulder. A sling locks the rifle into your body. A rest will steady both.

Last fall I crept to a knob above a herd of elk working their way up a timbered draw in Montana's Bitterroot Mountains. A diffuse gray light slowly painted over the stars as I wriggled into a prone, sling tight and my left hand hard against a rock. The sling and the rock together stilled the crosswire in my 3–9x Leupold. It hardly shivered as I waited. And waited. Dawn followed the elk up the hill, and by the time I could verify the bull's antlers and clearly see the reticle against his ribs, I'd been poised to shoot for several minutes. But the rest not only kept the rifle from moving, it kept me from tiring. This 300-yard shot was longer than I like to take, but the rock and sling made it easy. So did my years of shooting .22 rifles in prone matches, and those summer days in 'chuck pastures sneaking within rimfire range. Had the elk been a gallon jug, I'd still have hit it.

A rest—and practice using one—makes everyone a better marksman, in the field and on the range. Any device or technique that helps steady your rifle is an investment in accuracy.

A variety of clever, inexpensive, and effective rests are available.

BOWLING BALLS AND OTHER SUPPORTS

What do you get when you marry a vise to a bowling ball and plop it into a wooden socket? A rifle rest! It might not look like one, but this clever device not only supports your favorite .22, it grips the rifle with padded hardwood clamps. The result is more consistent shooting, because you play a smaller role in each shot. Like the Ransom rest for pistol shooters, the Ball Shooting System is part vise. Incidentally, you'll likely want to use it with hard-kicking centerfires too, as the ball's mass and rocking motion absorb recoil. Marty Lytle, the Montanan who came up with this product and now manufactures it, recommends that you *not* hold a hard-kicking rifle tight against your shoulder. "Just let the ball handle the punch."

The oak base has a rope-lined hole to accommodate the modified bowling ball. The vise (really a padded clamp, also of oak) is permanently affixed to the ball and designed to secure your rifle at both the receiver and forend. Just snug it with a turn of the handle. What keeps the ball from turning? Nothing but its own mass, and therein lies the beauty of this rest. It is cleverly built to keep most rifles perched on top

The bowling ball central to the Ball Shooting System provides stability and absorbs recoil.

without help from your hand; the ball's weight compresses the rope in the socket below. But to move point of aim, all you do is nudge the rifle. Unlike other rests that adjust separately on vertical and horizontal planes, the ball allows you to move the rifle in an infinite number of planes at once, to change not only windage and elevation but also cant. Instead of fussing with knobs and latches, you just apply a little pressure to the rifle stock; the rifle tilts to your bidding, then stays put.

Does it work? Yup. The ball does indeed hold a rifle securely. And you can easily adjust point of aim. The clamp accommodates most rifles, though you'll need extra padding to snug the oak fingers up front around slender forends. You probably won't have to snug the clamp with .22s, as you should periodically with hard-kicking centerfire rifles. Tip: Take care when setting up that you don't *drop* the ball into its socket. You might get a split.

Here's a short list of places with useful shooting rests. Some are manufacturers; some are distributors or retailers that carry one or more brands.

Bill Hicks
15155 23rd Avenue
Minneapolis, MN 55447
1-800-223-0702
Carries the Decker gun vise.

Ball Shooting System
Aim-Right
446 Lumpry Road
Arlee, MT 59821
406-726-3598

Brownells
200 South Front Street
Montezuma, IA 50171
515-623-5401
Carries Protecktor, Ransom, Bench Master, Bullshooter, and Wichita.

Cabela's
One Cabela Drive
Sidney, NE 69160
1-800-237-4444
Carries Bench Master, Benchmark, BenchBuddy, Lohman, Uncle Bud's, Hoppe's, Outer's, and Cabela's.

Hoppe's
A Brunswick Company
Airport Industrial Mall
Coatesville, PA 19320
610-384-6000

Hornady Manufacturing
P.O. Box 1848
Grand Island, NE 68802-1848
1-800-338-3220

Midway USA
P.O. Box 1035
Columbia, MO 65205
573-446-6363
Carries Protecktor, Hoppe's, and Midway.

Outers-Blount
P.O. Box 38
Onalaska, WI 54650
608-781-5800

Sinclair International
2330 Wayne Haven Street
Fort Wayne, IN 46803
219-749-5136
Carries Protecktor and Sinclair.

Storehorse
16607 Blanco Road, Suite 100
San Antonio, TX 78232
210-492-8405

Target Shooting
P.O. Box 773
Watertown, SD 57201-0773
605-882-6955

Chapter 23

GETTING TO ZERO

You can miss a target from a solid rest if your rifle is not sighted in or zeroed. You'll hit where you aim *only* if you've first aligned the sight with the bullet's path. The rifle manufacturer can roughly align iron sights, but final zeroing is up to you. Factory technicians can't know which load or ammunition you're going to use, or at what range you want to zero; and they may not look at the sights the way you do. When you mount a scope on the rifle, you'll have to zero from scratch.

A bullet never flies straight; it begins to drop as soon as it leaves the muzzle, and the arc steepens as the bullet travels downrange. Your line of sight, in contrast, is straight. It will contact the bullet's arc in one or two places. While it's possible to adjust the sight so your line of aim is tangent to the bullet's arc, a better tactic is to thread the line of sight *through* the arc. Two intersections give you a zero range at the second crossing. Imagine the bullet's flight path as an arc. Now imagine a straight line angling into the arc from above but almost parallel to the arc's shallow end. The line will cut the arc, travel beneath it, then cut it again at the arc's steep end. That's your sightline. Between intersections, you want the line, your sightline, to stay close enough to the arc that you can ignore the gap.

If you're a target shooter, you must adjust your sight to zero for every yardage on the course. As a hunter, that's impractical because shots can come quickly, and you'll seldom know the exact yardage. So before zeroing, you pick a maximum distance you'll allow the line of sight to dip below the bullet's arc. For big game hunting, a reasonable

For competitive bull's-eye shooting, zero at the target distance and shade for light variable wind.

maximum is three inches. If your bullet hits three inches above point of aim when you're shooting at a deer's chest, you'll still kill the deer. And, of course, that much error occurs only at one distance, a little over halfway to the second intersection of your sightline and the bullet's arc.

By the same logic, you should be able to "hold center" on big game animals to the range at which your bullet drops three inches *below* sightline. This is maximum point-blank range. You determine maximum point-blank range when you zero your rifle. Fast, flat-shooting bullets have a longer point-blank range than slow bullets that drop quickly, but the actual yardage is determined by your zero. Point-blank range also depends on how much gap you'll allow between trajectory and sightline at midrange. Varmint shooters get less latitude here than big game hunters. Sending bullets three inches above point of aim will allow prairie dogs to live another day, unless you hold low.

The steep arc of a .22 Long Rifle bullet and the fact that it's used on relatively small targets makes a short zero mandatory. You won't want more than an inch of vertical deviation at midrange if you expect to keep your crosswires "on fur" when shooting at squirrels. The rule of thumb when I was young: zero the high-speed solids or hollowpoints at seventy-five yards, for a one-inch midrange peak, and a point-blank

Dead on. Appropriate zero range depends on anticipated shot distance and the bullet's trajectory.

range of about eighty-five yards. The bullet's first crossing of your sight-line would fall at roughly twenty-five yards. This advice is still sound, and in my view works as well for hyper-velocity .22 Long Rifle ammo. You can reach a bit farther with rifles in .22 WMR, which I'd zero at a hundred yards. The .17 HMR can handle a 125-yard zero.

If these distances seem short compared to centerfire zeros—typically 150 yards for the .30-30 and kin, 200 for the vast majority of modern big game rounds, and 250 for fast-steppers like the .257 Weatherby—well, they are. Speed flattens flight. So does a high ballistic coefficient—that mathematical expression of a bullet's ability to cleave the air. Most centerfire hunting rounds fire sleek, ballistically efficient bullets. Excepting the polymer-tipped .17 HMR, most rimfire bullets have blunt noses and ribbed shanks (to hold lubricant and engage the rifling). Such bullets generate lots of air resistance, which means a high rate of deceleration.

Because gravity acts over time, the faster a bullet can get from the muzzle to the target, the less it will drop between those two points, all else equal. If you held a bullet in your fingers alongside the horizontal barrel of a rifle and dropped the bullet at the same time that you fired the rifle, the bullets would strike the earth at the same time. The difference, of course, is in point of impact. One would fall at your feet. The other,

You'll need different zeroes for big game rifles and .22s.

depending on initial velocity and ballistic coefficient, would hit far away. A traditional rimfire bullet starts slow and decelerates quickly.

Incidentally, sight height affects zero because it determines the angle of the sightline to the bullet's arc. A flat line of sight will make a second crossing sooner (closer) than a line of sight that's steep by virtue of, say, high scope mounts. Keep that in mind when you are comparing points of impact with the data in ballistics tables, some of which specify a 1.5-inch gap between bore center and sightline at the muzzle.

After deciding on a zero, you'll want to bore-sight your rifle. Place it on sandbags or any rest that holds it still. You don't have to be at the range, only somewhere that gives you a long view toward a small, distant target. I use a padded chair in my living room and look through the window to a rock on the far side of the Columbia River. Remove the bolt and line up the target in the center of the bore. Brace the rifle so it does not move. Adjust your scope so the reticle centers the target. It's that easy. The rifle is now bore-sighted and should plant bullets close to your point of aim.

Bore-sighting saves time and ammunition at the range. Lever, slide, and autoloading rifles require a collimator, an optical device you

To score with any rifle, you must first bore-sight it, adjusting the sight so you're looking where the rifle is shooting.

attach to the muzzle with a bore spud. The collimator shows you a grid that takes the place of a distant target. If you shoot with iron sights, zeroing is a live-fire proposition.

Before you toss the rifle in the pickup, check guard screws and scope screws to ensure that they're tight. Then make a list of what you'll need at the range. Here's a good place to start:

- Sandbags and adjustable shooting rest
- Spotting scope and bench tripod
- Targets, with pasters or tape to cover bullet holes
- Stapler and staples, or tape, to attach targets
- Troubleshooting kit, with screwdrivers to fit every rifle and scope-mount screw
- Rifle-cleaning kit
- Old sweatshirts to pad your elbows on the bench
- Shooting glasses and hearing protection (remember that other shooters may be using loud rifles)
- Notepad and pen to record sight changes and general observations

In your haste, don't forget the rifle and ammo—I once ran off without the bolt.

Try to pick a still day for zeroing. You don't want to fight the wind for control of the rifle, and you don't want to zero for a right or left drift. You can chronograph loads while zeroing, and test them for accuracy. But it's best if you first zero with one load, then focus on other things. If you must change zero for different ammunition later, it won't take long.

My range isn't developed. It has a bench but no target boards. I substitute large cardboard boxes with white paper squares affixed. These white squares are my favorite targets. I size them according to the sight. For iron sights at a hundred yards, they're a square foot, or bigger. For a 4x scope, I'll use a six-inch square, for a 6x scope a four-inch square. If you're shooting a varmint rifle with a 16x or 20x scope, you'll want a much smaller block. The white paper shows up plainly against a brown box, and holes are easy to see no matter where the bullets land. Black lines and target faces hide little bullet holes. I prefer square over round targets because they're easy to quarter with a crosswire. With a dot or a front bead, the corners of the square remain visible, clearly indicating if the sight is off-center. I also like these targets because they're as cheap as typing paper.

Your first shots should be at the first crossing of sightline and bullet arc: twenty-five yards for rimfires, thirty-five for centerfires (whether or not you've bore-sighted). Shooting at long range, you may miss the backer with that first round. Then you'll have no clue as to proper sight correction. No sense wasting even one bullet off the backer, or hitting a target frame. When you've brought point of impact to within an inch of center, take the target to seventy-five yards for your .22, to full zero range for centerfires. At long range, fire at least two shots before making sight corrections. If those holes are more than an inch apart, fire another shot. Small groups tell you with greater certainty where to move the sight.

To hit the diminutive vital area on small game, you need a precise zero.

Group size is partly a function of rifle and load. But mainly it's a function of how still you hold the rifle and how well you execute the shot. Even with a benchrest, it's easy to make a bad shot. In fact, a bench can give you a false sense of stability, prompting fast, sloppy shooting. Take time to be sure each shot is engineered just like the one before it.

An adjustable rest helps you make a good shot because with it you can "dial in" the exact position you want the rifle, bringing its natural point of aim to the bull's-eye. Sandbags simply take more time to position. The rifle is best supported just behind the forend swivel and just ahead of the stock's toe. Protect forward sandbags from the swivel stud on recoil by wadding a washcloth in front of the bag. Never zero a rifle with the barrel touching a rest. The barrel will vibrate away from the rest and throw the shot wide. Unless you're shooting a rifle of very heavy recoil and must hold it down lest it jump off the rest, keep your left hand off the forend. Use it instead to pinch the sandbags or beanbags that support the toe of the stock. A little hand pressure here can shift the rifle just enough to bring the sight to the exact center of the target. Your right hand should keep steady but light pressure on the grip as you pull the trigger straight back.

After you've zeroed a rifle, get off the bench and shoot a couple of groups from each of the positions you most often use when hunting. I shoot a lot from the sit with a tight sling. I've found that the sling pulls the rifle down and left, so my shots don't hit where they would if the rifle were benched. One .30 magnum put a sitting group nine inches below the centered group I'd fired from the bench. A barrel-mounted sling swivel exacerbates this problem, but a stud on the forend is no guarantee that groups will stay together. A forend that applies lots of pressure to the barrel can be pulled free by a sling. A big change in point of impact may result.

Keep the barrel cool. With centerfires, I take no more than ten shots before setting the rifle aside, bolt open, to bring the bore temperature down. If I have to take more than thirty shots, or if the groups open up, I clean the bore. Having two or three rifles at the range is a good idea. The second and third keep you occupied while the first cools. If

You won't have a benchrest with you in the field, so check zero from hunting positions while you're at the shooting range.

you simply twiddle your thumbs, you won't let the barrel cool long enough. But a rimfire rifle won't heat up fast enough to delay you at all when zeroing.

Unless you visit a backwoods range like mine, you'll likely have to share the line with other shooters. A few tips: Stay as far away from them as possible. If you must talk to another shooter, walk behind and wait quietly until he or she has an unloaded rifle. Don't interrupt a shot; don't yell across the line. Obey all firing line commands instantly, no matter how inconvenient. If there's no range officer, ask individual shooters for permission for a cease-fire, then wait until all rifles are empty before calling a cease-fire. Leave your rifle on the bench, action

The most accurate bullets may not have the flattest trajectories.

open, whenever someone is downrange. When everyone has returned from the targets, wait until someone declares that the line is hot before loading up. Or ask if the line is ready before calling a hot line yourself.

Post enough targets to occupy your rifles for at least half an hour. Frequent cease-fires waste time. At long ranges, set targets on adjacent frames if they're vacant. The walk may be good for your health, but it also raises your pulse and delays your shooting after you're back on the line. If someone calls a cease-fire too frequently, offer to loan targets or set up another frame for the shooter. If he or she doesn't have a spotting scope, offer to look at that target periodically.

After zeroing, thoroughly clean your rifle and run a lightly oiled patch through the bore. If you have time to let the barrel get stone cold, shoot later that day to check point of impact. Pay attention to the first and second shots: where they land and how close they are. Those are the shots that count when you're hunting. Save that target. Visit the range at least once more before the hunt to see if the zero has shifted, again firing from a cold barrel. A composite group from different days should form a tight knot. Changes in conditions can, of course, affect point of impact. Note wind speed and direction so you can compensate when necessary.

Zeroing a rifle is like calibrating a precision instrument. It's a first step to accuracy, an essential function of any rifle. If you don't zero carefully, or check zero occasionally, your rifle is all but useless. And in the field you'll be hunting for a shot you can't make.

Chapter 24

HOLDING A RIFLE STILL

I've missed a lot of easy shots. That's because missing is easy. The mental and physical routines that deliver hits are hard-won by disciplined practice. Nobody is born a marksman. You may be blessed with fine vision, lightning reflexes, and extraordinary hand-eye coordination. You may have built great muscles. But to shoot accurately, you still must learn how to hold a rifle steady, and control your breathing and trigger squeeze.

Shooting fundamentals are few. You needn't be very bright to learn them or in the best physical shape to hone them. But you must master them. A crack field shot is not someone who makes an astonishing hit, because anyone can get lucky. Even consistent success on hunts can fail as a measure of marksmanship, because even little animals are big targets. Real marksmen are those shooters who can print tight groups on paper from hunting positions quickly.

If you shoot little groups only from the bench, or if you need a rangefinder or wind flags to put bullets where you aim, or a minute to prep for every shot, the animals will win most of the time.

Shooters who are confident of hitting right where they aim take full advantage of their bodies, both as shooting platforms and as the link between eye and striker.

The foundation of every shot is body position. The key to any solid position is bone structure. Bones, not muscles, best support you and the rifle. Muscles are elastic, and they tire. Muscles contain blood that surges, and nerves that twitch. Bones are like bricks: If you can align them so your muscles don't have to work to keep joints from slipping, you'll build with bones a platform that's as still as the human body can be. Bone alignment must also allow the rifle to point naturally at the target. If you force the rifle on target, you'll have the same problems as if you depended on muscles to support your body's weight. When the trigger breaks, your body wants to relax. If it is already relaxed, the rifle stays on target. If you have muscled the rifle where it doesn't want to go, it will come off target at the shot.

Bones can help in all positions. The most stable is prone, mainly because it is the lowest. It gives you the most ground contact and puts your center of gravity mere inches above the earth. Your left arm should be almost directly underneath the rifle. Your arm muscles will hold the elbow at the correct angle (with a lot of help from a tight sling), but they should not support the rifle. Count on your bones for that. Reduce stomach contact with the ground by cocking your right leg, rolling your body onto your left-side ribs. Those bones then support your torso, while your stomach is held clear of the ground to mitigate

The author demonstrates the correct prone form that won him two state championships.

pulse-bounce. Your right elbow is like the leg of a tripod jammed into the ground on the side. No muscle tension necessary here, because your hand on the rifle holds the elbow at a constant angle.

Sitting is not quite as steady as prone, but it's more versatile because it puts your muzzle above grass and low brush, and it allows you to swivel to follow a moving animal. It is also more useful on uneven terrain. I often fire from sitting, my legs tentlike in front of me, heels hard into the ground. It's important to lean well forward, the rear flat surfaces of your elbows against the fronts of your knees. Muscles in the small of your back stretch to put elbows against knees. But the stretch is held by bone contact, elbow to knee, so there's no effort required to maintain this position. Your lower torso rests, through your spine, on your tailbone. Some weight, including that of the rifle, rests on your left arm, which is held by friction and muscle tension (and a sling) against your knee. Leg bones support a lot of forward weight, but your leg muscles are relaxed, the bones held at their proper angle by the solid contact of heels and buttocks on the ground.

Alternative sitting positions are the crossed-leg and crossed-ankle variations. Competitive shooters like them. However, they're not as

Sam Shaw demonstrates the sit, which is readily adaptable to uneven or sloping ground.

useful as the "tent" position on uneven ground. They also put the rifle on a lower plane, which can fill your sight picture with tall grass and brush. Though crossed-leg sitting can give you the best results on paper, it requires more practice to stretch thigh and back muscles. The crossed-ankle option is faster; I use it in the rapid-fire stage of the National Match course. But your "base" on the ground is not as broad.

Kneeling, a quick position from standing, delivers a higher sight-line than sitting—and more wobble. The sight typically moves in an elliptical pattern from nine and ten o'clock to three and four. Shooters posting the best kneeling scores minimize that movement and reduce fa-

An erect posture is essential for good results while kneeling. Remember to use bone support.

tigue by keeping their weight over their bones. I'm careful to center my torso weight on my tailbone, planted squarely on the heel of my right foot, which is bent underneath to contact the ground through sole and toes. Literally from head to toe, that stack of bone supports half my weight. Practice conditions your foot to the muscle stretch. A vertical left shin carries about 35 percent of my weight, and supports the rifle. My left elbow rests just in front of my left knee. Again, "flat-on-flat" is the rule.

As with sitting, if you put the point of your elbow on your kneecap, you'll get wobble. To minimize horizontal sway in kneeling, angle your left foot parallel with your right leg, comfortably off to the side and bearing little weight. (Ground friction will hold your foot in place, despite muscle tension in your calf.) Place the rifle butt high on your clavicle, so you look directly forward. Don't hunch or lean forward. Given proper bone alignment, an erect kneeling position is both steady and easy to maintain.

Whether prone, sitting, or kneeling, a shooting sling helps. My pick, the Brownell's Latigo, has an adjustable loop that pulls taut between your upper left arm and the front swivel, while the rear of the sling remains slack. Result: Sling tension pulls the rifle into your right shoulder and reduces wobble.

Getting into a sling is harder to describe than to do. With the rifle facing away from you, give the loop a half turn out and slip your left arm through it, then snug it down above your triceps with the sliding keeper. Flip your left hand over the sling and grip the forend. The sling should lie flat against the back of your left hand, and, properly adjusted for length, tighten up like a bowstring when the rifle butt meets your shoulder. A two-piece military sling can be made to work the same way, but it has double claw hooks that can bang against the rifle. The Whelen sling, seldom seen now, employs a hook and a thong latch. Target shooters typically like 1¼-inch slings, but 1-inch slings are more common, partly because hunters prefer their lighter weight. Also, most modern swivels are made for 1-inch slings.

Standing, or offhand, is the position of last resort, because your center of gravity is so high and you have so little ground contact. Your

Kneeling puts your line of sight higher than sitting.

left arm is unsupported, so a sling is of little use—there's nothing to brace your arm against its tension. Albeit unsteady, offhand is both flexible and very fast, and thus worth practicing.

Good offhand shooting starts at ground level. Plant your feet shoulder-width apart, equal weight on each and a line through your toes at about a thirty-degree angle to sightline. (The thirty-degree foot angle works for me; you may find a more open or closed stance more comfortable.) To find out, tack several targets close together side-by-side on a backing board. With the idea of aiming at the center target, shoulder the rifle with eyes closed. Relax. Now open your eyes. Note where the sight is. Do it again. Again. You may find that the sight wants to hang not on the center bull's-eye, but near another. Change foot position until the sight is pointed at that middle target when you open your eyes. As you move your feet, changing the angle of your body to the line of targets, you may also notice a change in the angle of your feet to one another. The most comfortable angle is best.

Stand flat-footed. I prefer slight forward pressure on the balls of my feet. My knees are straight but not locked. To make the most of bone support, you may incorporate some "lean." Adjust lean to fine-tune balance, keeping center of gravity over your feet.

Offhand, you have only two points of ground contact, and no left arm support. This is the most difficult position to master.

"Most successful shooters lean back and slightly right to counter the rifle's weight," says Gary Anderson, an Olympic shooter who has won two gold medals. "They support the rifle by bracing the left arm against their ribs." Try that with a heavy rifle, and you'll agree with Gary. But hunting rifles lack the mass to stay still with your left hand supporting the forend far to the rear. Wind and heartbeat bounce a lightweight rifle resting against your ribs. You'll get better results holding the forend near midpoint, where you can actively direct and steady it.

Stand upright. Lones Wigger, another Olympic double gold medalist, stands as straight as a new corner post. "Hunching over the rifle puts you off balance and adds tension to back muscles," he says. Keep your head upright too, even if bringing the stock to your cheek puts the rifle's butt above your shoulder. You see best when you look straight ahead. With the rifle ready to fire, your right elbow is best horizontal. There, it puts some strain on your wrist, but like back tension in sitting, wrist tension offhand requires no effort to maintain. The friction of your hand on the grip does that, and the tension can help steady the rifle. A high (horizontal) right elbow also puts a pocket in your shoulder, a place for the butt to settle naturally. Grip the forend lightly but with full hand contact. Pull the stock more firmly with your right hand.

Let your left elbow support the rifle from underneath, not out to the side. Pulling that elbow left strains your shoulder muscles and tires your arm. My left elbow falls directly forward of that shoulder, in a straight line from shoulder to front swivel stud, just in front of my hand. That elbow is almost directly above my left little toe.

In offhand, muscles in both arms come into play, but even where there's no bone support to the ground, you can make the best of bones by aligning them so the muscle loads fall as nearly as possible in line with major bones. If you must swing with a moving target, anticipate where the shot will occur and position your body for maximum bone support and degree of relaxation at that point. In other words, mimic accomplished shotgunners.

Keep your left arm well underneath the rifle, your right elbow almost horizontal.

Whatever your shooting position, when you get a quick shot in the field, point your feet before you point the rifle. Bring it smoothly to your cheek (not cheek to the rifle) as you breathe deeply to bring oxygenated air to your brain and eyes. Shoot with both eyes open if you can, pressuring the trigger as you exhale slowly. Keep up the pressure when the sight is on target. Hold pressure when the sight bounces off target or if your position falls apart (that is, if you lose bone support). The rifle should fire when your lungs are emptied but not purged. Don't jerk. You'll disturb the rifle if you try to fire quickly as the sight dives toward center.

You won't like shooting at paper from unsupported positions. It's easier on the ego to shoot little groups from the bench. But to shoot well in the field (and boost your hunting success), you must often shoot with only your body as a platform, doing everything right, every time. Good shooting follows established habit. When that rabbit catapults from cover, you won't have time to think about shooting. Your body must be conditioned to react reflexively in the right way—so that an aimed shot comes off without conscious effort.

Exhibition shooters show great fluidity and a wonderful economy of movement as the rifle tracks an aerial target. But though it may appear

No matter what position you're shooting from, paying attention to fundamentals will provide greater accuracy.

effortless, every shot reflects discipline. The shooter's body looks natural in its routine because long training has purged superfluous movement and sifted out bad habits. And because bone support eliminates all the strain.

THE HASTY SLING

Most slings these days aren't really slings at all. They're carrying straps, without a shooting loop. A strap *can* help steady your rifle, though not as effectively as a shooting sling.

The hasty sling is the most common single-strap technique. It is indeed a technique, not the strap itself. You won't buy a hasty sling. You can employ a shooting sling as a hasty sling, just by keeping the loop flat and using the entire assembly as a single strap. Poke your left arm between strap and rifle, then wrap your left wrist once around the strap's front end. The hasty sling has some utility offhand because it puts tension on the rifle, deadening jiggles. It won't prevent the rifle from dipping and bobbing offhand, though, because your arm is still without support.

The hasty sling works within a narrow range of strap lengths. If the strap is too long, it will not snug up unless you cock your arm out to the side or grab the strap up front instead of gripping the forend. If the strap is short, you'll find a hasty sling anything but hasty, as you worm your left arm around the strap while attempting a natural bend in your elbow. With a too-short strap, you may have to forgo a front wrap altogether, simply using the strap as a brace.

The broad "cobra" straps that distribute rifle weight nicely for trail carry are too bulky and stiff to wrap around your wrist. Cobra straps can even be liabilities. A friend once threw his rifle up for a quick shot and saw nothing but black. The wide strap had flopped over the barrel, blocking the scope.

A target-style stance mandates a different hasty sling: Jab your arm between the strap and rifle as before, then form an upside-down pedestal with your left thumb and forefingers. Place them just in front of the trigger guard, or with thumb on the guard, fingers forward. Rest your upper left arm on your ribs and lean back. The rifle's weight lies on its balance point. The strap tightens above your triceps, against your pectoral muscle.

A hasty sling is a technique, not an accessory.

Straps work well as shooting aids if both swivels are in front of the trigger, "Scout Rifle" fashion. Slip your arm between strap and forend, then bring the strap against your triceps as you shoulder the rifle. Properly adjusted for length, the strap permits a comfortable arm angle. Because one swivel is just forward of the guard and the other up front, the pull is rearward on both ends of the strap. A strap on a Scout Rifle acts like the working end of a shooting sling, but without loop or keeper. A forward-mounted sling forces you to carry the rifle muzzle down—not as bizarre an alternative as you might think.

In general, a strap is inferior to a shooting sling as a steadying device in prone, sitting, and kneeling. The hasty sling technique is quicker than deployment of a shooting sling, though with practice any rifleman can don a shooting loop in seconds. Offhand, you may discover a hasty sling gives you a steadier rifle than no sling at all, whether you use a strap or a shooting sling with the loop flat.

The key to better shooting, with or without a sling, is practice. If sling or strap use is not second nature, you might find yourself in a tangle when you should be squeezing the trigger.

This Scout Rifle has a "Ching sling" that can be used quickly offhand—with practice.

Chapter 25

PREPPING FOR THE FIELD

Shooting at animals is easier than shooting at bull's-eyes, because most animals are much bigger. On the other hand, animals don't have concentric rings to help you aim. Neither do you know the target distance. You may have to shoot uphill or down, from a spot that's wet, rocky, or steep. The wind could be gusting with enough force to splinter palm trees, or just enough to bounce your reticle gently out of the vitals when you pull the last ounce from the trigger. You'll be excited, and maybe out of breath. Your hands may be cold, or mittened, or both. You may be too stiff for a low position, or swathed in clothes that won't let you bend or use a sling quickly. Add target movement, brush in the bullet's path, backlighting, or barely enough light to aim, and suddenly the variables target shooters never see can make even a short shot tough. Maybe so tough that you'd do best to pass.

You can't practice beating all the gremlins that might someday scuttle a shot. But you *can* practice shooting fundamentals until they're second nature, and until under good conditions you can hit little targets most of the time. You can practice in hunting clothes and jog before shooting so you learn how to shoot when you're short of breath. You can put yourself at the mercy of the wind on breezy days, and shoot in poor light or against the sun, through thick mirage and gusty wind, at unknown distances and steep angles.

You may not have much time to engineer a shot while actually hunting, so practice under time constraints.

Incidentally, steep shot angles don't affect point of impact as much as ordinarily thought. If the angle, up or down, is less than thirty degrees and the target is within point-blank range, forget about it. Just shoot. The bullet may strike a bit high, but it won't miss vitals. At longer range, the effect is greater. Ditto for very steep angles, where you need to aim low because the bullet is not traveling perpendicular to the tug of gravity. So it will be less affected by gravity than if it covered the same distance horizontally. Only the horizontal component of the bullet's flight matters. Hold for that distance.

To better get the picture, visualize a bullet fired straight up or straight down. There is no arc, because gravity pulls only on the nose or heel of the bullet. The horizontal component of the bullet's flight is zero. No matter how far the shot, the bullet will not cross the line of sight a second time. Result: you must hold low to hit at any range beyond the first crossing of sightline and bullet path.

A day in the field with a .22 prepares youngsters for the hunt and teaches them important life lessons.

Most botched shots afield have less to do with miscalculations than with poor marksmanship. Almost none can be laid to inadequate or malfunctioning equipment. A primary tenet for every hunter is to know his or her effective range under hunting conditions. The probability that you'll hit a squirrel's head, aiming against strong back-light, in a stiff wind, at a steep uphill angle, is lower than the odds that you'll connect if you had the same-size bull's-eye target tacked to a board at a shooting range on a bright, calm day. A rabbit bouncing through corn stubble can make a fool of anyone who claims mastery of skeet.

Remember that with living creatures, every shot has an ethical component altogether absent when you're punching paper or shattering clay targets. A bad shot may not miss, but cripple. You don't make a bad shot if you don't shoot. My rule of thumb is that if I can't be 90 percent sure of cleanly killing game, the safety stays on. Hoping for a lucky

For hunting, practice cycling the action and shooting quickly, leaning slightly forward.

hit is irresponsible. No shot is lucky. The shooter makes the shot what it is. The rifle does our bidding. A bullet flies in predictable fashion. The hit or miss is our doing. Cripples result from shots we couldn't make but didn't miss badly enough to spare the animal. They're shots that experienced, conscientious hunters don't take.

An inexpensive, unadorned .22 rifle can help make anyone a crack marksman. Practice is the key.

Chapter 26

SURPRISE! THE BULLET'S GONE

It happened in a rimfire rifle match years ago. Squirming into position, I accidentally touched the trigger. The rifle fired.

In the long seconds that followed, two possibilities emerged. The bullet had missed the paper and I'd get another chance; the shot would be dismissed as a "sighter." The more probable outcome was that I had hit the paper peripherally; the shot would be scored a miss. Peering through the spotting scope, I was astonished to see a hole in the middle of the record target. Exactly in the middle.

I've never again been that lucky. But luck was only partly responsible. If you're almost ready to shoot, the rifle should be pointing at the target more often than it's pointing anywhere else. One measure of a solid shooting position is the difficulty you have in pulling the sight *off* the target. Though I hadn't yet looked into the sight when I bumped the trigger in that match, my position had kept the muzzle very near where it should have been, even as I reloaded the single-shot rifle.

Consistently fine shooting has less to do with intrinsic rifle accuracy than with the shooter. Specifically, you want to do three things well: find a position that brings the rifle naturally on target; control breathing so the sight doesn't pitch like a ship on high seas; and crush the trigger as you would an egg that you didn't want to leak. Triggering the shot seems the simplest of these duties. It is, in fact, exasperatingly difficult.

The shot should be a surprise, but not a shock.

You may have been coached to squeeze triggers so smoothly and gradually that every shot comes as a surprise. A great plan if the sight stays still. Alas, neither you nor I can hold it still. It dips and hops and bounces from side to side. It moves like a turbo-charged figure skater or caroms from point to point like a base runner. It is *never* still. When occasionally it pauses near the middle, quivering, we know that it will dash off again just before the last ounce comes off the trigger. Our only hope for a hit comes from a solid position. It makes the target center a pivot-point, the place the reticle comes back to, if only briefly, more

It's tempting to jerk the trigger—don't. Pull when the sight is on target, hold off when it wanders.

often than any other place in its travels. Odds are that a steady squeeze will drop the striker when the sight is near where we want it.

But often the sight wanders farther, and moves with more vigor, when we pressure the trigger than when we're simply waiting for the sight to settle. Any increase in the range of sight movement reduces the time our reticle spends in the middle. Faster sight movement makes the sight picture hard to assess.

Some years ago, in typical North Woods second-growth, I spied a deer foraging in a small clearing. There was lots of brush between us, and crunchy snow made approach impossible. From the sit I found an alley for my bullet. Slowly I squeezed. *Too* slowly. The whitetail turned away before I finished. I completed the squeeze and called a good hit. But nearly two hours later, after a tough tracking job, I considered it a stroke of undeserved luck when the buck gave me a follow-up shot.

My first hit had been about four inches to the right of where I'd held. Not much. But given the steep quartering angle, enough to cause a crippling hit. The failure reminded me of an easy shot I'd blown a couple of autumns earlier. The elk lay eighty yards below me on a

Bring the rifle firmly into the pocket of your shoulder, and keep your elbow level. Control the trigger.

timbered north face. I fired right away because the shot looked so easy. The bullet missed low. A fast second shot clipped a spinal process high. The elk dropped but bounced back up and thundered off with its companions, leaving no blood.

I should have done better. After all, I've botched a lot of shots the way I botched those, starting in my youth with .22 rifles. I recall missing a sitting rabbit at such short range that I'm embarrassed to admit it in print. And I've yanked the trigger when taking too long to fire at a soup can. Missing with a .22 is more instructive than missing with a big game rifle, because there's no recoil to obscure your mistakes. Still, we remember most vividly those shots that would have delivered up a trophy, had we only made one good shot.

For example, a recent late-season deer hunt put me in country with lots of big bucks. After several days of passing up deer with average antlers, I was down to the final hours. I slipped into heavy cover on a north slope and eased through deep snow and deadfall. In a grid of lodgepole shadow the glistening black nose of a grizzled mule deer caught my eye. The shot sent him away, downhill in giant leaps. I followed fast, certain the bullet had been lethal. But the track suddenly cut back up the mountain. It occurred to me then that either a .280 Improved couldn't be trusted or I had bungled the shot. The chase ended in a meadow. The buck had almost made it to the other side when a 154-grain Hornady confirmed that there was nothing wrong with that .280.

My problem is that I don't always pull the trigger smoothly. In fact, I often yank it. When in its dance the sight hops toward center, my brain screams "Now!" Of course, "now" is not really when the rifle will fire, but when I *wish* it would fire. "Now" is a handful of milliseconds—or a bushel of milliseconds—before the bullet leaves the barrel. During that time the sight may move smartly in another direction or stay on course but accelerate past the target. Naturally, I don't want to give it time for either option. While I can't shorten lock time, I *can* abbreviate the trigger squeeze. This urge is as strong as the sex drive; it is less choice than

You may have to shoot quickly in the field, but the trigger pull must still be smooth.

instinct, as compelling as the need to pull your hand from a fire. The result, however, always disappoints. Yanking the trigger moves the rifle. Riflemen who hit consistently have mastered not the trick of speeding up a trigger squeeze, but of extending the "now" by cajoling the trigger.

Triggers are a bit like teenagers. Some can be cajoled. Others require a heavy hand. A few need replacing, though that's not always possible. Unfortunately, legal concerns have prompted manufacturers to increase both sear engagement and trigger spring tension. It's unfortunate because a rifle that's hard to discharge accidentally is also hard to discharge accurately. The more muscle you must apply to the trigger, the more movement you impart to the barrel. A stiff spring (heavy trigger) or excessive sear engagement (long pull) also increases lock time, leaving that "now" somewhere in the distant past.

A trigger with a crisp three-pound letoff is commonly considered a good trigger. It's heavy for black bull's-eye target shooting but reasonable afield, given that your fingers might be cold or gloved. Excitement can dull senses too, so you don't want the two-ounce triggers popular on prone guns. Sadly, many rifles come from the factory with triggers stiff enough to lift five-pound dumbbells. A few I've tested have scaled over six pounds, as much weight as is in the rifle you're trying to hold still.

The lack of perceptible movement that makes a trigger feel crisp results from keeping sear contact to a minimum. Crisp pulls are good not only because they minimize finger movement but because they tend to be more consistent than long pulls. Even if you believe that every shot should be a surprise, you'll shoot better if the surprises come at the same level of finger pressure each time you squeeze.

Adjustable triggers let you set the weight and sear engagement, as well as overtravel (movement of the trigger after letoff). Overtravel doesn't matter much, in my view. But if a trigger is too hard to pull easily, or if sear engagement is so great that you get a mushy, gritty, or two-stage pull, either you or your gunsmith needs to tinker. If warranties matter to you, be aware that trigger work can void them.

Because litigants now lurk in the most unlikely places, I'll not tell here exactly how to dig sealant from sear stop and trigger spring screws

You can test the accuracy of a rifle from a vise, but you can't learn trigger control there.

on "factory-adjustable" triggers. Nor how to apply a stone to those triggers without adjustments. Still, to shoot accurately, you need a consistent trigger pull, and a letoff that comes easily. If you can't predict a trigger or pull it through without disturbing the rifle, you'll miss. On a recent hunt, I stoned the trigger on a borrowed rifle because even with the weight adjustment on the edge of reliability, the pull was very hard. Removing some of the sear lip reduced its "bite" while shortening the take-up or creep. Result: the trigger not only felt crisp, but lighter as well. The owner hasn't sued me yet.

Set triggers respond to a light touch while keeping sear engagement comfortably safe until you decide to shoot. Pulling the front trigger of a double set trigger (popular in Europe) doesn't fire the rifle. Instead, it mechanically reduces weight of pull for the rear trigger. You can fire quickly without touching the front trigger simply by pulling the rear trigger. Single set triggers incorporate a small lever in the finger pad or are designed so that pushing forward on the pad sets the mechanism for a light pull. I don't like set triggers, because they are complex. Many are slow, extending lock time. Set triggers are also expensive, and a double set trigger requires you to shift your hand slightly between pulls.

High-quality single-stage replacement triggers are available for most popular bolt-action centerfire rifles and match-grade rimfires. They are not, alas, commonly manufactured for sporting-class .22s. So if you're looking for a .22 rifle that will shoot accurately afield, insist on one with a good trigger. Among aftermarket triggers, Carl Kenyon's were tops when I shot on the smallbore prone circuit. Canjar made a popular single-stage set trigger. Both were designed for target guns. Timney (www.timneytrigger.com) may now have the largest selection of sporting rifle triggers, most of which are reasonably priced and easy to install yourself. Shilen and Jewell have a strong following on the match circuit.

Whether you tune your own or buy an aftermarket trigger, try cajoling it. You'll probably like the results, even when the shot comes as a surprise.

Chapter 27

CANT

If you do things in a natural sort of way, you hold a rifle with the sights on top and the trigger on the bottom, just as you drive a car with the shiny side up. But unlike automobiles, rifles aren't connected to the ground. Rifles can be tipped as easily as you tip your hand. They can be fired at a tilt or even upside down. While most shooters keep the sights on top, many do not. Those who tip their rifles are said to be canting.

"A cant isn't bad," a shooting coach told me long ago, "so long as you do it the same each time." Doing it the same each time presupposes that you know you're doing it in the first place. Riflemen who don't think about cant either tip the rifle at pretty much the same angle out of habit, or they allow the angle of the sights to change slightly with each shot.

It's pretty easy to spot a cant if you're coaching, just as it's easy to see the tilt of a truck loaded too heavily on one side if you're driving behind it. In the truck's cab, you might not be able to tell; and when you're looking through the sights you often can't tell either.

A canted reticle will not cause a miss. In fact, you can rotate the scope so the crosswire looks like an "X" and use it as effectively as before. A small disadvantage is that you won't have a vertical wire to help you hold off for wind deflection or show you the line of bullet drop at long range. And you won't have a horizontal wire to help you lead running animals.

A canted *rifle*, however, is another story. Regardless of how the reticle appears, if the rifle is tipped, you'll have problems hitting beyond

A cant won't necessarily impair your ability to hit the target, but canting consistently is difficult.

zero range because the bullet path is not going to fall along the vertical wire or directly below the intersection. If your sightline is directly over the bore, a long shot requires you only to hold high. If your sightline is forced to the *side* of a vertical plane through the bore by a canted rifle, you'll not only have to hold high, but to one side.

Here's the reason: Given that your scope is mounted directly above the bore, your line of sight crosses the bullet path twice. The first crossing happens at about twenty-five yards for rimfires, thirty-five for centerfires. The second crossing is at zero range—seventy-five yards for the .22 Long Rifle and two hundred for most popular big game rounds, if you follow common practice. If the rifle is rotated so the scope falls to the side of the barrel, the sightline will cross only once, because gravity sucks the bullet straight down, while the line of sight has a horizontal component. Whether the scope is on top of the rifle or a bit to the side, the line of sight will converge with the bullet path, slice through it, then angle away. If the scope is on top of the rifle, gravity pulls the bullet in an arc back into and through the straight line of sight. If the scope is not on top, the bullet path still dips below the horizontal *plane* of the sightline, but when this happens the trajectory is well to the side of where you're looking.

The best way to avoid a cant is to start training early with a scope reticle aligned vertically.

How much practical difference will canting make? Not much. A cant that escapes your notice won't cause a noticeable shift in bullet impact at normal hunting ranges. As the targets get smaller and the range longer, and as you impose stricter accuracy standards, cant starts to matter.

When I was on the Michigan State University rifle team, I marveled at a colleague who shot very well but used a cant that would have spilled coffee. Standing, he looked straight ahead through sights that fell into his natural line of vision when he rotated the Anschutz rifle on his shoulder. The adjustable butt let him do that without changing the contact angle of the butt hook. So his sights tilted in toward him. Not only the line of sight, but also the rifle's center of gravity fell closer to the centerline of his torso. From a mechanical perspective, this made perfect sense. I tried shooting that way and found it darned near impossible.

In traditional bull's-eye competition for .22 rimfires, targets are very small and rifles supremely accurate, so shooters must correct for cant. (Some globe sights for target rifles have tiny bubble levels that show you the slightest cant at a glance.) On the other hand, my teammate on the smallbore squad didn't have to worry about horizontal

Target shooters sometimes employ a slight cant, but you'll want to hold the rifle vertically when shooting afield.

angles because his shooting was done up close at one distance. It is easy to accommodate cant at a single distance. You simply move the sights to put the bullets where you look. Forget about how sightline and trajectory converge, and what they do beyond the target. It doesn't matter.

But we hunters don't shoot at just one distance. So although small degrees of cant seldom affect our performance on game, it's a good idea to shoot with the sights squarely on top of the rifle. Cant is just one more thing to worry about, one more distraction, a small but thorny threat to the self-confidence that can help us shoot well.

It's easy to see if you have a cant. Simply loosen your scope rings and line up the vertical wire with the butt of your rifle. Now tighten the rings. Throw the rifle to your shoulder with your eyes closed. Then open them. The wire should appear vertical. If it does not, you're tipping the rifle. Practice holding it right side up.

Chapter 28

A BULLET'S WAY THROUGH WIND

There's an ambush in front of your muzzle. The wind is a diabolical character waiting to snatch your bullet from its intended course and rob you of center hits. Shooters adept at reading the evidence of wind in leaves, grass, flags, and mirage have become clever at adjusting their sights and aim to compensate. But wind is not steady. It surges and subsides. Sometimes it leaves altogether or sneaks around and attacks from the opposite direction. You can miss as easily in a letup as in a pickup. A sudden reversal doubles the error if you've compensated.

A Wyoming wind can get your attention. It has a breadth and depth that makes the earth itself hunker down. A Wyoming wind bends thick trees and shaves the edges off big rocks. It drove settlers mad and killed their cows in winter. It blows trucks over on Interstate 80. It certainly has its way with little things like bullets.

I thought about that as I bellied into the short sage on the ridge, wind-tears blurring my aim. The sling snug, I held the horizontal wire just over the antelope's back, then pulled my rifle to the left, against the wind. The Remington 722 bounced, and its 90-grain Remington soft-point sped away. As my sight picture came back after recoil, the animal jetted off. The sprint was short. As the *thwuck* of a hit floated back, the buck nosed into the sagebrush.

Wind is a constant concern in pronghorn country. The author doped it well on this hunt.

I'd held on the animal's nose. Gravity had pulled my 6mm bullet about eighteen inches low, and wind had moved it almost as far. The result: a heart shot.

My first lessons in wind drift came in rimfire prone matches. Having started on indoor ranges, I felt as though I'd been plucked from a swimming pool and dropped into the North Atlantic. Indoors, the medals went to shooters who held the rifles still and executed their shots well. Outdoors, you had to hold, execute, *and* dope the wind. If you ignored the wind, you lost. A .22 bullet seemed as compliant as a shuttlecock at a hundred yards, and it was easily driven two scoring rings out of the X by light breezes at fifty.

At first, I thought wind flags unnecessary. I dismissed as gadgets the ubiquitous "windicators"—small, wind-driven fans with tails that swung atop stems on ball bearings. Then I found myself watching the flags and listening to the hum of the windicators. Wind speed and velocity were affecting my shots. If I zeroed during a predominant wind condition and the wind suddenly picked up or slacked off, my bullets would stray. A reversal would hurl my shot far out of center.

Sometimes the windicators wouldn't tip me off. They'd hum lazily with nary a flip of their tail, while my bullets jumped in and out

This competitor's spotting scope is focused at midrange to monitor wind not moving at the target.

of the 10-ring. The flags at fifty and one hundred yards told me that downrange, the wind was capricious. Sometimes wind at the target would be opposite that at the line. I'd see flags in full flap at a hundred yards, and limp at fifty. Occasionally the windicators would spin furiously to the left, while the midrange flag lifted to the right, and the hundred-yard flag kicked out left again. A bullet sent through that gauntlet would fly a zigzag course. Shooting when you got mixed signals was pretty risky. I noticed that when the wind was visibly contrary or undecided, the spatter of shots at the line would die out as shooters waited for more favorable conditions.

Favorable didn't necessarily mean still. It is possible to shoot very well in a stiff breeze, as long as you're zeroed for that condition or "shade" (compensate) for it properly. Savvy shooters make notes about the wind on a range so they know predominant drift. The Spokane range, for example, is built on a riverbank. Wind typically angles across the firing line from seven or eight o'clock but then bounces off the bank and crosses the target line from four o'clock. If you minded only wind at the line, you'd make a big mistake. Zeroing for predominant drift gives competitors more shooting time without sight changes

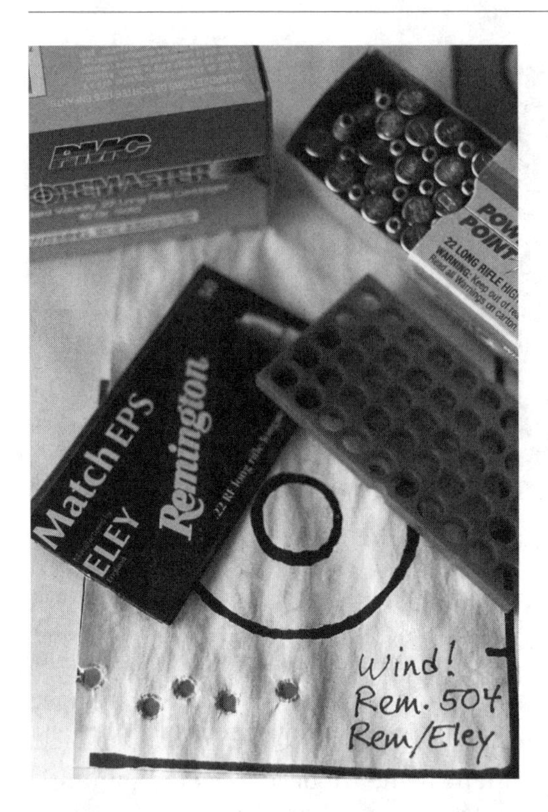

Wind can open groups to embarrassing dimensions.

during a match. They can then afford to hold their fire during letoffs, pickups, and reversals, or at least reduce the number of shots they must fire in those conditions. They note differences between morning and afternoon drift, and they watch flags on both ends of the line, because wind conditions can differ between firing points.

Even at the fifty-yard line, bullets from .22 Long Rifle cartridges yield readily to the slightest breeze. That's why we who squandered our Saturdays shooting .22s watched the mirage as well as the flags. Lazy breezes that would hardly lift a flag could make mirage run and frighten bullets into the big rings. At modest ranges, bullets from most centerfire rifles can drive through pretty strong winds without significant deflection. Then again, "significant" is relative. A couple inches of drift will lose a match for you if you're shooting a .22 at a hundred yards, but it's of no consequence if your target is as big as a deer's chest.

A 170-grain flat-nose .30-30 bullet drifts less than two inches in a 10-mph sidewind at a hundred yards. A 25-mph wind, which is strong enough to sway trees, pushes that .30-30 bullet only about four inches off course. Bullets from most other big game cartridges buck the wind better. So at woods ranges, you really needn't think about wind. Remember too that deflection is generally figured for wind at right angles to the bullet's path. Even wind that picks up small children can have little effect on your bullet if the angle is acute.

But distance makes a lot of difference, because bullets slow down. Just as the trajectory of a bullet becomes steeper the farther it gets from the muzzle, so wind deflection becomes greater at long range. You might think of drift as a horizontal trajectory. A constant wind is, in effect, very much like gravity. Bullets scribe a parabolic arc under the pressure of wind for the same reasons their trajectory is parabolic.

Double the wind speed, and you double the drift. Halve the wind speed, and you halve the drift.

Reduce the wind's angle from ninety degrees, and you reduce drift proportionately. A full-value or crosswind blowing at right angles to the bullet's path has twice the effect on it as a quartering wind.

You can ignore headwinds and tailwinds unless they are very strong.

Change the shot distance, however, and the drift may surprise you. For example, a .22 Long Rifle match bullet that starts at 1,050 fps and drifts an inch at 50 yards may, in the same conditions, strike 4 inches off course at 100. A 130-grain .270 bullet launched at 3,000 fps is shoved just ¾ inch at 100 yards by a 10-mph wind. But it is 3 inches off course at 200 yards and 7 inches off at 300. Figure 13 inches at 400. Why?

Well, there's little drift at short range because the bullet reaches the target quickly. There's not much drop from bore-line up close either. From 50 to 100 yards for rimfires, and beyond a hundred yards for centerfires, drift and drop increase significantly. The operating factor is bullet deceleration.

It may be of academic interest that drift quadruples between 50 and 100 yards for the .22 Long Rifle and in the second hundred yards for many centerfires. The important thing to remember is that it increases with distance but not at a constant ratio. In fact, wind drift for the .270 bullet at 500 yards is only about 60 percent greater than at 400. Remember that rate of deceleration changes as the bullet moves downrange, and that while speedy bullets can get through wind a little better than slow bullets, ballistic coefficient becomes ever more important in determining drift at long range. A handy rule of thumb is to assume an inch of drift at 100 yards, and double that at 200; triple the 200 drift at 300, and double the 300 drift at 400.

Bullet velocity, weight, and shape all affect wind deflection. A bullet the shape of a soup can is not well adapted for flight. There's a lot of air pressure on the nose and a high rate of deceleration. Because a bullet's form contributes to its ballistic coefficient (the numerical expression of its ability to cleave air), the .22 Long Rifle bullet will always fare poorly in its battle with drag and wind.

The broad range of bullet shapes in centerfire ammo makes predicting wind drift problematic. A .30-30 flat-nose has a low ballistic coefficient, or C. But lightweight spitzers—say, 70-grain .243s, or the 17-grain bullets in .17 HMR cartridges, also have low ballistic coefficients. Their low sectional density (ratio of a bullet's weight to the square

A light breeze blew these 17-caliber bullets farther off course than gravity pulled them down.

of its diameter) acts like a blunt nose to reduce ballistic coefficient. In other words, a bullet that is streamlined but short for its diameter can be as aerodynamically inept as a bullet that is longer but has a blunt nose.

Nose shape, by the way, has less effect on trajectory and drift than you might think. Ballistician Alan Corzine, currently with Federal Cartridge, says that the first tenth of an inch of the nose can be flat, round, or pointed without affecting trajectory or drift. The ogive—the leading curve of the bullet between tip and shank—*does* matter. You'll hear arguments for "tangent" ogives and "secant" ogives. These engineering terms have to do with the placement of the center of the circle, of which the ogive forms a segment. That center determines the segment's profile. A round-nose bullet with a sweeping ogive may fly along nearly the same track as a pointed bullet. Similar trajectories mean the bullets lose velocity at about the same rate, and that they'll respond similarly to wind.

Boat-tail bullets have been touted as "slippery" projectiles, giving gravity a run for its money. At normal hunting ranges, however, boat-tail (tapered-heel) bullets offer little advantage. Say that we start a 140-grain 7mm bullet at 2,700 fps. No matter whether it is a flat-base bullet or a boat-tail, it passes the 100-yard mark clocking about 2,500 fps. At 200 yards, the boat-tail bullet is clipping along at 2,320, just 15 fps

Sleek bullet profiles definitely minimize wind drift—ogive shape is most important.

faster than its flat-base counterpart. At 350 yards, the boat-tail bullet is leading by 35 fps. Now, 350 yards is a very long distance, but the difference in drop between these two bullets amounts to only about half an inch. Expect the same difference in wind drift. Boat-tail bullets become an asset only at very long ranges—or in gale-force winds. A 30-mph wind that shoves our flat-base 7mm bullet 17 inches at 350 yards moves the boat-tail bullet 15½ inches. Obviously, there's no significant advantage to a tapered heel on a jacketed .22 WMR or .17 HMR rimfire bullet at the ranges these rounds are normally used. Some manufacturers say they prefer to produce flat-base bullets because there is only one angle at the heel, and therefore less chance for dimensional error.

Determining bullet drop is as easy as estimating range, because gravity acts in a constant and predictable way. For any given load, drop is the same at any given yardage on any day at any place. (Even substantial differences in elevation have little practical effect on drop.) Just memorize your bullet's trajectory and practice estimating distances until your eye becomes adept. Wind is different because it changes day to day, and sometimes spins on its heel in a second. It varies by location and topography. Like gravity, it is invisible, but there's no formula avail-

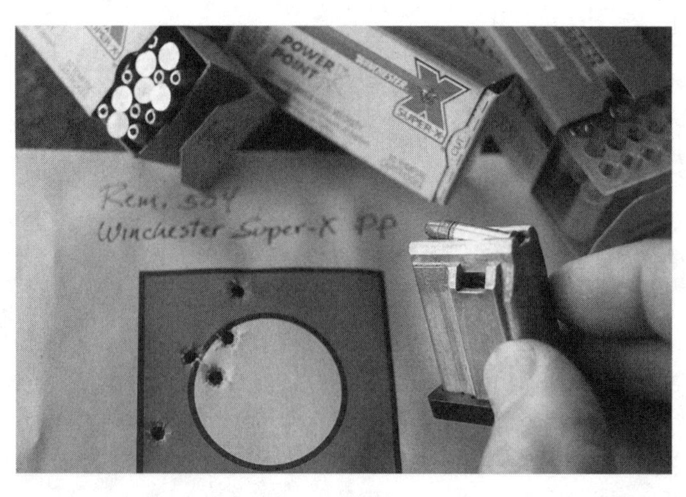

Wind from the right typically pushes bullets up; wind from the left brings them below center.

able to describe it or show you its effects until by some mechanical measure you determine its precise speed and direction. Even then, compensating can be hard. Wind is seldom the same at the muzzle as it is downrange.

Just recently I shot a couple of Kenny Jarrett's super-accurate rifles at six hundred yards. Paper targets occasionally were ripped from the backing by a wind strong enough to sway the tops of sturdy loblolly pines. The little 65-grain Shilen bullets in the .243 Catbird (a .270 case necked down) would get through a couple hundred yards on their blistering speed alone, but I expected to have a tough time keeping them on paper at six hundred. To my astonishment, I fired a three-shot group under four inches. The reason: Our wind, gusting to twenty-five miles per hour, came from seven o'clock. And those pines sheltered my bullets to nearly the five-hundred-yard mark. Total drift amounted to less than six inches. Heavier bullets at lower speed from a .308 gave me similar results.

Reading wind is an acquired skill. When I started minding windicators and range flags, I thought myself pretty sophisticated. But still bullets strayed, even when I called the shot well. Dick Nelson, a fine rifleman who also helped Boeing engineer the first moon vehicle, took me aside one day. "You'll have to read the mirage. Do that, and those bullets will hop through the 10-ring like trained pigs." I had never seen trained pigs, but the part about the 10-ring got my attention. Here's what Dick and other savvy smallbore shooters taught me about mirage:

Mirage is a visual distortion caused by heat waves rising from the earth's surface. If you don't see it, it isn't there.

Mirage does not move bullets; its dance shows you wind that does.

You can't see mirage at all distances at once. You'll either see the strongest mirage or the mirage at the range for which your scope is focused. To get the most information about wind that most strongly affects their bullets, match shooters typically focus their spotting scopes to read mirage a little short of the targets.

Mirage that's really bumpy and moving slowly indicates a light breeze. Mirage that's flat and fast indicates a stronger breeze. When mirage disappears suddenly with no change in light conditions, it's often because the wind has picked up. Mirage that boils vertically shows you a still condition. But beware—a boil commonly precedes a reversal in wind direction. Many competitive shooters zero for a light

Doping wind with a .22 will prepare you for making long, accurate shots at big game in windy country.

prevailing breeze, then hold their fire during boils and reversals, shading and shooting during pickups and letoffs.

Mirage can make you shoot at a target that isn't there, by "floating" the target in the direction air currents are moving. The displacement isn't enough to worry about when you're shooting at game, though it can costs points on the small targets in a rifle match.

In the field, you may seldom see mirage. Fall hunting seasons bring cold weather, which all but cancels mirage. To read wind, you'll have to rely on coarser signs: nodding trees and grass, the leaves and snow and mist that yield to wind.

Remember that wind at the target is as important as wind at the muzzle. In fact, it can be more important, because the bullet is moving slower, and over any given distance wind has more time to work its mischief. Wind at the muzzle has the advantage of leverage. That is, it can start a bullet on a new course, and distance will magnify the displacement of that bullet from bore-line. If it strikes two inches to the left at a hundred yards, it will not come back to center even if conditions are dead calm at two hundred yards and beyond. In fact, the bullet will move ever farther from bore-line at long range, if at a reduced rate, because wind at the muzzle has established an angle between the bullet's path and bore-line.

Not long ago I spent half a day shooting at prairie dogs with a .223. I don't shoot a lot of prairie dogs, because it seems to me that shooting and hunting are different. When I shoot a lot, it's at paper. But this day, a couple of friends and I bellied to within two hundred yards of a small dog town and battled the wind with our little 50-grain spitzers. We counted few hits, especially after the 200-yard sod poodles got wise and we were forced to stretch the rifles to 250, then 300. A stiff breeze from eight o'clock carried the bullets from three to six inches, depending on distance and our timing. Shooting between gusts, we sometimes over-corrected. In spotting for one another, we learned more than if we'd been alone, trying to see bullet strikes during recoil.

Late in the morning, we moved to another rise so the wind came from seven o'clock. Immediately we saw wind deflection shrink. It confirmed an old target-shooting rule: Unless it is very strong, ignore wind from between eleven and one o'clock, and from between five and seven o'clock. It's hard, when you feel wind on your face or neck, to remember that a bullet moving 3,000 fps is encountering tremendous wind resistance even in still conditions. It is generating its own headwind—a 2,000-mph gale! What difference do you think a 20-mph headwind or tailwind will have on this bullet's flight?

It's foolish to assume every breeze you feel will affect your bullet's point of impact. On the other hand, wind is a compelling force. At long range, with inefficient bullets in a full-value wind, you may have to aim where you don't want the bullet to go.

Chapter 29

WHY HUNTERS MISS

If you've never bungled a shot at big game, seek out someone in your community who hunts and ask him to show you a rifle. Shooting can be a lot of fun.

If, like me, you've missed often, you're apprehensive every time the crosswire dances tentatively into a shoulder crease. You know that when the trigger breaks, the die is cast, and you don't trust yourself to hit. Missing easy shots can shatter your confidence and predispose you to missing. Expect to miss, and you probably will.

So the first step to better shooting at big game is better shooting at big game. Here's a quick review.

Acknowledge that you're in charge of each shot. Hunters with alibis set themselves up to miss. If you know that wind and gravity and pine boughs bend a bullet's path, it's up to you to compensate or decline the shot. Remember: If you don't shoot, you can't miss. Filling the air with bullets when you merely *hope* to hit something boosts your odds for a hit from zero to just above zero, while the odds that you'll miss or cripple an animal rise from zero to nearly 100 percent.

Be ready to shoot, always. And when the possibility of a shot pops up, act as if you *will* shoot. To decline a shot is easy; you can do that anytime. Hitting usually requires that you make the most of every second. So carry the rifle as if you expected to shoot at any time, and when you spot game within range, look at it through your sights first. I've lost opportunities examining animals with a binocular before shouldering the rifle.

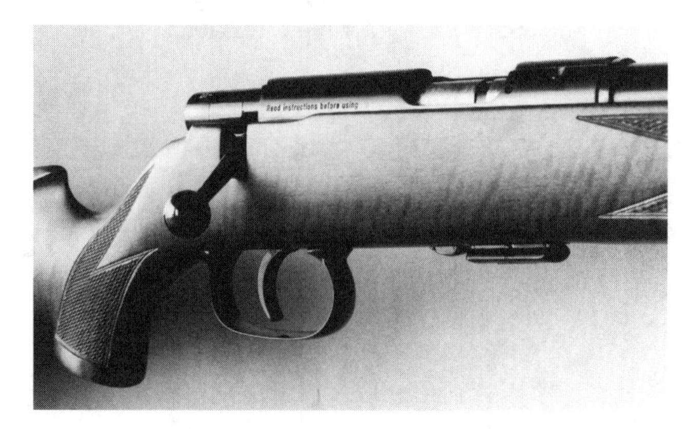

Rarely is a miss attributable to the rifle. This Anschutz sporter will print one-hole groups at fifty yards.

Anchor the rifle. That is, shoot from the steadiest position available. Use a rock or limb as a rest, but pad the forend (never rest the barrel) with your hand to reduce the rifle's vibration away from the surface. Use a shooting sling, whose adjustable loop transfers rifle weight from your left hand to the muscles of your left shoulder, which can better support the weight. As discussed earlier, a carrying strap doesn't work because it pulls from the rear swivel too, tugging the rifle from your shoulder and twisting it.

Sometimes we miss because we shoot too fast, sometimes because we're too deliberate.

Iron sights on a short-barreled gun must be perfectly aligned.

Focus. Concentrate on the reticle, as muscle memory from long practice brings the rifle on target. Breathe deeply a couple of times to deliver oxygen to brain and eyes for clearer aim, then let your lungs relax as you pull the rifle firmly into your shoulder with your left hand and begin the trigger squeeze. Add trigger pressure when the reticle comes on target; hold pressure when it wanders. If your position falls apart or the reticle is bouncing too hard or you run out of breath, start over.

Go gently on the trigger. A hit takes a tiny slice of time. The bullet has only one chance in its headlong flight to find the mark, and as you squeeze the final ounce from that trigger, you seal the outcome. All the rifle movement you see in the scope field before a shot matters not; what counts is the position of the reticle when the bullet leaves. If you hold a rifle still, then jerk the trigger, you're pulling the rifle off target during the eyeblink in time that locks in the bullet's flight path.

A lot of hunters set themselves up to miss even before there's a shot to take. They don't practice.

Shooting is like any other activity. The more often you do it, the more natural it seems. Now, firing away at soup cans on a sand bank is

Mostly, we miss because we simply don't shoot enough. Practicing with a .22 will sharpen your eye.

only helpful if you mind what you're doing. A few careful shots benefit you more than full magazines sprayed without regard to shooting fundamentals. Paper bull's-eyes help you most because the bullet holes tell you where your sight was when the rifle fired. Calling your shot, or predicting where the bullet will land before you see the hole, is an important skill.

The real mark here is about the size of a big marble. Don't take the shot unless you can consistently nail it in practice sessions.

You'll want to know as an animal runs off where the bullet struck. Paper targets confirm your calls—or show that you didn't pay attention.

If paper bores you, try rimfire metallic silhouettes.

Once you have the fundamentals of marksmanship in hand, it's a good idea to practice under the clock. You may find, as I have, that speeding up your cadence a bit can actually help you shoot more accurately. Remember, though, that accuracy is more important than speed, and if you don't have time for a good shot, you really don't have time for a shot.

A few more tips, if you don't like to miss: When hunting in cold weather, wear wool mitts that free your fingers through a slit. They're warmer than gloves; besides, it's hard to shoot accurately with gloved fingers. Before the season, make sure that you can shoot well when dressed in hunting gear. A heavy jacket or a backpack strap can increase your effective length of pull. Practice getting into a sling or using your bipod or shooting sticks, so you can steady your rifle without taking your eyes off the target.

Chapter 30

MEASURE YOUR MARKSMANSHIP

Whether your rifle is a nail-driver or has a musket's wanderlust, you won't know if you can hit anything with it until you document your shooting skill. Without skill, the most accurate rifle is useless as soon as you lift it off the sandbags. A skilled marksman can make the musket lethal.

Repetition tests marksmanship just as it does accuracy. The place to start repeating your hits, oddly enough, is on the bench. There you can refine your breathing and trigger squeeze and learn to read the wind. You'll learn to call shots there too—"freeze framing" the sight picture at the instant of firing to accurately predict where your bullet will land. Bench groups will be small, engendering confidence and encouraging you to shoot more. If this exercise seems elementary and beneath your dignity, skip it. But I still find it useful. The other day I practiced my fundamentals with a Remington 40x in .22 rimfire, at fifty yards, using new match ammo made for Remington by Eley. You can do this with any rifle, but one that's very accurate and doesn't kick hard is best. You must know that the rifle will shoot where you point it.

I fired a series of five-shot groups, trying to make each a little smaller than the last. Trigger and breath control were all that mattered; the bench held the rifle. On average, the groups ran a little over 0.60. The best, my last, measured about 0.40. You don't have to shoot groups

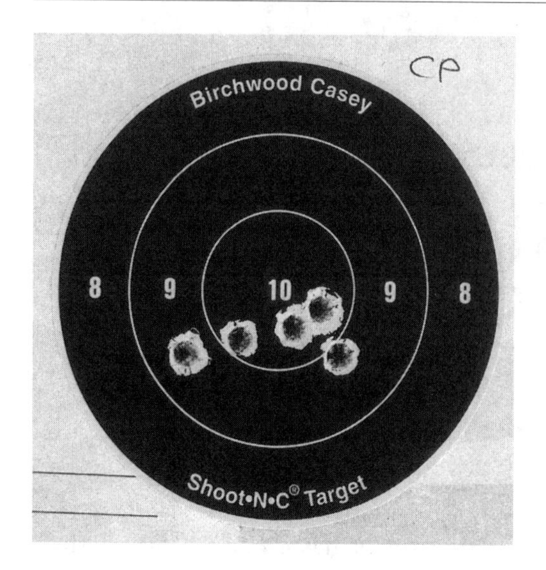

Until you print bullet holes on paper, you can't measure your progress as a marksman.

that tight, though, because not all rifles and cartridges will. But deliver enough shots into a group, and replicate the group often enough, and you'll soon figure out which marginal shots resulted from your incompetence. Give yourself plenty of time with this exercise.

Next, shoot from a bipod or an improvised rest (not a bench). Shoot half a dozen five-shot groups. They'll be bigger than those you shot from the bench, but if you control the trigger not *that* much bigger. Wild shots are bad news here. If they happen, dry-fire until they don't, taking care to make each "shot" a good one. Call each, and score yourself.

The last step in documenting your skill is tough, because it forces you to *hold* the rifle and take responsibility for all errant shots. You know the rifle will shoot into, say, three minutes of angle. Shots outside that perimeter can't be blamed on the rifle or ammunition. Fire six groups, two each from sitting, kneeling, and offhand. A sling is okay here, but no bipods, stumps, posts, packs, or other supports that may be unavailable when you see an animal and must shoot quickly.

If results here fall short of appalling, you deserve a milkshake. Mine usually point out the need for more dry-firing. Whatever the outcome, you'll know how far you can fire effectively from field positions. If you're

Don't just shoot under ideal conditions; use paper targets in field situations to improve marksmanship.

shooting a centerfire rifle, use the results of shooting at a hundred yards to calculate your maximum effective range on deer. Toss out your worst shot from each position, then take the average spread of each pair of groups (one 4-shot and one 5-shot from each position) and divide that figure into twelve. Multiply by one hundred, and you get maximum effective range.

For example, say that, from kneeling, you print two 6-inch groups. Deleting your worst shot, you come up with one 6-inch group and one that now measures just four inches. Average group size: five inches. Divide 5 into 12, and you get 2.4. Multiply by 100, and you get 240, the maximum distance in yards at which you should be able to plant nine of ten shots inside the twelve-inch vitals of a deer. Small animals like rabbits and squirrels aren't as forgiving; but then, with rimfire rifles you won't be shooting far either.

This formula gives you the *maximum* practical limit, because on a hunt many things conspire to make shooting more difficult. Wind, for example. Dope it wrong at long range, and you're in trouble. You won't know the actual range either—a real problem where the bullet's arc is steep. Shivering or panting, you'll make the rifle shake, sending bullets all over the hill. Get excited, or hurry because time is short, and even if you don't jerk the trigger, your pulse and nerves can throw the bullet off target.

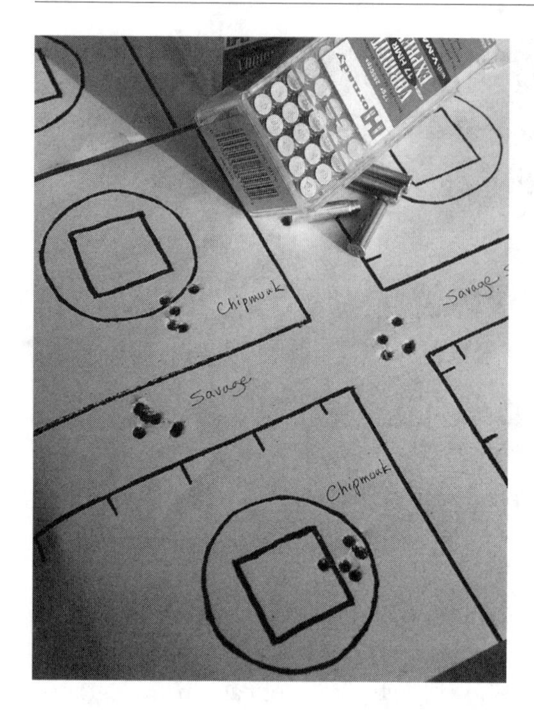

Even inexpensive rifles shoot better groups from a bench than you can from hunting positions. Get off the bench and improve your marksmanship.

One accomplished hunter put it this way: "If you can't be certain of a first-round hit, there's no point in shooting." Don't count on backup from the magazine. Those bullets are as ignorant as the first, and no more able to overcome your inadequacies.

Shoot when you're sure. Decline when you have doubts. Before the season, document your skill so you know what you can and can't do with that rifle. By the time you've determined your limits, you will probably have extended them. Getting your own measure gives you invaluable practice, as you concentrate on the fundamentals that make you deadly in the field.

Replicating shots from a bench, we know a rifle is accurate. Replicating shots without support, we confirm our skill. On the hunt, rifle accuracy matters a lot less than marksmanship.

Chapter 31

A STAND-UP GAME

Early in the last century, Pancho Villa and his bandits pillaged Mexican farmsteads. Violence was a problem only when it happened within ranks. After one raid, a couple of Pancho's henchmen evidently argued over who was the better shot. Burying both would have been hard work in the afternoon heat, so their leader suggested a contest. A couple of steers, curiously still alive, were rounded up and staked far away . . .

Shooting livestock at long range eventually drew more reputable marksmen. Dr. Mario Gonzales wrote about a fiesta in Jalisco where contestants fired at chickens a hundred meters away—with pistols. Any hit drawing blood claimed that chicken for that shooter. In 1946 Gonzales joined a club in Guadalajara and attended weekly chicken shoots. For variety, turkeys were added as targets at 150 and 200 meters, pigeons at 50 meters. Riflemen could shoot at chickens 200 meters away, and try to hit turkeys at 400. Sheep were staked 500 meters downrange.

This sport didn't last long. Animal suffering had less to do with its demise than did cheating. Riflemen learned you could hit a big rock next to a small target to draw blood with the shrapnel. Or pay an official to overlook blood from a previous hit, to count later. Animals were not the same size, and some moved more than others, prompting complaints. Softnose bullets damaged meat. Rounding up and staking the livestock was lots of work.

In 1948 Don Gonzalo Aguilar organized a rifle match in Mexico City, substituting metal silhouettes in the shape of animals. Four years

The author shoots a rimfire Metallic Silhouette course with a Kimber SVT.

later Mexico held its first national *Siluetas Metalicas* championship. This course of fire included 30 shots: 10 each at *gallinas* (chickens) at 200 meters, *guajalotes* (turkeys) at 385, and *borregos* (sheep) at 500. Riflemen with .22s could shoot *palomas* (doves) at 50 and 100 meters, and pint-size steel *gallinas* at 150.

Into the early 1960s, *Siluetas Metalicas* remained a Mexican sport. Then, in 1967, Roy Dunlap and others at the George Paterson Rifle Club of Nogales, Arizona built a silhouette range. The targets were like those used by Mexico's Northern League, but Roy put horns on the sheep. The club added a bank of *javelinas* (pigs), to be shot at 300 meters. On April 12, 1969, the first American Metallic Silhouette match happened at the Tucson rifle range. An entry fee of thirty pesos, or $2.40, included all the pit-barbecued beef you could eat. Matches that followed stateside were for centerfire rifles only, maximum weight changed from Mexico's 4.0 kg (about 8.8 pounds) to 4.6 kg (10.2 pounds) to accommodate scopes. Still, all shots had to be taken offhand (standing), without a sling or artificial support.

I shot my first silhouette match in 1974, on a strip of featureless New Mexico sand. Distant *borregos* weaved unsteadily in mirage that floated them off their steel pedestals. "Teeny, ain't they," grinned a man

"Swinger" silhouettes set up in your yard provide practice when you can't get to a range.

scuffing a level spot in the prickly pear to my left. Teeny! It was like trying to hold on animal crackers riding surf.

"*Listo!*" I slipped a cartridge into my .270. "*Fuego!*" The following fusillade was punctuated occasionally by pings, clangs, and far-away bongs. Between shots I'd see the odd turkey or sheep melt into the desert. They didn't fall; they just disappeared. The sound of the strike floated back later. Closer, the pigs toppled, or skittered off their pedestals. Chickens took a beating at two hundred meters, leaping off their perches and spinning into the sand.

When the rifles at last fell silent, only one gap had appeared in my line of five *borregos*.

The stout man who won that day hit about half his eighty targets. He shot them with a Winchester Model 70 .30-06 and a Weaver K-4 scope, an off-the-shelf rifle you'd hunt with. Later, when shooters began building custom artillery, a "hunting class" would evolve to maintain the original spirit of the sport. Rifles for hunting matches would be held to less than nine pounds overall weight, with a two-pound trigger and functional magazine.

Metallic Silhouette shooting has spread north in these last thirty years, and expanded to included more than centerfire hunting rifles.

These porkers look easy to hit, but it's a different story when you see them from the firing line.

The National Rifle Association has developed courses of fire for black-powder cartridge rifle, long-range pistol, short-range pistol, smallbore (rimfire) rifle, even air rifle and air pistol. Rules are similar; gun specifications, target sizes, and distances vary.

In the popular centerfire and rimfire rifle matches, competitors fire 40, 60, 80, or 120 shots in five-round strings, with no sighting shots. Targets are taken left to right; any hits out of sequence are counted as misses. A second-round hit on target number 3 would be a *double* miss because target #2 is safe and the hit on target #3 cannot be scored. No coaching is allowed. If wind knocks down a target, you skip it and return to the left-most remaining target for your last shot. Equipment failure may qualify you for an alibi string, thirty seconds per shot, at the close of that relay. Ties are broken by "sudden death" shoot-offs.

The only cartridge restriction in the centerfire event is a bullet 6mm or larger, but most shooters favor bigger missiles, because *borregos* hit low by a lightweight bullet sometimes don't fall. Unnecessarily powerful cartridges are bad business because they make you flinch. Early on, the most popular factory rifle for Metallic Silhouette shooting was the varmint-weight Remington 700 in .308. Custom-built rifles for Metallic Silhouette usually feature short, heavy barrels and lightweight synthetic stocks. Vertical grips and tall combs are the rule, because shooting is off-hand only. You won't see many 4x scopes these days. Some shooters use magnification as high as 24x, though I prefer about half that. (Wind can make a high-power scope very difficult to control.) Target-style turret knobs help you switch from one distance to another. I zero on pigs at three hundred meters, aiming low on the chicken and just above the turkey. I crank the elevation dial only for the sheep. An adjustable objective enables you to focus sharply when using high magnification.

A silhouette range requires no target frames, pits, or cement firing line. But you do need space. A 500-meter shot is 547 yards. Add fifty for parking, scoring tables. That means 600 yards of relatively flat land with a hill tall enough to catch bullets and a road to the targets so you can carry them in a vehicle and set them up in a hurry during a match.

In places too suburban for long shooting, rimfire Metallic Silhouette shooting evolved. Scaled to roughly one-fifth the size of standard silhouettes, rimfire targets are set at 40, 60, 77, and 100 yards. They save a lot of steel. Bases for centerfire sheep are as big as sheep *targets* for the .22s, which require only quarter-inch plate. You can throw eight banks of .22 targets in your trunk, with pedestals and sight-in gongs. At the range, just drive the pedestals in the ground. Centerfire targets fill a U-Haul van, and you need a crew of stevedores to set them, plus permanent pedestals.

Ammunition for rimfire shooting can be any .22 caliber Short, Long, or Long Rifle cartridge. However, hypervelocity rounds don't qualify. Match ammo isn't necessary, but groups bigger than one inch at fifty yards could cost you. Rimfire rifles must hew to the 10.2-pound weight limit of centerfires, and the same limitations concerning barrel length (30 inches), comb height (bore-line), and forend dimensions (no more than 2¼ inches deep or wide). Any safe trigger is permissible. Early on, Anschutz built a silhouette rifle on its Model 54 action, with a trigger adjustable to 2.1 ounces. Blue-collar beginners who shot against such hardware soon howled for a "hunter" class. The NRA modified centerfire hunter-class rules, settling on a 7.5-pound weight limit and allowing single-shot actions.

Many common rimfire rifles can be competitive. One fellow I know made his debut with a battered Mossberg, using a hacksaw blade in place of its missing bolt stop and taping the splintered stock together. The scope was a cheapie. This young man worked hard on fundamentals, however, and won a club championship.

Metallic silhouette shooting can help you become a good shot. While hunters covet new equipment, the truth is that ordinary rifles, optics, and ammo are better than they'll ever know because they lack the skill to test them. Silhouette shooting is a way to gain that skill. Francisco Doroteo Arango "Pancho" Villa probably never had a better idea.

Paint can help you see the targets (these are bigger than rimfire size).

Chapter 32

CLEANING RIMFIRES

The outside-lubricated or plated bullets of traditional .22 rimfire ammunition baby rifle and pistol bores. There's no jacket to cause copper fouling, and the bullets travel at relatively low speed. The small amounts of quick-burning powder in .22 cartridges don't eat throats, and there's little propellant residue to draw moisture or affect accuracy. Lube left from bullets protects the bore as effectively as oil or grease on the final patch used for cleaning centerfire rifles.

For these reasons, I rarely clean .22 rimfire sporters. In competition, I clean the bore every forty record shots, at the most. Sometimes I'll fire eighty, plus sighters, between bore cleanings. And these are just to ensure a slick bore and top-end accuracy.

Cleaning more often that necessary is not only extra work; it can be counterproductive. Every time you introduce a cleaning rod into the barrel, you run some risk of damage. Proper use of high-quality rods, jags, and brushes won't damage bores, but a tight patch can cause a rod to flex or tip, and contact the chamber or muzzle. Any grit picked up by a rod, patch, or brush can be transferred to the bore.

Be especially careful with rimfire ammo not to let any outside-lubed bullets out of the box until you load them. If you drop one, set it aside for a thorough cleaning before you load it. Lubed bullets collect grit much more easily than copper-jacketed bullets; grit in the bore acts like sandpaper on its finish.

To keep centerfire bores free of jacket deposits, clean after every range session. You may have to clean even more often—say, every

If your rifle is shooting well, you may not need to clean it. Just use an occasional patch with solvent.

twenty shots—if the bore shows fouling or accuracy deteriorates. So it's a good idea to take cleaning supplies to the range. You'll come up with your own cleaning routine, but here's how I scrub out a bore.

1. Saturate a patch with bore solvent and swab the bore one way; remove the patch at the muzzle.
2. Replace the patch with a clean one, saturate it, swab the bore both ways; remove the patch.
3. Set the rifle aside for a minute or more to give the solvent time to work.
4. Saturate a brass or nylon brush and scrub the bore three times both ways.
5. Run dry patches through the bore until they come clean.
6. If patches come out green or blue, repeat the entire process until this evidence of copper disappears.
7. Swab the bore with an oily patch to prevent rust on the clean steel.

Of course, this procedure also works with .17 HMR rifles and pistols, as well as with centerfires. Getting the bore "squeaky clean" isn't

Typical .22 rimfire, outside-lubricated bullets driven slowly by a pinch of powder leave little residue.

imperative if you're shooting most jacketed softpoints. In fact, a minimal amount of fouling may *improve* accuracy by filling microscopic pits and tool marks in the bore. After cleaning their rifles, competitive riflemen almost always fire "fouling shots" before moving to a record target, because the first shot out of a clean bore is apt to fly wide. On the other hand, the people at Barnes Bullets advise that before shooting any bullet with a soft copper exterior, you should make sure the bore is very clean. A little residue from gilding metal jackets may have a significant effect on the accuracy of Barnes X-Bullets.

I like to have the rifle in a cradle when I clean. You can get one from Midway, Brownells, or Cabela's. For lack of anything better, clean your rifle on sandbags. Put something under the muzzle to catch soiled patches and solvent drippings. Keep solvents—especially ammonia-based solvents—off wood stocks. Such chemicals can even harm some metal finishes. Solvents are not lubricants or preservatives!

Clean from the breech, and use a bore guide, available from shooting supply houses. A bore guide is a plastic sleeves that fits in the bolt race and centers the cleaning rod in the bore so the rod doesn't bang against the chamber. One size fits most centerfire rifles. I acquired my bore guide from Sinclair International. At the time, it cost less than fifteen bucks—a small price to pay to prevent barrel damage.

If you're shooting a lever-action, pump, or autoloader, you'll have to clean from the muzzle. Be careful not to nick or egg the muzzle with a cleaning rod. Any irregularity at the muzzle gives gas a detour around the bullet base just as the bullet is getting airborne. Tipping results, which ruins accuracy. Use a small plastic funnel or a rod guide from Dewey to protect the muzzle.

One-piece cleaning rods are kinder to your bore than jointed rods. Among shooters who use one-piece rods are those who favor steel rods, like the old Belding and Mull, and those who prefer coated steel, like those from Bore Tech and Dewey. Uncoated steel is stronger for its out-

One-piece cleaning rods are the best choice for bores.

side diameter than is coated steel, so it flexes less. Coating cushions contact between rod and bore, but it also picks up grit. Even soft aluminum rods can carry nasties into that expensive rifling. That's why it makes sense to wipe off any rod with an oily cloth before you swab the bore. Store rods in plastic or cardboard tubes.

Some hunters use slotted tips for their patches, while others prefer jags with a point on the end, to center the patch. Spearing patches, you avoid the temptation to pull soiled patches back through the bore. I think it's best to push your first patch out the muzzle and retrieve the rod empty, rather than tug the powder and primer residue back across the rifling and into the action. Later, to speed things up, you can swab both ways. Nylon brushes are easiest on the bore, but I prefer the aggressive action of brass. Used prudently, it will not harm a barrel or shorten its life. Steel brushes are too harsh, in my view.

A coated cleaning cable is easy on the rifle. However, cleaning a bore with a cable is slow, and a cable won't dislodge an obstruction in the bore. One cable that does a quick cleaning job is the BoreSnake by GunMate (503-655-2837 or 208-743-3919). This device is really a rope. It has its own copper brush embedded in a thick woven section sized to fit the bore. A more slender leading section has a brass weight that you drop down the barrel. After applying solvent to the brush and thick section, you pull them through the bore. No assembly required; no lost brushes or rod tips. And no muzzle damage.

Like ordinary cables, the BoreSnake can swab pumps, autoloaders, and lever guns from the chamber forward, pulling debris out the muzzle instead of depositing it in the action. The ropes, which can be cleaned in ordinary detergent, are caliber-specific, in diameters from .22 to 10-gauge. A BoreSnake, cable, or compact segmented rod makes sense if you're backpacking into hunting camp. Make sure cleaning solvents are in tightly sealed bottles.

A high-tech way to remove copper and lead is available in the "Foul Out II" kit from Outers. This device uses electrical current to lift metal deposits from the rifling and bring them through solution to a rod in the bore's center. It works like electroplating. The bore must first be cleaned and degreased; same goes for the jointed steel rod supplied in the kit. The rod is very slender; you fit it to the bore by installing four O-rings of appropriate size. The idea isn't to get a tight fit; you just want to keep the rod from touching the bore. Space the O-rings from the throat to half an inch short of the muzzle.

Before inserting the rod, plug the chamber with a tapered stopper. Then, with the rifle muzzle-up, pour copper- or lead-specific cleaning solution into the bore (both solvents are in the kit). When the bore is about half full, insert the rod carefully until it rests on the rubber stopper. Then add solvent until the bore is full. The electrical unit has two leads, one of which you clip to the rod, and the other to the rifle's front sight or other steel part. Switch on the device and leave it alone. If the bore is heavily leaded, the rod will quickly accumulate lead residue. You'll have to remove the rod to clean off the deposit. Reinsert it and

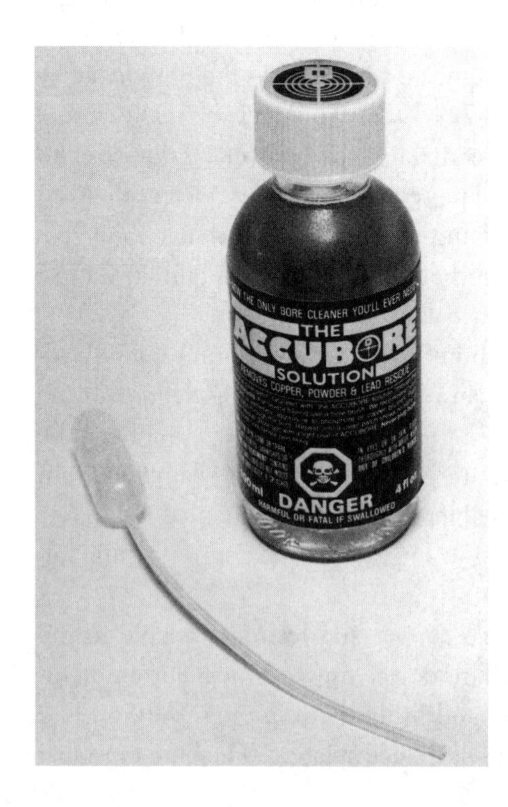

Swab with solvent on a patch or nylon brush. Finish with a dry patch, then one that's lightly oiled.

again bring the solvent level up to the muzzle. Copper deposits transfer more slowly. After four hours (or when the "clean" light comes on), you've gotten as much as you can out of that solvent. If more time is required, you'll need fresh solvent.

When cleaning the bore, don't forget the chamber. While it's true that a chamber doesn't get blasted with fuel residues or smeared with lead or copper, it can pick up moisture. If you don't keep the chamber dry, you're inviting rust. A neglected chamber may show rust; you'll want to attack it with a tight-fitting brass brush dipped in Hoppe's No. 9. After swabbing the chamber until patches come clean, give it the same light oil treatment that you do the rifling.

Before you fire the rifle again, however, pull that oil out with a dry patch. Reason: You want the case to grip the chamber wall when it expands. Reduce that grip with a film of oil, and you increase backthrust against the bolt face.

If you're storing your rifle in a damp climate, coat the bore with gun grease. But remove it *all* before shooting, as grease in the rifling can boost pressures.

Cleaning other parts of the gun doesn't need to be done as often as cleaning the bore. After each hunting season, I pull the barreled action from the stock and disassemble what's easy to disassemble (bolt, friction rings, simple triggers like the Model 70's). I spray all these parts with a degreaser or an all-purpose solvent like WD-40. If there's any rust, I scrub it with a brass brush dipped in Hoppe's No. 9. Then I wipe all metal surfaces clean and apply a very light coating of gun oil before reassembling. The stock gets a rubdown with a dry rag or, if it is oil-finished wood, with boiled linseed oil. I work the linseed oil in until my hand is hot, then wipe the stock dry. A toothbrush cleans out the checkering.

A clean rifle shoots more accurately than one that is fouled. A rifle that you've disassembled to clean has no secrets. You'll have confidence in a clean rifle, and confidence leads to better shooting.

Appendix

RIMFIRE BALLISTICS

Cartridge	**Wt. (grs.)**	**Bullet style**
American Eagle .22 Long Rifle HV	38	HP Copper-Plated
American Eagle .22 Long Rifle HV	40	Solid
CCI .22 Short	29	HS
CCI .22 Short	27	HP
CCI .22 Short Target	29	
CCI .22 Short	29	CB
CCI .22 Long	29	HS
CCI .22 Long	29	CB
CCI .22 Long Rifle Stinger	32	HP
CCI .22 Long Rifle Quik-Shok	32	
CCI .22 Long Rifle Mini-Mag	36	HP
CCI .22 Long Rifle SGB	40	Lead FN
CCI .22 Long Rifle Mini-Mag	40	HS
CCI .22 Long Rifle Sub-sonic	40	HP
CCI .22 Long Rifle Standard-V	40	
CCI .22 Long Rifle Green Tag	40	Comp
CCI .22 Long Rifle Silhouette	40	
CCI .22 Long Rifle Pistol Match	40	
CCI .22 Long Rifle Velocitor	40	HP
CCI Long Rifle Shotshell	31	#12 shot
CCI .22 WMR TNT	30	HP
CCI .22 WMR Maxi-Mag-V	30	HP
CCI .22 WMR Maxi-Mag	40	HS
CCI .22 WMR Maxi-Mag	40	HP
CCI .22 WMR Gold Dot	50	HP
CCI .22 WRF	45	JHP
CCI WMR Shotshell	52	#12 shot
Fed .22 Long Rifle Target	40	Solid
Fed .22 Long Rifle HV	40	Solid
Fed .22 Long Rifle HV	36	HP
Fed .22 Long Rifle HV	40	Solid Copper Pl.
Fed .22 Long Rifle HV	38	HP Copper Pl.
Fed .22 Long Rifle Hyper-V	31	HP Copper Pl.
Fed .22 Long Rifle Bird Shot	25	#10 lead shot
Fed .22 WMR	30	Speer TNT JHP
Fed .22 WMR	30	Jacketed HP
Fed .22 WMR	40	FMJ
Fed .22 WMR	50	Jacketed HP
Hornady .17 Mach 2	17	V-Max
Hornady .17 HMR	17	V-Max
Rem .17 HMR	17	V-Max BT

Velocity (fps)			Energy (ft-lbs)			Trajectory (inches)		
Muzzle	50 yds.	100 yds.	Muzzle	50 yds.	100 yds.	50 yds.	100 yds.	150 yds.
1280	1120	1020	140	105	90	0	−6.3	−20.6
1260	1100	1020	140	110	90	0	−6.5	−21.0
1132	1004	920	83	65	54	1.0	−4.1	
1164	1013	920	81	62	51	1.0	−4.3	
830	752	695	44	36	31	1.0	−6.8	
727	667	610	34	28	24			
1180	1038	946	90	69	58	1.0	−4.1	
727	557	610	34	28	24			
1640	1277	1132	191	115	91	1.0	−2.6	
1640	1277	1132	191	115	91	1.0	−2.6	
1280	1126	1012	131	101	82	1.0	−3.5	
1255	1110	1019	138	104	88	1.0	−3.4	
1255	1110	1016	140	109	92	1.0	−3.6	
1070	984	914	102	86	74	1.0	−4.2	
1070	996	936	102	88	78	1.0	−4.1	
1070	996	936	102	88	78	1.0	−4.1	
1255	1110	1016	140	109	92	1.0	−3.6	
1070	996	936	102	88	78	1.0	−4.1	
1435	1238	1095	183	136	107	1.0	−2.2	
950								
2200	1750	1373	322	204	128	0	−1.4	
2200	1750	1373	322	204	128	0	−1.4	
1910	1490	1325	324	197	156	0	−1.7	
1910	1490	1326	324	197	156	0	−1.7	
1525	1331	1176	258	197	154	0	−2.0	
1300	1127	1015	169	127	103	0	3.0	
1000								
1080	1000	930	105	90	75	0	−7.2	
1260	1100	1020	140	110	90	0	−6.5	−21.0
1255	1100	1000	125	95	80	0	−5.6	−19.9
1260	1100	1020	140	110	90	0	−6.5	−21.0
1280	1120	1020	140	105	90	0	−6.3	−20.6
1550	1280	1100	165	115	85	0	−3.8	−14.7
2200	1720	1340	325	200	120	0	−1.5	−8.1
2200	1760	1400	325	205	130	0	−1.3	−7.3
1910	1600	1330	325	225	155	0	−2.9	−10.7
1650	1450	1280	300	235	180	0	−3.6	−12.5
2100	1799	1530	166	122	88	0.7	0	−4.4
2550	2212	1902	245	185	136	0.1	0	−2.6
2550	2212	1901	245	185	136	0.1	0	−2.6

Cartridge	Wt. (grs.)	Bullet style
Rem .22 Short HV	29	Golden Lead
Rem/Eley .22 Match EPS	40	Lead FN
Rem/Eley .22 Club Xtra	40	Lead RN
Rem/Eley .22 Target Rifle	40	Lead RN
Rem .22 Long Rifle Subsonic	38	HP
Rem .22 Long Rifle Target	40	Lead RN
Rem .22 Long Rifle HV	40	Golden Lead
Rem .22 Long Rifle HV	36	Golden HP
Rem .22 Yellow Jacket Long Rifle Hyper-V	33	TCHP
Rem .22 Viper Long Rifle Hyper-V	36	TC Solid
Rem .22 Long Rifle Thunderbolt	40	Lead RN
Rem .22 Long Rifle Cyclone	36	HP
Rem .22 WMR	33	V-Max BT
Rem .22 WMR	40	Jacketed HP
Rem .22 WMR	40	Pointed SP
Win .22 Short	29	LRN
Win .22 Short	Bk pwd	blank
Win .22 Long Rifle Power-Point	40	PP
Win .22 Long Rifle	40	LRN
Win .22 Long Rifle	37	LHP
Win .22 Long Rifle T22	40	LRN-SV
Win .22 Long Rifle Wildcat	40	LRN
Win .22 Long Rifle	40	LHP
Win .22 Long Rifle XPERT	36	LHP
Win .22 Long Rifle Bird Shot		#12 shot
Win 22 WRF	45	LFN
Win .22 WMR	40	JHP
Win .22 WMR	40	FMJ
Win .22 Mag Supreme	34	JHP
Win .22 Dyna Point WMR	45	DP

Velocity (fps)			Energy (ft-lbs)			Trajectory (inches)		
Muzzle	50 yds.	100 yds.	Muzzle	50 yds.	100 yds.	50 yds.	100 yds.	150 yds.
1095	982	903	77	62	52	1.0	−4.5	
1085	1006	941	105	90	79	1.0	−4.5	
1085	1006	941	105	90	79	1.0	−4.5	
1085	1006	941	105	90	79	1.0	−4.5	
1050	965	901	93	79	69	1.0	−4.7	
1150	1048	976	117	98	85	1.0	−4.0	
1255	1113	1017	140	110	92	1.0	−3.4	
1280	1117	1010	131	100	82	1.0	−3.5	
1500	1247	1075	165	114	85	1.0	−2.8	
1410	1198	1056	159	115	89	1.0	−3.0	
1255	1113	1017	140	110	92	1.0	−3.4	
1280	1117	1010	131	100	82	1.0	−3.5	
2000	1730	1495	293	219	164	0.6	0	−4.3
1910	1610	1350	324	230	162	0.9	0	−5.7
1910	1600	1340	324	227	159	1.0	0	−5.8
1095		903	77		52		−4.5	
1280		1001	146		89	1.0	−3.5	
1255		1017	140		92	1.0	−3.6	
1280		1015	135		85	1.0	−3.5	
1150		976	117		85	1.0	−4.0	
1255		1017	140		92	1.0	−3.6	
1150		976	117		85	1.0	−4.0	
1220		956	122		75	1.0	−4.0	
1300		1023	169		105	1.0	−3.2	
1910		1326	324		156	0	−1.7	
1910		1326	324		156	0	−1.7	
2120		1435	338		155	1.0	−1.4	
1550		1147	240		131	1.0	−2.6	

INDEX

Index